D0848057

VISCOUNT MAUÁ
AND THE EMPIRE
OF BRAZIL

A BIOGRAPHY OF

IRINEU EVANGELISTA DE SOUSA

(1813-1889)

BARON AND VISCOUNT MAUÁ AT THE AGE OF FORTY-THREE

VISCOUNT MAUÁ AND THE EMPIRE OF BRAZIL

A BIOGRAPHY OF

IRINEU EVANGELISTA DE SOUSA

(1813-1889)

BY

ANYDA MARCHANT

UNIVERSITY OF CALIFORNIA PRESS

BERKELEY AND LOS ANGELES   1965

F
2536
·M2675
1965

University of California Press
Berkeley and Los Angeles, California

Cambridge University Press
London, England

© 1965 by The Regents of the University of California
Library of Congress Catalog Card Number: 65-10773

Designed by Harry Marks

Printed in the United States of America

TO MY BROTHER

ALMA COLLEGE
MONTEITH LIBRARY
ALMA, MICHIG

T HE MODERN FACE of Brazil, its present aspirations, the achievements of the past twenty years, are more widely known abroad than its previous life, the evolution of its people, the derivation of its culture. The present-day foreign reader with an interest in books about Brazil must be left with an impression that Brazil began a few years ago and that before then there lay only years without incident. If he is interested in the economic history of the New World, he will certainly have encountered Alan Krebs Manchester's *British Pre-eminence in Brazil*. He may be familiar with the activities of Brazil's agreeably eccentric emperor, Dom Pedro II, through Mary Wilhelmine Williams' full-length biography in English, *Dom Pedro the Magnanimous*. Or with Dom Pedro's immediate ancestors, who, as members of the Habsburg dynasty, have provided material for scandalous narrative, as in Bertita Harding's *Amazon Throne*. An agricultural country, so vast and empty that most of its terrain was unknown even to the inhabitants of the littoral, without a record of bloody revolution or constant international war, had no history. It was inert, featureless, and without dramatic effect on a reading public, such as that of the United States, accustomed to thinking of its neighbors to the south in terms of Mexican history or of the vague, ceaseless, apparently causeless turmoil of the other Caribbean countries.

Because Portugal has always been of major interest to English traders and because the first act of the refugee Prince João on arriving in the New World was to invite foreigners into Brazil, there are a number of valuable accounts, travelers' tales, that paint a picture of the Rio de Janeiro that the boy Irineu Evangelista de Sousa, later Baron and Viscount Mauá, first saw in the 1820's.

The most indefatigable and all-observing of these visitors was John Luccock, an Englishman, who arrived, for the first time, on the heels of the royal family in 1808. He lived not only in the capital but traveled through the provinces, seeking information on the commercial prospects for English businessmen. He was apparently not a man of much cultivation and certainly did not expect to mingle in court circles. He was conservative, unexcitable, with strong opinions easily aroused by the moral laxities he saw at such close quarters in all classes of society. Especially did he notice the appalling absence of creature comforts. He describes the physical appearance of the new court, and the habits of life of this handful of people living on the shore of a vast and mysterious continent. He published his observations in his *Notes on Rio de Janeiro*.

Maria Graham, on the other hand, who stopped in Rio when her husband's frigate-of-war (he was a captain in the Royal Navy) put into the harbor in 1821 and returned for a longer visit in the following years, saw the shops and the shopkeepers from the point of view of a lady who was used to the best of London and who was familiar with continental Europe and with India. She went horseback riding up the Corcovado Mountain, visited the ladies of the royal household, recorded the method and problems of supplying Rio with vegetables, meat, bread, and milk, and gave a spirited account of the happenings in Rio after Dom João's eldest son proclaimed Brazil an independent empire and himself its first emperor, as Pedro I. Her account of these visits is in her *Journal of a Voyage to Brazil and Residence there during Part of the Years 1821, 1822, 1823*.

The Reverend Robert Walsh, coming several years later as chaplain

to the British envoy, brought a more astute political mind to the problems of the period, but, like Luccock, he had a sharp eye for the
details of life in the streets. He saw Brazil in its first decade of independence and published his observations as *Notices of Brazil in 1828
and 1829.*

There was a goodly company of such travelers who recorded their
impressions of their stay in Brazil during the period of Mauá's life.
There were the English naturalists, George Gardner, Charles Darwin,
Sir Henry Chamberlain, John Mawe. There were William Edwards
who visited the Amazon, Herbert Smith, William Scully, the Americans D. P. Kidder and J. C. Fletcher, and Edward Ewbank. There
was Mrs. Agassiz, who kept a journal of the Harvard scientific expedition which her husband led up the Amazon.

In fact, the number is endless, nor were they all English and Americans. Germans, Frenchmen, Italians—all came and took away impressions of the new empire thriving under the Southern Cross. They told
about the way of life among all classes of people, about the institution
of slavery, about the problems of population and transportation in so
vast a land, about the means of livelihood of the inhabitants, about the
new industries, the new railroads, the wealth, and the luxury to be
seen as the century passed.

The foreigners were not the only ones who left descriptions of
Brazil of the time of Dom Pedro II. There were also several Brazilians,
men of family, wealth, and political position, who in their last years
cast back to their active days and wrote their recollections for the
benefit of posterity. Recently their descendants have been diligently
rescuing from the limbo of old bookstores and family bookshelves
these memoirs and printing them, often with valuable annotations.

Among these last may be mentioned the daybook kept by Felix
Cavalcanti de Albuquerque Melo, an outstanding member of one of
the great oligarchic families of the north of Brazil, edited and pub-
lished by his greatgrandson, Gilberto Freyre, the sociologist, as
Memórias de um Cavalcanti. The man who was perhaps Mauá's most
bitter personal enemy was another of these chroniclers. Albino José
Barbosa de Oliveira married a rich heiress of the province of São
Paulo and lived a busy life in the midst of the gaiety that surrounded

the second Emperor's sober court. When he was old and about to die
he jotted down the principal recollections of his day—the arduous
journeys to and from São Paulo, before the building of the railroad,
in coaches over terrible roads or in litters carried by slaves or on horseback—recollections republished by his descendant, Americo Jacobino
Lacombe as *Memórias de um magistrado do imperio.* Councilor Albino's distant connection, Francisco de Paula Ferreira de Rezende,
also left his memoirs, republished by his son, Cassio Barbosa de
Rezende, *Minhas recordações.*

Dom Pedro II always displayed respect for the principle of the freedom of public opinion. He never inhibited the expression of criticism
of himself. One of the most celebrated instances of this scrupulous attitude arose in connection with the publication by Tito Franco de
Almeida in 1867 of the critical opinions of Councilor Francisco José
Furtado, who had been President of the Council of State for a brief
and unsatisfactory period in 1864. Dom Pedro did not fail to read the
book and to annotate it with his own comments, thus creating a price-
less document which has been edited in modern form by Carlos Fontes
and published as *O conselheiro Francisco José Furtado.* For the later
years of the Emperor's reign and life, there exists now in published
form the diary, *Diário e notas autobiográficas,* kept by André Rebouças, an intelligent and imaginative young Negro who achieved a position of modest renown as an engineer trained in the Emperor's Military School.

The German colonists who came to Brazil in large numbers during
the Emperor's reign left behind at least two important books recording the tribulations and impressions of these immigrants who came to
combat not only a wilderness but the institution of slavery. Thomas
Davatz first published his memoirs in 1850. They are now available
in a Portuguese edition, *Memórias de um colono no Brasil.* Thirty
years later, Karl von Koseritz gathered into book form his newspaper
impressions of Rio de Janeiro and São Paulo, now published in a Portuguese edition under the title *Imagens do Brasil.*

Koseritz wrote his account of the times for his contemporaries. He
was editor of a newspaper popular among his fellow colonists and a
power in the German colony. Coming from the southernmost prov-

ince of Rio Grande do Sul, the same province from which Mauá migrated as a boy of nine, he noted the security of life in the capital, where, in spite of insufficient police, "no one carries arms, not even in lonely places and at any hour of the night." This, he remarked sadly, would not be true in his home province, with its long history of banditry and family feuds.

Filial respect has led the sons and grandsons of a number of the great men of Dom Pedro II's world to write the biographies of their fathers and grandfathers, using family archives and caches of letters otherwise inaccessible to the general reader. None of these equals in value and scope Joaquim Nabuco's *Um estadista do imperio*, the biography of a brilliant father by a brilliant son. Among the others must be mentioned: J. J. Silveira Martins' biography of his father, Gaspar Silveira Martins; Wanderley Pinho's first volume on the life of Baron Cotegipe, *Cotegipe e seu tempo*, as well as his edition of letters by the Emperor addressed to Cotegipe, *Cartas do imperador ao barão de Cotegipe*, and his collection of anecdotal history of the figures and events of court society, *Salões e damas do segundo reinado;* José Antonio Soares de Sousa's life of his grandfather, *Vida do visconde do Uruguai;* Luís da Câmara Cascudo's life of the Marquess of Olinda, *O marques de Olinda e seu tempo;* Baron Rio Branco's life of his father, the Viscount, *Biografia de José Maria da Silva Paranhos, o visconde de Rio Branco.*

Beyond these sources there are others, fragmentary studies of special aspects of Brazilian nineteenth-century history. The late Alberto Rangel has provided a penetrating discussion of the contemporary accounts from which we can learn of Dom Pedro II's upbringing, *A educação do príncipe.* Americo Jacobina Lacombe has made several contributions to the history of the founding of the imperial summer resort of Petrópolis, of principal interest being his *Paulo Barbosa e a fundação de Petrópolis.* In Vicente Licinio Cardoso's *A margem da história do Brasil,* and in Nelson Werneck Sodré's similar study, *Panorama do segundo imperio,* discussions of Mauá in relation to his period and especially to the Emperor, may be found.

Other volumes of particular interest are: Batista Pereira's vignettes of many of the principal men of Dom Pedro II's government, *Figuras do imperio;* Argeu Guimarães, *Em torno do casamento de Pedro II,* based on research in Spanish archives; Afonso Celso's *Oito anos de parlamento. O poder pessoal de D. Pedro II;* Pedro Lamas' reminiscences of his father, Mauá's great friend, the Uruguayan minister to Brazil, Andrés Lamas, *Etapas de una gran política;* Arthur Cesar Ferreira Reis's study of the navigation of the Amazon, in *Panorama econômico-financeiro do segundo reinado;* Fernando Saboia de Medeiros' *A liberdade de navegação do Amazonas;* Lawrence Hill's *Diplomatic Relations of the United States and Brazil;* Lídia Besouchet's biography of the first José Maria da Silva Paranhos, *O visconde do Rio Branco;* Pelham Horton Box's *The Origins of the Paraguayan War;* Renato Mendonça's life of Baron Penedo, who for many years was Brazilian minister to London, *Um diplomata na côrte do Inglaterra;* and Heitor Lyra's biography of Dom Pedro II.

A detailed and annotated list of some of these sources, and many others besides which bear directly on Mauá, is appended to the Claudio Ganns edition of his greatgrandfather's statement to the creditors of Mauá and Company, mentioned below. The list contains not only many Brazilian and foreign books and articles published up to 1943 which contain some reference to Mauá and his work, but also a detailed indication of other sources, such as files of letters available in the Archivo Publico, the Biblioteca Nacional, the Instituto Histórico e Geográfico Brasileiro, and so on. It is likely that there are still further undiscovered sources, such as letters, reports and contracts of the companies of which Mauá was a founder or shareholder, and documentary material of various kinds. I am indebted to Lídia Besouchet for the information that a so far unused archive of Mauá's letters addressed to the Argentine General Urquiza is preserved in the Estancia de San José, copies of which she was able to supply me. The Estancia de San José in the Argentine province of Entre Rios was once the General's country estate and is now a museum.

I had the good fortune of meeting Claudio Ganns in Rio. He has gathered together a private library bearing on his greatgrandfather's life and achievements. As the result of his generous coöperation I have been able to examine books not available in the United States; a bulky

package of letters by Mauá to his partner in Montevideo, Ricardo
José Ribeiro, originally in the possession of Mauá's last surviving
daughter, Dona Irene de Sousa Ribeiro and donated by her to the
Instituto Histórico e Geográfico Brasileiro; other bulky packages of
letters to other people; relics of Mauá himself (his gold-rimmed
spectacles, the silver-mounted spade and small wheelbarrow used by
the Emperor in ceremoniously turning the first clod in the building
of Brazil's first railroad, and so on), preserved in the Instituto's headquarters.

Most valuable of all was the *copiador* in Claudio Ganns's possession: a bound volume of copies of letters made by the old-fashioned
method of passing a sponge over the original and passing the damp
page through a press—the businessman's only resource for preserving
facsimile copies of his correspondence in the days before the type-
writer. This volume, rather battered by the passage of time, is apparently the only such file of Mauá's professional correspondence surviving, and it covers the first six-month period of 1861, which fortunately
was a year of considerable importance in Mauá's life.

Among these letters I discovered many addressed to Mauá's partners in England, Alexander MacGregor in London and J. H. de Castro
in Manchester. Most precious of all, I found two letters addressed to
Richard Carruthers, the old Englishman who had educated Mauá and
had given him his start in life; these are letters of great value, for they
immediately preceded and succeeded in date the only letter from
Richard Carruthers to Mauá known to exist and which also was in
Claudio Ganns's custody. The letters in the *copiador*—some of them
half obliterated by fading or the corrosion of the paper by the ink—
are not letters addressed to public men, full of the reservations and
formality that must necessarily clothe such communications. They
are the informal, candid, detailed instructions and explanations offered
to his business partners and, in the case of De Castro, to one of his
closest friends. I am certain that never was Mauá more himself than
when, late at night in his private room, the commotion of the business day finished and his family asleep in the quiet house, he sat down
to cover pages and pages with his neat, rapid writing, telling his

partners what his plans were or his other business associates what was best to do in the management of the many companies whose affairs were in his hands.

It is also through the kindness of Claudio Ganns that I received a copy of the brochure of reminiscences of Mauá written by his youngest daughter, Dona Irene de Sousa Ribeiro, in her last days.

Not all such first-hand sources as I had occasion to use were in private hands. To the former Director of the Public Archives in Rio, Dr. E. Vilhena de Morais, I owe the full text of the letter written by Mauá to the Viscount São Vicente in 1869, which is referred to in the chapter dealing with Mauá's claims against the Uruguayan government and also a photostatic reproduction of the decree, carrying the signature of Dom Pedro II, granting to Mauá the title of Baron in 1854.

The essence of the Second Reign is preserved in all its exotic flavor in the Imperial Palace in Petrópolis, now the Imperial Museum. It is not a great mansion but a simple building, painted bright pink and trimmed with white stone, set in a spacious tropical garden full of palm trees, tropical lilies, dense green vegetation confined between pebble walks, with a statue of the Emperor at one end. This was Dom Pedro II's favorite home, the place to which he summoned statesmen, common folk, and foreign visitors when he wished to distinguish them with a little extra attention, for an audience a little less formal than those in the palace of São Cristovão. To the director, Alcindo Sodré (whose wife is a descendant of Mauá), I owe the sight of an iron railway sleeper, said to have been invented by Mauá himself to conquer the difficulties presented by the use of wood in a destructive tropical climate.

An advertisement in the *Manchester Guardian* brought a responsive letter from Edith Lambert Harding of Bolton, in Lancashire. She told me in it that she was a descendant of Richard Carruthers on both sides of her family and that she remembered seeing, when Carruthers' house and effects were sold, "several portraits and pictures of family groups, obviously of foreign origin—possible Baron Mauá and his family." She had often heard her father speak of the connection with the

Baron. From her I learned some of the details of Carruthers' life on his return to England.

The principal sources for biographical material on Mauá are: The edition of Mauá's own statement to his creditors at the time of his bankruptcy, *Visconde de Mauá: Autobiografia*, with introduction and notes by his greatgrandson, Claudio Ganns; *Mauá*, by Alberto de Faria, a detailed, eulogistic account of Mauá's life and activities; Lídia Besouchet's excellent biographical study, *Mauá e seu tempo* (or, in Spanish, *Mauá y su época*), her edition of Mauá's letters to his friend Andrés Lamas, entitled *A correspondência política de Mauá no Rio da Prata* (also published in a Spanish edition), and her essay on Mauá's habits of thought, *O pensamento vivo de Mauá*; Edgardo de Castro Rebelo's critique of Mauá as a figure of national and international finance, *Mauá: restaurando a verdade*; J. F. Normano's excellent economic study of Brazil, *Brazil, a Study of Economic Types*, or, in Portuguese, *A evolução econômica do Brasil*; Renato Costa's monograph, *Síntesis de una vida: Mauá*, and a series of newspaper articles by the same author which appeared in the *Correio do Povo* of Pôrto Alegre, Rio Grande do Sul, in 1945; a volume issued by the Instituto Histórico e Geográfico Brasileiro in 1940 to commemorate the fiftieth anniversary of Mauá's death, *O visconde de Mauá*, which contains addresses delivered by Rodrigo Octavio Filho, Gustavo Barroso, and Alcindo Sodré; Rodrigo Octavio Filho's short study of Mauá included in his *Figuras do imperio e da republic;* and Gustavo Barroso's unsubstantiated attack on Mauá in *História secreta do Brasil*.

THE SPELLING OF BRAZILIAN NAMES

In 1931 Brazil adopted, by a decree of law, a new orthography for her language. Its purpose was to modernize and systematize the spelling of Brazilian Portuguese, and its effect is generally to suppress unsounded consonants and most double consonants and to indicate the phonetics of words by the greater use of accents.

The spelling of Brazilian proper names is likewise governed by the

new orthography. Therefore, the reader who delves into the source
material of such a study as the present one will note considerable dif-
ferences in the spelling of the names of the figures of Brazilian history. Mauá spelled his name thus: Irenêo Evangelista de Souza. Under
the new rules this becomes: Irineu Evangelista de Sousa. Viscount
Itaborahy becomes Viscount Itaboraí. When the new orthography
was first instituted, some names considered too traditional to be
changed were retained in the old spelling, as for example the name
of the state of Bahia. In more recent times, even such exceptions are
receiving the modern usage, Bahia often becoming Baía. Some exceptions still remain, however. Gilberto Freyre, the wellknown sociologist, still spells his name with a "y" instead of an "i".

In the present study names have been modernized, even in passages
quoted directly from books published in the old orthography.

In Brazil, both men and women are commonly addressed and referred to by their given names rather than by their surnames. This
implies no familiarity on the part of the speaker. Thus, Mauá, before
he received his patents of nobility, was correctly addressed as Senhor
Irineu. Men in political office likewise were so addressed, as Zacarias,
for instance, instead of Góes e Vasconcelos, and Eusébio, instead of
Queiroz. Again, there are some exceptions. The elder Rio Branco,
when not called by his title, is frequently referred to in Brazilian pub-
lications as Paranhos, Baron Bom Retiro as Couto Ferraz, and Viscount
Sousa Franco as Sousa Franco, his title being the same as his family
name.

ACKNOWLEDGMENTS

It was my brother Alexander Marchant who first suggested to me that
Mauá needed a biography in English. Without his encouragement and
practical assistance in finding the people, books, and other sources
from whom and from which the material for it was obtained, the
present study would never have come into being.

My second debt of gratitude I owe to Alan Manchester, who has
read the manuscript in its various revisions. He has never failed to

give me the benefit of his knowledge of Brazil in the period covered and his critical evaluation of what I have attempted to do.

To Claudio and Laíde Ganns I owe much for their kindness and hospitality in Rio and the generosity with which they gave me access to Mauá's personal papers and their family's recollections of him. The illustration for the frontispiece is a photograph, taken in 1856, that first appeared in A. Sisson, *Galeria dos contemporâneos ilustres* (Rio de Janeiro, 1857), the first biography of Mauá to be published. The present copy was made from Lídia Besouchet's *Mauá y su época* (Spanish edition, Buenos Aires, 1940), where it is stated that the photograph is in the drawingroom of Mauá's *estancia* in Mercedes, Uruguay.

The note on my sources shows that many people have had a hand in this re-creation of a man and an era. To them all I acknowledge my gratitude and appreciation for their help and for the good fellowship with which they imparted to me whatever they were able to contribute to the finished work.

CONTENTS

WHO WAS
MAUÁ?

IT MAY fairly be said that the history of nineteenth-century Brazil is nearly a closed book to English-speaking readers. The reason, of course, is chiefly the language barrier. Eça de Queiroz, Portugal's great novelist and satirist, once remarked that his finest thoughts were entombed in the Portuguese language. Unfortunately he was right, for only recently has Portuguese attracted attention as a language to be studied, thus unlocking the treasures of literature produced both in Portugal and Brazil, once Portugal's chief colony.

In the course of the past forty years a few books have been published in English that give a picture of some aspects of Brazil in the nineteenth century. From them the general reader can learn the major outlines of the historical events. At the beginning of the century Brazil emerged suddenly in the main stream of European history through a fortuitous circumstance. The Portuguese royal family, seeking refuge from Napoleon, migrated across the Atlantic to Rio de Janeiro and there established the court for about a decade. By the time Napoleon had been exiled to St. Helena and the king of Portugal had returned to Lisbon, Brazil was too far along the road to nationhood to revert to the status of colony.

The second decade of the eighteenth century saw the colonies of the Spanish crown in South America revolt and declare their independence. Brazil followed suit and in 1822 became an independent country. But instead of becoming a republic, like its Spanish-speaking neighbors, it became a monarchy, with the eldest son and heir of the king of Portugal as its first emperor.

The reign of the first emperor was brief and ended in his abdication in 1831 in favor of his five-year-old son. Brazil was governed by a regency until her second emperor was crowned at the age of sixteen in 1841.

Throughout this early period of the First Reign and the Regency, Brazil was in a state of political ferment. It is remarkable that she escaped both widespread civil disorder and fragmentation into more than one country, on the model of her Spanish-speaking neighbors. However, the fact that this did not take place and that Brazil remained one huge, sparsely populated nation, Portuguese-speaking and with a tradition of constitutional monarchy, has given her a character entirely different from the other countries of South America. The Second Reign, that of Dom Pedro II, which lasted from 1841 to his abdication in 1889 in favor of his daughter, the Princess Isabel, whose reign was brief, provided Brazil with a political stability that was able to withstand the sometimes open rebellion of local chiefs in some parts of the country and a disastrous foreign war, that with Paraguay in the 1860s. Throughout this part of her history Brazil was an agricultural country whose considerable wealth was based first on sugar and then on sugar and coffee, raised on great plantations by slaves imported from the Portuguese colonies in Africa. This opulent slavocracy produced a society, in which the political as well as the economic power was in the hands of large, closely knit landowning families, the firm support of the imperial throne. It was a society in which the emphasis was on highly polished manners and a disdain of business as an occupation for a man of substance and cultivation, and in which a gift for political oratory was one of the marks of a gentleman.

That much of the scene of nineteenth-century Brazil may be known to the general reader. But the personalities of the chief actors in that scene are almost entirely unknown. Probably the only one known at all is the second emperor himself. He was half a Habsburg, his mother being the daughter of Francis I of Austria and his aunt Napoleon's second empress, Marie Louise. From his mother he inherited a taste for bookish pursuits, and the strict upbringing he received from European tutors gave an intellectual bent to his mind and a strait-laced character to his moral outlook. In 1876 he visited the United States as a "modern Haroun-al Raschid, wandering about to see the great world as a simple traveller" (the description is Longfellow's). At the Philadelphia Exposition his intellectual curiosity gave Alexander Graham Bell his first chance to demonstrate his invention, the telephone.

One of the most remarkable of the men who surrounded the Emperor and determined the economic progress of his empire was a man who was not typical of his age nor of imperial society. He was born a poor boy, Irineu Evangelista de Sousa by name, in the part of the country least loyal to the imperial government. He nevertheless made himself the wealthiest and sometimes one of the most powerful men in Brazil. In Brazilian history he is known as Baron and Viscount Mauá, the title the Emperor gave him in reward for building the first railroad in Brazil, taking the Indian name of the town where the line began. When Mauá eventually went bankrupt, it was partly because, in the end, he failed in his long struggle against the economic environment of the empire of Dom Pedro II.

Even to modern Brazilians, Mauá is a vague figure. The American historian Alan Krebs Manchester has called him the shadow of Viscount Rio Branco, the Emperor's great minister of empire. Brazilians usually recall that he had something to do with railroads and banks and that there was a spectacular bankruptcy—a sort of Brazilian echo of Baring Brothers. He is not a figure that springs to most people's minds when they think of that part of the New World that has received a predominantly Mediterranean culture. The well-sung heroes of Spanish and Portuguese America are the discoverers and seekers after gold and precious stones, the missionary priests, the conquistadores. Columbus, Cabral, Magellan, Balboa, Pizarro, Cortez; Las Casas, the friend of the Indian engulfed by the white man's ambition;

Bolívar, the champion of liberty who achieved independence for half a dozen modern states; all these fit into the traditional concept of Latin American history. Men of business, innovators in industry, self-made men who gained power through the amassing of great wealth in commercial and industrial pursuits—these are taken to be more at home in North America, to be more naturally the product of that part of the New World originally settled by the English.

Nevertheless, Mauá was one of the latter, a man as completely and extraordinarily a man of affairs as any produced in France, Germany, England, or the United States in the same period. During his life he was everywhere in Brazil and Uruguay, providing the money for, and holding the purse strings of, every major financial undertaking between 1850 and 1875. Yet he is not remembered, except vaguely, as a name only. It is as if the very versatility of his activities had so dissipated his own personality that no recollection of it survives, except, anonymously, in the enterprises he founded and which outlived him. Had he built but one railroad, he would perhaps be known as the man who first built a railroad in Brazil. Had he only laid the first submarine cable connecting South America and Europe, he would perhaps be as well-known as Cyrus Field. But he did so many things, crowded so many achievements into twenty-five years that today he is practically unknown, overwhelmed by his own creations.

Mauá lived through the brief reign of Dom Pedro I (1822-1831), through the regency that governed Brazil during the childhood of Dom Pedro II (1831-1840), and through the Second Reign, the empire of Dom Pedro II (1841-1889). In that time, Brazil changed from a backward colony to an independent agricultural empire dependent on slave labor, to an independent republic in which industry was beginning to develop and slavery was abolished. Not a little of that change is directly attributable to his activities.

The modern visitor to Rio de Janeiro will find Mauá very much in evidence as a name. One of the first things he will see is the Praça Mauá (Mauá Square), which lies at one end of the principal avenue, the Avenida Rio Branco or Central, at the beginning of the docks, where the headquarters of the Brazilian Touring Club are situated. A little to one side of the stream of traffic (formerly it was in the very midst) that flows through the square from the Avenida to the dockside and on to the northern suburbs, he will see, high on a tall column, the statue of a gentleman in a frock coat, nonchalantly grasping a walking stick. This, the plaque on the pedestal will tell him, is Irineu Evangelista de Sousa, Viscount Mauá, thus commemorated by the Brazilian Engineering Club.

The visitor will discover, if he goes by train to Petrópolis, in the mountains behind Rio (where he can still see the only house that Mauá ever built for himself), that there is a railway station for suburban trains of the Leopoldina Railway (the modern descendant of Mauá's first railroad) called the Barão de Mauá Station. He will notice a bank, a radio station, industrial establishments of all descriptions, technological schools, shops—all graced by the name of this ubiquitous, if mysterious, gentleman.

Mysterious because he was not understood even by his contemporaries among his own countrymen. As a man wielding great financial power he was necessarily a part of the political history of Brazil in the nineteenth century, yet he was alien to it, and as such suspect.

The purpose of the following pages is to recapture the man himself and set him in the midst of the scene in which he spent his life and among the people with whom he dealt. Since he was not a typical man in that scene nor among those people, his manner of treating both his environment and his associates is the surest mirror of his personality and his inner drive.

PART ONE

THE
MERCHANT

CHAPTER I

LUSITANIA TRANSPLANTED

IN THE last years of the fifteenth century, Vasco da Gama sailed to the East Indies around the Cape of Good Hope at the tip of Africa, the first European to find his way directly to Asia by sea. From then on other Portuguese captains sailed to India, the Moluccas, the South China Sea, Ceylon and Burma to trade for spices and other eastern luxuries for the European market. On April 22, 1500, one of them, Pedro Alvares Cabral, sailing far to the west in the southern Atlantic, sighted the coast of Brazil. Thus Portugal acquired her largest and most valuable colony, which she was to hold, even against the French and the Dutch, for three hundred years.

Brazil had thus been discovered in Portugal's heroic age, when as navigators and sailors the Portuguese had few peers. But in the three hundred years of colonial life, while Portugal decayed, her daughter was not permitted to enhance that fading grandeur nor give new blood to the old glory. To the Portuguese crown Brazil was the supplier of wealth, first in dyewoods, then in sugar raised by slave labor on great plantations, and then in gold and precious stones. But as a colony it was to have no free intercourse with the rest of the world.

Everything that went from Brazil must go to Lisbon and everything that came must come from Lisbon. Like an aging matriarch, half-aware of the decline of her powers, Portugal would brook no competition, encourage no successor, suspicious of every new generation as of the usurper.

Agriculture and industry in Brazil were allowed no free development. The crops and manufactures were restricted so as to form a complement to the economic structure of Portugal and the Portuguese empire. The cultivation of grapes, for example, was prohibited, in order not to produce competition for Portuguese wines, though only the poorer quality of the home product was ever exported to Brazil. Cloth could not be woven nor glass manufactured. Even a good supply of tools and implements commonly in use in the rest of the world could not be imported. The natural consequence of such restrictions was a standard of living considerably below that of the countries of western Europe.

The closing days of the year 1807 saw the first great breach made in this primitive lethargy. There are certain scenes in the world's history which, though in themselves the stuff of tragedy, are invested by their protagonists with a ludicrous air. The flight of the Portuguese court from the fear of capture by Napoleon's armies was such an episode. The reigning Queen of Portugal, Maria I, was demented. Her son João, a corpulent, timid, procrastinating man, governed as Prince Regent. João was married to a virago, the sister of the King of Spain, who despised her husband and the Portuguese and whom João suspected of plotting against his kingdom and possibly his life. João vacillated, uneasy in his palace, as Napoleon gained success after success, won battle after battle. Should he endure the war in captivity? or should he take the advice of Viscount Strangford, the British minister, and flee to Brazil, safely out of the Monster's grasp? He procrastinated so long, in fact, that when Napoleon's General Junot entered Lisbon, November 27, 1807, the royal fleet was escaping, with the last puffs of a favorable but dying wind, out of the harbor under the escort of a British cruiser. On March 8, 1808, the city of Rio de Janeiro, stirred into an excitement unequaled by any previous disturbance save possibly the last attack by the French a hundred years before, welcomed the royal flotilla sailing in under Sugarloaf Mountain.

The city, when the court arrived, was incredibly primitive. It extended back from the beach a bare half mile and was situated on a low, flat piece of ground, surrounded in part by marshes. It had a population of possibly eighty thousand people, no sewage system, and a water system dependent on the great aqueduct built by one of the viceroys, which fed a small number of public fountains.

What had seemed a canny governmental policy in Lisbon did not make for comfortable living in Rio. Prince João and his court had a unique opportunity of reaping the rewards of their ancestors' repressive measures. Not even royalty could be well served under the circumstances, no matter how willing and well-disposed the Prince's subjects might be. Prince João and his family and retainers were lodged in a building that had housed the mint and the prison. It had been hastily connected, by a sort of covered way, with the Convent of the Carmelites, to provide a more ample temporary palace. Even so, it was not large enough, and the houses on the opposite side of the Largo do Paço (Palace Square), the largest square in the city, were taken as lodgings for the Princess Carlota Joaquina's ladies in waiting. The arrogant peers of the realm and court officials requisitioned without ceremony the houses of the local gentry, a high-handed proceeding not calculated to endear them to their unwilling hosts.

The demented old Queen who, lost in a supernatural world of shadowy terrors, was unaware of these new surroundings, had only a small chaise in which to ride abroad. Her servants wore old and discolored livery. Her guards wore patched jackets, no waistcoats, gloves, or stockings, and their worn-out boots were never blacked. There were not enough carbines to go around; in place of these, several guards carried old pistols and swords of different designs. Their horses' trappings were pieced together with rawhide. Their helmets and cartridge belts were of so old-fashioned a make that the type had vanished from Europe and could not have been matched even in Portugal.

The Prince Regent had for his own use only an out-of-date single-horse chaise, without the royal arms, and his children used a family carriage said to have been the gift of the King of England. On the old Queen's birthday, when a state ceremony was held, only six carriages could be found in the whole of the city to transport the wealthy families to the feast, and these were all open vehicles, two-wheeled and drawn by mules, driven by dirty Negro slaves. The only other means of conveyance for the well-to-do—everyone else must walk—was a sedan chair suspended from a pole and carried by two slaves.

The town itself was a half-awake place, with a few narrow streets paved with the granite of the surrounding mountains. The houses had one or two stories, made of stone covered with plaster and white-washed. They were roofed with semicircular tiles, the edges laid within each other to form natural channels to carry off the heavy rains. The typical dwelling had a good-sized room floored with boards laid upon beams on the ground. Behind this room were alcoves con-taining beds, for the colonial Brazilian guarded against any danger from the night air by making sure that there were no windows in his sleeping room. The beds were medieval in construction, and the dearth of furniture was noticeable even in houses of the well-to-do. There was usually a sofa of ceremony and some old chairs painted red and white and decorated with wreaths of flowers. The family gathering place was a verandah at the back of the house, and there the women sat, as they sat at dinner or in church, on the floor on mats, lace-making, if they were industrious, or eating sweetmeats, if they were not. At table they ate with their fingers, while the gentle-men, when they visited one another, brought along each his own knife to eat with. The kitchen was at the back of the house, with an enclosed yard. If the master of the house owned a horse, it was stabled in that yard, and quite often there was no other way to get there except through the principal room. Some English merchants who lived above their shops had their floors caulked like the deck of a ship, so that the water used to wash them would not trickle down on the goods stored below. In that hot, humid climate and marshy terrain, a smell of damp characteristically pervaded the house.

The crowds that filled the city's streets were made up largely of half-naked, sweating black slaves, who frightened and disgusted the visiting foreigners. Slaves were not only servants and unskilled laborers; they were also, in many cases, artisans and provided the only means of carrying on what public utilities existed. Frequently they hired out their services to earn money to take home at night, for the income of many a white Brazilian was entirely what his slave could earn. White women were never seen in the streets, except on their way to church, heavily veiled or shouded in covered sedan chairs.

The lawyers and the businessmen congregated in their favorite meeting place, the corner of the Rua do Ouvidor and the Rua da Quitanda (Judge Street and Market Street). They wore rusty old black coats, ill-fitting and patched, gaily colored embroidered waist-coats with deep pockets, tight breeches fastened with square buckles of sham brilliants, stockings of homespun cotton, and enormous buckles on their shoes. On their heads they wore powdered wigs and fantailed hats, and carried old dirks in the place of swords. Even the artisans who were not slaves dressed in this fashion. No one except a slave or a foreigner carried anything in his hand. The only vehicles for transporting merchandise were ox carts and a sort of four-wheeled truck pulled by ten or a dozen Negroes.

The numerous churches and convents and other religious buildings were the only public buildings of note. In their multiplicity and prominence and in the number and variety of religious images set up at street corners and the quantity of ex-votos hung up in the churches, was to be seen another characteristic inheritance from Portugal and of the narrow life forced upon the colony. The only community and social life the inhabitants knew was centered on religious ceremonies.

Dom João VI of Portugal—Prince João, as he was when he landed in Brazil—has not gone down in history as one of the more glorious of the world's monarchs. Yet in an unexpected and effective way he displayed an openness of mind and a generosity of spirit for which Brazilians can be grateful. For all his silent, procrastinating ways, his coming across the water was, for Brazil, a boon and a deliverance. Within a week of his arrival he signed the decree that permitted Brazil to deal directly with the rest of the world. Immediately the harbor of

Rio de Janeiro filled with vessels laden with the products of European countries. Under his rule, the royal government completely reversed its former policy and, instead of inhibiting all chance of a national life, set to work to promote its development. The reasons for this reversal were obvious. Portugal was in the hands of the enemy and its ports were blockaded by the British Navy, which controlled the seas. Anti-Christ ruled Europe and there was some doubt about the eventual return of the Portuguese court to Lisbon.

Under Dom João, the city acquired more of the air of a sophisticated society, not only through his efforts but also as the result of the flood of emigrants, whose coming he encouraged, from Portugal and from the rest of Europe, uneasy with the upheavals of the Napoleonic wars. He was friendly to the idea that Brazil differed from Portugal and not always to the disadvantage of the new country. He was fond of music, and he had brought his own string orchestra to play in the royal chapel and his band of players to give theatrical performances at the Palace. He founded schools, set up a royal printing press, opened a library and a national museum and school of fine arts. He also founded the Botanical Garden, ever since a jewel among the beauties of Rio, set up for the useful purpose of acclimating new plants intended for the colony's agricultural development. He established a post office by means of which communication was at least possible, if not easy, with all parts of the Portuguese dominions. He repealed regulations which hampered the industrial activities of the gold and diamond mines.

The Brazilians had greeted him on arrival with sentimental affection, which grew, fostered by the many changes he wrought, in spite of the arrogance of his Portuguese courtiers. By 1816, when the court held a function, the wealthy and the great came in court dress, new and even splendid, and in well-made carriages drawn by horses and attended by white servants instead of black slaves. On state occasions Dom João held his levees on a balcony of the Palace, so that he might be seen by the crowd that gathered beneath. He was less afraid of the Brazilians, less fearful of assassination, than he had been in Portugal; he knew he was much more popular with his colonial subjects than he had ever been at home. Because he required it, Brazilian women began to appear at social functions, awkward, illiterate, ignorant as they were from centuries of a harem-like existence. Rio was a much gayer place after his arrival. He abolished the dreary-looking shutters that masked the fronts of houses; his political caution made him fear ambuscades. There were now three booksellers in the city, and an official newspaper was published every week in the royal printing house. The city itself had doubled in size. The illiteracy rate among the white people had fallen, for the migration of refugees from Europe had provided a good supply of school teachers.

The influx of newcomers from Europe helped also in improving the city's food supply. Many of these emigrants settled in the suburbs and became market gardeners. By 1820 the diet of the Cariocas (the inhabitants of the city of Rio) had become varied and plentiful, as well as substantial. The inevitable black beans and rice and farinha (the flour made of the mandioca root) were still the staff of life, but fruit was good and cheap, and vegetables, poultry, and meat of good quality were to be had. The oysters and crabs, said well-traveled visitors, were as good as any found anywhere else in the world, and the Cariocas were particular about their bread, which was made of flour shipped from the United States.

Perhaps no one element was more responsible for the new sophistication in the city than the large French colony. The French had come first in 1813, the year the Bourbons had been restored to the throne of France, and again in 1816, when the American ship, the *Caliph*, had brought a number of families from Le Havre. Among them were professors for Dom João's new academy of arts and sciences. There were also jewelers, dressmakers, pastrycooks, watchmakers, booksellers, and various other craftsmen skilled in the crafts for which the French were famous. By 1818 there were said to be fourteen thousand of them in Rio. Altogether they had a hundred and forty shops, where such things as mirrors, ornamental clocks, enameled china vases, brocade curtains could be obtained for the first time in Rio. These gave an elegance and a touch of the great world especially to the Rua do Ouvidor (Judge Street) and the Rua dos Ourives (Goldsmiths' Street) which these streets never afterward entirely lost, even when their French shopkeepers had long since gone.

By 1822, Queen Maria I of Portugal was dead, Dom João had reluctantly gone back to Portugal, and his son Pedro ruled in Brazil as Regent. Pedro was a clever, impulsive, capricious man who had spent most of his life in Brazil. He resented the attempt of the Portuguese parliament, now that the menace of Napoleon was removed, to shut off Brazil again behind the customs house at Lisbon, once more a colony entirely dependent on the mother country. He refused to return to Lisbon when summoned and instead seized the opportunity to proclaim Brazil an independent empire and himself its first emperor. He began his reign with the enthusiastic support of the Brazilians.

In the following decade he was to lose that popularity and become more and more embroiled in the intrigues surrounding the succession to the throne of Portugal. In the end these troubles, compounded by the political restlessness growing in Brazil itself, would result in his abdication in favor of his five-year-old son and the establishment of another regency. But for the moment all was dramatic optimism, affectionate acclaim in a capital city gradually acquiring a worldly sophistication.

CHAPTER II

YOUNG
AMBITION'S
LADDER

THE SUN of a morning late in 1822 rose on Guanabara Bay. The haze, dispersing, was like a curtain rising on one of the most spectacular stages of the world. The calm waters sparkled, a deep blue as vivid as the high clear blue of the sky, accented by little fleecy clouds that came and went near the horizon. All around rose abruptly the granite peaks, tinged purple in the hazy light, the Hunchback, the Sugarloaf, and the lesser hills covered by a dense and deeply green subtropical vegetation. In the western crescent of the bay, well-sheltered from the sea, lay Saint Sebastian's city, the modern Rio de Janeiro, its churches and monasteries, forts and houses, gleaming whitely against the green of the mountains rising perpendicularly behind it, while at its feet shone its fine, curving, sandy beaches. The mirror-like waters of the bay were dotted with white sails—throngs of them, which in their number constituted the first vital modern fact in the history of the city: the opening of the ports of Brazil to the world's trade.

Even a nine-year-old boy could feel the splendor of that scene, which many travelers, familiar with other magnificent corners of the earth, have praised as beyond their powers adequately to describe. Irineu Evangelista de Sousa watched the morning break and the mountains appear as he stood on the deck of his uncle's bark out in the roads. What thoughts were his at that moment he never afterward recorded, but his feelings must have been a mixture of awe, dismay, and the exhilaration that novelty produces in adventurous youth.

He had come from far, from the south, to begin a new life. His old life was gone, down in Rio Grande do Sul. There he had been born on December 28, 1813, on his father's small ranch in the parish of Nossa Senhora da Conceição de Arroio Grande (Our Lady of the Conception in Arroio Grande). That parish was in what was then the captaincy (for Brazil was still a colony of Portugal and was divided into administrative areas called captaincies) of São Pedro do Rio Grande do Sul, a few miles from the border of the modern Republic of Uruguay.

His father, João Evangelista de Avila e Sousa, had died by violence, either murdered by cattle thieves on a journey south to sell his animals or killed by an accidental bullet, fired from ambush at a friend riding at his side. Irineu's mother, Dona Mariana Batista de Carvalho, had remarried. Perhaps—but this is on the whole unlikely—Irineu had had two years of schooling in the city of São Paulo, the capital of what by then had become the province of São Paulo and the principal city of southern Brazil. Family tradition declares that his mother was of Dutch extraction, probably the descendant of settlers from the Low Countries who had populated the Azores during the reign of Charles V, the Holy Roman Emperor and inheritor of most of the thrones of western Europe. People from the Azores had been among the first settlers, in turn, of the great plains in the southernmost part of Brazil. There was also the legend that his grandfather had lived to be a hundred years old and in the end died by a fall from his horse. These facts and surmises are all that is known of the childhood and ancestry of Irineu.

It was his uncle, a captain in the India trade, which linked Portugal to her overseas empire, who brought him to Rio. Captain João Batista de Carvalho stopped regularly in the Brazilian ports on his passage between Portugal and the East. This time he had his small nephew with him, and though he had his cargo and was ready to sail on the voyage that lasted, in its entire length, about eight months, he dallied a day or so. It was his intention to apprentice the boy to a trade, to give him a start in life.

Apprenticeship to some trade was the only way to independence for a boy who had neither important family connections nor money. Schooling was out of the question, unless the boy was to go with the priests and friars. Uncle João was a mariner and perhaps he suggested that Irineu should follow the sea. Perhaps Irineu's mother did not wish her son to be a sailor. Perhaps, when Uncle João's vessel had left the south and reached Rio, Irineu had himself decided that a sea-faring life would not suit him. The only other means of livelihood his uncle could readily find him was as a clerk to a merchant. As captain of a trading vessel, Uncle João was no doubt well known to the merchants of Rio. He would soon find a berth ashore for the youngster.

Even for a boy of independent spirit the outlook was grim. When his uncle's bark sailed for India, he would be on his own, placed among strangers in a strange city, which, for all its slovenly ways, was still a great metropolis to a boy from the sparsely settled cattle country of the south. Not only was he to live among strangers, with no friend and no kin within easy reach of letters, but he was to work for his living fifteen or sixteen hours a day as a clerk in a shop.

For the moment the novelty of the situation probably disguised for him the gloomier side of things. Here there was a great bustle on the quay side, great crowds of people in the streets, more vessels in the harbor than he ever imagined to exist. He and his uncle went ashore early; once the cool of the morning was past it was well to put aside the thought of doing business. The day would become hot and airless. Perhaps in the afternoon a violent storm would break, first with large splashing drops and the crackle of lightning, then in torrents of water that would deluge the streets, while the thunder rolled mightily from mountain to mountain. Like all other travelers of that day, they had to be rowed ashore, for Rio had as yet no dock-side at which ocean-going vessels might tie up.

They used the common landing, the stairs of the Customs House, which led them at once into the heart of the city. It was not the Rua do Ouvidor, with its new French shops, that they sought, but the Rua da Quitanda, the principal street of the Portuguese merchants. Formerly these Lusitanians had had a monopoly of the retail trade of the city, and even now their habits had not changed, although they felt the competition of the newcomers, the crowds of Europeans who had followed the Portuguese court from Lisbon to Rio in flight from Napoleon. The Portuguese shops were characteristic. At each shop door was a long bench, in the daytime covered with goods on display. In the evening this became a seat for the merchant and his cronies as they played backgammon, often for high stakes. Gambling of one sort or another was the characteristic vice of Brazilians, said visitors. At seven in the morning the merchant went to the warehouse and there he chose his stocks from the new merchandise brought in by the English importers. After breakfast he sat in his shop, but business was desultory. After an unceremonious meal at noon, he took a *sesta* or nap, as did most of his fellow citizens.

So deep and unshakeable was the conservatism of the average Portuguese merchant that even the great changes made in the city during the past few years had failed to make any essential difference in his habits. Rio had acquired a little of the bustle of a European city. Its new houses were larger and more spacious than the old. There were a few English retail shops, chiefly saddlers and fancy grocers, besides the French shops with their luxuries. But the Portuguese merchant remained apathetic under the new pressure of business. If he was engaged in talking politics or reading his newspapers or perhaps only enjoying a cool seat in the back of his shop on a warm day, he would often say to his customer that he did not have the article called for, rather than get up and look for it. If the customer, anxious to have the article and doubtful of finding it in any other shop in the city, insisted, the merchant, as likely as not, would tell him to find it for himself among the wares and to lay the money down on the counter.

These Portuguese merchants had in general a reputation for honesty and correctness in their dealings, of being good if strict husbands and fathers, and generous to the local charities. But in their business dealings they betrayed the deep effects of the semibarbarous darkness in which it had served Portugal to keep her Brazilian colony. The use of any new article had to be explained to them, no matter how simple and obvious its operation. Their stocks were scanty and they were unused to any commercial bustle. Their shops, occupying the whole front of their houses, were usually eighteen feet square, with two doors as the only means of letting in light and air, doors which were never shut except while the merchant ate dinner and at night. The front of the shop was empty and the counter at the back always ran from wall to wall, parallel with the street. A strong old table stood behind the counter and on it goods were displayed or stored. The sides of the shop, to the height of three feet, were usually fitted with drawers and above these were glass cases, gaudily painted, one of the few uses to which window glass was put in Brazil.

The shopkeeper and his servants ate and slept in the close damp rooms that were the shop. The master sometimes had a bed. His clerks and slaves slept on the counter or on the floor. The counter was also the table for the noonday meal, sent up from the kitchen and eaten in a hurry.

It was just such a shop in which Uncle João placed Irineu. No record remains of the name and character of his first master, but family tradition declared that the shop was a very small affair, dealing in candles and tea. Whatever it was, it was to be home and school for the boy from the south. Tradition also preserved Irineu's own reminiscence, told to his children and grandchildren, that he sent his mother his small wage, that he slept on the counter of the shop, and that a kind customer of his master's, doubtless seeing a spark in the boy, lent him books which he studied at night under the fish-oil lamp before his master's door. That same friend, now anonymous, also helped him to learn accountancy, French, and other things when his master was not by.

He did not stay long in this first place. When he was eleven he became clerk to a dry-goods merchant, João Rodrigues (sometimes called Antonio José) Pereira de Almeida, listed in the businessmen's almanac of the Brazilian empire of that period (1824-1827) as having his place of business at number 155 Rua Direita (Straight Street, today called the Rua Primeiro de Marco, First of March Street). Irineu was with Almeida for four years. By the time he was thirteen he had become cashier, a trusted clerk who had charge of the keys of the strongbox. For a boy left on his own in a strange city, ignorant and friendless, he had done very well for himself.

Another change soon confronted him. In 1829 Almeida went bankrupt. His shop was closed, his goods sold up to satisfy his creditors. In the bankruptcy proceedings Irineu met the man who was to make the biggest change in his life, an English merchant by the name of Richard Carruthers.

CHAPTER III

THE ENGLISH MERCHANT

D OM JOÃO VI may well be called the first modernizer of Brazil. But he did not act alone in bringing new ideas and new manners to the colony. One of his most powerful allies was the English merchant, to whom he opened wide the door of trade with his principal colony.

The English merchant in Brazil inherited a long history of privilege in Portugal. In fact, Portugal had had an interest for English traders ever since the twelfth century, when the English crusaders, in helping to establish the new kingdom of Portugal, opened the way for trading relations between the two countries that went through many vicissitudes but never actually stopped during the next eight hundred years.

The opening of the ports of Brazil to the commerce of the world, which was Dom João's first step on arriving in the New World, meant really that they were opened to English commerce, since the British Navy controlled the seas and had blockaded Europe. English trade with Brazil boomed. In London the Portuguese minister called upon merchants who wanted to do business with Brazil to attend a meeting at which he would preside. One hundred and thirteen London merchants joined the association so formed, and later a permanent committee of the Association of English Merchants Trading with Brazil was elected, composed of sixteen members, two of whom were members of Parliament.

On February 19, 1810, after long negotiations and in spite of threats from the papal nuncio, Dom João signed a treaty with England which gave her the position of the most favored nation. Goods imported into Brazil from England were to pay much lower duties than those from other countries. One provision of the treaty established special judges conservator to try all cases involving British subjects. Another, to which the papal nuncio had objected strongly, provided that the English should have the right to worship as Protestants in their houses or in churches and chapels built by them, although such places were to be disguised as private dwellings and could not have bells. The treaty, though useful to the English merchants, was a source of irritation in the relations between England and Brazil for many years. It had been intended by Dom João merely as a protective measure for his throne, which needed its only prop, England. It did not fit conditions when Brazil became the seat of the court. Nevertheless, when Dom João returned to Lisbon the treaty still stood. Under it English merchants had transferred to Brazil all the special rights they had enjoyed in Portugal.

In spite of the disadvantages of the 1810 treaty, Brazil benefited from the commerce it encouraged. The Brazilians eagerly bought stout broadcloth, hats, boots, earthenware, glass, mirrors, silks, cottons, linens, and woolens. Cheshire cheeses, hams, salt, and drugs were items of luxury they much appreciated. In the crowd of foreigners that followed Dom João to Rio were many Englishmen, madly speculating in this flourishing new market. They came in such numbers and brought such a strange assortment of goods that before long the market at Rio was overflowing with imports, many of them unsuitable for the people and the country that were supposed to absorb them. The Brazilians who visited the customs house goggled and laughed at the blankets, the warming pans, and even ice skates that arrived in the boxes from London and Liverpool. Many a merchant, in haste to make a fortune, had shipped out to Brazil the last sweepings from the shops and warehouses of London, which he had ransacked in his eagerness to find stock. Some of these things, it is true, found uses their makers had not intended. Warming pans were used for boiling sugar in the sugar mills, and ice skates were hammered into knives and other hard-to-come-by objects, for they were made of iron and well-tempered steel, unobtainable in Brazil.

It seemed a heaven-sent opportunity for the trader. First, there was the perfect harbor, a matter of the highest importance to the masters of sailing vessels. The Sugarloaf marked the entrance through the broad, bold, deep channel into the landlocked bay, secure from gales at all seasons of the year. So safe was the passage into the bay that Rio was the only harbor in the world where pilots were not used. The land and sea breezes were so regular, strong, and steady that a sailing vessel might be almost certain of being able to sail in with one in the evening and out with the other in the morning. Though in the tropics, it did not suffer from all the fevers that harried sailors in other tropical ports, and water, wood, and provisions were to be had easily. Besides all this, there was its position, strategically on the most convenient route westward from the Atlantic to the Pacific by way of the Horn. No wonder the English merchants flocked to the new trading post.

The newcomers joined the old inhabitants of the colony of English merchants already established in Rio. During the more than one hundred years that had elapsed since the first treaty permitted English merchants to enter Brazil, these English had continued to live in the ports of the country, often with their families. With the mixture of tenacity, hardiness, and faith in the ultimate support of the British fleet with which English merchants throughout the queer corners of the world endured the reverses and neglect of their own government, they had survived to form, during the first years of the nineteenth century, a nucleus for a thriving colony in Brazil.

Brazil benefited from the confusion that prevailed in post-Napoleonic Europe. She achieved her independence with little disturbance to the every-day life of the country. Neither Portugal nor any other European power, except England, was in a position to prevent the establishment of Dom Pedro's empire. Even the Brazilians were surprised at the failure of the British to help the Portuguese in America.

But the British, with their mercantile interests foremost and always acutely aware of the fact that their role as a great power was entirely dependent on the flourishing of their trade, favored an independent Brazil, a new market free from the trammels of a colony.

The question of recognition of the new empire by foreign powers was another matter. The United States was the first to recognize the new nation. President Monroe made his official declaration on May 26, 1824. Recognition by Portugal was more complicated. There was nothing Portugal could do to prevent Brazil from being independent, but the matter of the succession to the throne of Brazil was bound up with the succession to the throne of Portugal. The Portuguese had required Dom João to come reluctantly home from his more easygoing, more comfortable court in Rio. Now his son and heir had tied himself up with the future of Brazil in a way that seemed to make it impossible for him to return to Portugal. On the other hand, Dom João and his ministers were willing to go to any lengths to prevent the king's second son Miguel, his mother's darling and the champion of absolutism and the Holy Alliance, from mounting the Portuguese throne. Portugal was under British domination and frightened by Austria, whose emperor was the father-in-law of Dom Pedro I.

The master of the situation was the British prime minister, Canning, and he had with him in London the able Brazilian agent, Felisberto Caldeira Brant Pontes, later the Marquess of Barbacena. Barbacena had been given no funds and little authority, but he was the erstwhile boon companion of Dom Pedro I and a shrewd negotiator. Through the combined efforts of the Brazilian and the Englishman, the Portuguese were talked into recognizing Brazilian independence as a *fait accompli* and in joining with the British in sending Sir Charles Stuart to Rio as an agent for both governments. The treaty was signed on August 29, 1825. It was a spectacular triumph for Brazil, since article fifty declared that "His Most Faithful Majesty recognizes Brazil as an independent empire and separate from the kingdoms of Portugal and Algarves."

These services, naturally, were not to go without payment, so far as the British were concerned. After considerable negotiation, in 1828, Brazil and England signed a new treaty to take the place of the old one of 1810, which established the full price, in commercial privileges, that Brazil was to pay for her recognition by England as an independent power. Besides a most-favored-nation clause, it provided for an *ad valorem* duty on English merchandise of 15 percent, in contrast to the 24 percent required of all other foreign merchandise. The office of judge conservator, which had become extinct in 1818, was revived. As a result of the treaty of 1828, an immense flood of manufactured goods reached Rio. Cottons, ginghams, silks, caps, shirts, shawls, gloves, hats, stockings, shoes, dressing cases, looking glasses, knives, hammers, needles and pins, muskets, barometers, pianos, drinking glasses, decanters, and thousands of other things flowed through its port into the New World.

The 1828 treaty was the last of the skillful and patient maneuvers in which the urbane, imperturbable Viscount Strangford acted as Fate to the new empire of Brazil. A numerous train of official and unofficial persons followed him to Rio on this occasion. Among them was one Richard Carruthers, who, as an English merchant, well versed in commercial dealings with the Portuguese, thus represented several hundreds of years of history.

Carruthers came to set up in business as an importer, to take advantage of the privileged position that the 1828 treaty offered English merchants. The English merchants did not make as much impression on the life of the city as did the French people, for, though English goods were ubiquitous, the Englishman was not. Being chiefly a wholesaler, the English merchant did not go in for elegant shops and he made no display. His goods were either packed up in the warehouses or on display in shops run by the Portuguese.

Richard Carruthers was an exception to this last rule, because he had a shop in the Rua Direita. He had done business in Portugal. He had two brothers who were wine merchants in Portugal, and one of them, at least, had a Portuguese partner. Carruthers himself had extensive connections in the financial world of Manchester, the great English market place for trade with the New World.

A surviving photograph of Richard Carruthers shows him as a reserved, tight-lipped, unshakeable old man, his lined face framed in the semicircle of white whiskers fashionable for elderly Englishmen in the middle of the nineteenth century. Such a man would not have run off incontinently to the New World at the first sign of an open market, with a hastily assembled store of warming pans and ice skates to sell to the inhabitants of the tropics. His protégé Irineu described him in later years, when Irineu himself was an old man harking back to his own early beginnings: "One of the best types among humanity, in the character of an old English merchant, noteworthy for his absolute honesty and belonging to the old school of positive morality."

Just what he meant by "the old school of positive morality" is obscure. Perhaps he meant that Carruthers was, in economic philosophy, a disciple of Henri Saint Simon, the eccentric Frenchman who survived the terrors of the French revolution to invent a new theory of society, based on government by businessmen and scientists, in the place of statesmen and churchmen. "Positive morality," however, is a vague term, much invoked in the early nineteenth-century discussion of a new world emerging in the machine age. What is known of Carruthers leads as well to another conclusion. He was firm, not unkindly, but certainly not expansive, impulsive, or visionary. It is plain from the training he gave Irineu that he disapproved of impractical fancies, that he had a steady belief in a decent way of living for everyone, even his clerks, and generosity in providing for the younger generation. He also had the Scotsman's belief in the value of education and the indispensibility of material well-being as the basis for every other sort of well-being. It seems, therefore, more likely that, if he subscribed to any doctrine, it was to Benthamism and the utopia of the greatest good for the greatest number, based on honest, diligent work. He was also, in all probability, well acquainted with the theories of Adam Smith, whose influence had been felt in the Brazil of the last years of the eighteenth century. In his personal life, he belied any implication of dourness and want of sympathy for the impetuous, spontaneous, often passionate people among whom he spent a greater part of his life. For he maintained a Brazilian household and begot a Brazilian son whom he left behind him when he retired to Carlisle.

Carruthers was a creditor of Pereira de Almeida, Irineu's Portuguese master, when that worthy merchant went bankrupt in 1829. When

Almeida called a meeting of his creditors, Carruthers was one of those present to hear him, with the scrupulous care of a strictly honest man, offer all his assets, including his dwelling house and his wife's jewels, in payment of his debts. An awkward silence greeted the offer. In that small and closely knit community of merchants, where every man's reputation was known, Almeida was respected and his creditors were sympathetic. They were embarrassed, in fact, until Carruthers relieved the tension with a generous declaration. In England, he said, a man's home was his castle. It was the refuge in which he could gather his forces again to confront the world.

"You had better keep your house and your wife her jewels," said Carruthers. "We can do without them." Once phrased, the idea was agreeable to the other creditors. They were glad to see old Almeida save something for himself.

Gratitude to Carruthers mingled with another emotion in Almeida. His character being what it was, he felt a pang over the blighted future of his promising young clerk Irineu. He gave painful thought to the boy's prospects. Finally he solved the matter in a simple fashion. He took Irineu to the Englishman and said, "I give you an excellent clerk."

So simply are the lines of men's lives sometimes laid down. At fifteen Irineu not only had a new job and a new master. He had crossed the threshold of a career that was to take him far beyond the simple dreams and commonplace hopes that had been his when he first arrived in Rio. To Carruthers he soon was much more than a new clerk. He was a pupil, a prop for old age, almost a son, certainly an heir. By 1831 the firm of Carruthers and Company, at number 84 Rua Direita, was doing a thriving business. That year a new crisis arose in the history of Brazil. For Dom Pedro I, Dom João's eldest son, had finally abdicated the throne of the new empire of Brazil, overwhelmed by political troubles and anxious to secure the throne of Portugal for his daughter. He had abdicated and gone to Europe, leaving his five-year-old son Emperor of Brazil in his stead and the government of the country in the hands of a regency. The situation was touch-and-go, for the country was in a turmoil, the monarchy without prestige, and Brazil was surrounded on every side by peoples who had not only set themselves up as republics independent of Spain, but who, in doing so, had split up the old political divisions of the Spanish dominions. It seemed hardly likely that Brazil would escape a similar fragmentation. To the south, in Irineu's native province, civil war had broken out among men whose dislike of the central government in Rio was strong enough to lead them to secession.

But in the meantime, Carruthers and Company flourished, and its new clerk spent the last and most valuable years of his apprenticeship.

CHAPTER IV

SENHOR IRINEU

IRINEU was sixteen years old when he joined the firm of Carruthers and Company, a quiet, discreet boy, old for his years, with the smattering of an education that he had largely acquired himself. It was not long before he was old man Carruthers' devoted disciple as well as his clerk, absorbing from him the habits of thought of an English merchant.

The discerning old merchant was a careful husbandman where he saw good soil. In a few years the boy, who had grown up in a shop, working from seven in the morning until ten at night, when the bells of the nearby church told him it was time to close up, became a modern man of business. He learned to believe in the power of money. He learned to consider political interests purely in their effect on commercial and industrial enterprise. He learned to believe in economic liberalism. He learned to think, to read, to count, in English so thoroughly that it became his own language, the language in which he talked to himself in moments of business anxiety and the language in which he cursed. He excused this latter habit, in after years, by saying that he did not like so to abuse his native Portuguese.

Carruthers, in thus proceeding with Irineu's education, was neither haphazard nor capricious. He had a purpose well in mind.

"After I had given evidence," said Irineu, describing the situation in later years, "in his service, of ability, he chose me to be partner in his firm, when I was still a beardless boy, placing me thus early in my commercial career in a position in which I could develop those talents that perhaps lay hidden in me."

Within a year after Irineu was raised to the status of partner, Carruthers left for England. His thoughts had been turning toward home. He had been in Rio eight years, a long time for a man with business interests elsewhere. He had been a middle-aged man, a successful merchant, a bold speculator in new commercial fields, when he came to the New World to found this branch of his house. Now he was ready to retire, and he had beside him this trustworthy, intelligent, able young associate. He turned the business over to Irineu and sailed for Liverpool. He left behind him, besides his impress on Irineu's character and career, his firm, a reputation as an amateur painter in oils, and an illegitimate son.

He went home to Carlisle, where he built himself a fine house in what his relatives and neighbors considered to be a "Spanish" style, surrounded by forty acres of parkland. There on the banks of the river Eden he spent the rest of his days, fishing and dabbling in oil painting, to his less traveled relatives the traditional wealthy uncle whose riches had been gained in that mysterious and still outlandish part of the world known as South America. In the end he married his housekeeper and begot another son to inherit his worldly possessions.

In the meantime, the "beardless boy" in whose capable hands he had left his business dealings in Brazil, was not slow in striking out for himself. When the old man had first left for England, Irineu had had some doubt about how he would be accepted as manager of the firm by the other clerks, some of them Englishmen and older than himself. He attacked the problem boldly and with a dash of extravagance. First he rented and later bought a large house, with extensive grounds, on the still wild Santa Teresa Hill, a small mountain that rises sharply from the inner edge of the city.

It was an eccentric thing to do. Wealthy Brazilians, whose principal business was in Rio, might have country lodges up on the mountain, where the air was purer and the virgin forest did not harbor the fevers and distempers of the city in summer. The English merchants nearly all lived out of the city in the suburbs, if they could afford to relax supervision over their businesses, and traveled into town two or three times a week. But no one had considered the idea of commuting every day down the mountain and home again in the same day. There was not even a regular road. Horses or mules were the only means of getting up and down, unless one walked. Yet every evening Irineu climbed the steep passageway and stone steps by the side of the Convent of St. Anthony to reach his airy dwelling.

He liked the fresher air and had acquired new ideas about the benefit of better living conditions on the quality of work among the employees of a firm under his management. The house on Santa Teresa was run as a club, where the dirt and noise of the city were exchanged for the reviving quiet of the country. He instituted also the "English week," which meant the English weekend. To the Portuguese merchants Sunday was as much a day for business as any other. In fact, in Rio Sunday was preferred for auction sales. The English wholesale firms closed on Sundays, their owners being as fixed in their national habits as the Portuguese. Irineu went them all one better. Carruthers and Company closed at three in the afternoon of Saturday and the whole staff left the city to go up the mountain for the weekend.

Irineu himself used this leisure for reading. He was a young man with a purpose in life, and he had no time to waste. He studied English literature with one of the English clerks of the firm, an educated man with whom he could read Shakespeare and Milton. His custom on Sunday was to choose a comfortable corner of the wide verandah, from which he no doubt had a view of the magnificent bay sparkling quietly in the brilliant sun, surrounded by the abruptly rising, dark green, granite mountains, the freshening breeze reaching him from the ocean beyond. Here he would sit and read—read anything he could get his hands on, books in Portuguese, in French, in English, as well as magazines specializing in metallurgy, steam navigation, the railroads of England and the United States. He read, and his eager mind reached

out for more. The spirit of adventure and the determination to conquer his environment were native to him. He had, besides, a native
prudence that tempered this youthful eagerness. His head was full of
dreams, but he knew that to realize them he must first lay a firm foundation.

He did not remain obscure. He was the managing partner of one
of the soundest English mercantile houses in Rio, with a considerable
fortune for so young a man. He was the particular friend of the
businessmen in the English colony, to whom he was known, with the
characteristic imperviousness of the English tongue to the phonetics
of foreign speech, as Sinyor Irenneo. As early as 1835 his name
appears in an important commercial document. Together with his old
Portuguese master, Pereira de Almeida, and a number of other leading merchants, he signed as a shareholder a composition made by the
receivers of the liquidated Bank of Brazil. Besides this achievement of
an important place as a merchant in the city, he was, like many educated Brazilians of the day, a Freemason and as such inevitably active
in public affairs.

The world of Rio was broadening—politically as well as commer-
cially. The years of Dom Pedro II's minority, the 1830's, were uneasy
years for the new empire. Two problems, which were to remain until
the last decade of the century, were in constant ferment. That in international affairs centered in the slave trade. That in national affairs
was the powerful separatist movement, disguised as federalism, in
the southern province of Rio Grande do Sul, Irineu's native land. Behind the façade of the successful merchant, rumor had it, Senhor
Irineu had a finger in both these pies. He was a *farroupilha* (the nickname given the horsemen of the southern plains in allusion to their
cowboy's chaps with fringed edges, for *farrapos* literally means rags,
and *farroupilha*, ragamuffin), a partisan of the separatists in the War
of the Farrapos. Even years afterwards he was accused of giving
clandestine support to the separatist movement in his native province,
of cozening the Farroupilhas, among whom his own relatives might
well have been. His was said to be the "hidden hand" which in 1838
and 1839 fed and clothed thirty-three prisoners from the south who
had been shut up in the fortress of Santa Cruz, in the mouth of

Guanabara Bay, subsisting on a daily portion of watery soup and a handful of weevily black beans and farinha. It was said that in those convenient woods of his Santa Teresa property, the messengers of Teófilo Otoni, a leader in the republican movement in the province of Minas Gerais, escaped the police.

Much was made of this active but unavowed aid he was said to have given to the political movement that provided one of the most serious threats to the unity and integrity of Brazil during the difficult years of Dom Pedro II's minority. In 1842 he was still only a businessman, the managing partner of a foreign commercial house, but the legend of his political influence had become strong. So persistent and so open were such opinions that Irineu, now twenty-nine years old, felt called upon to publish a statement in the *Jornal do Comércio*, the most important newspaper in Brazil, denying that he had any influence with the great men of the conservative party, whom he named: The Marquesses of Paraná and Mont'Alegre, the Viscounts Uruguai and Itaboraí, and the senator Eusebio de Queiroz, shortly thereafter Minister of Justice; all of them men with whom he had many dealings when he first branched out into the career of an industrialist. In this statement he denied that he was a party man and declared that, if these men honored him with their friendship, he was equally friendly with some of contrary political views. He had vowed himself, he said, to the material betterment of his country.

Party politics, as old Carruthers would have said, were not for successful businessmen.

He was also an abolitionist. No more mischievous a source of irritation between England and Brazil than the problem of the slave trade could have been devised by the most malign spirit. The England of the early nineteenth century had a large and articulate middle class so imbued with the reforming spirit that it was convinced that traffic in human beings was a blasphemous sin whoever practiced it. At the same time, in the realm of economics, the English concept of a prosperous commercial world contained as a necessary premise the idea that slavery was uneconomic. The combination of these two points of view, the disinterested and the interested together, made for such

pressure on the British Parliament as could not be gainsaid by any
government. The former group, the moralists, felt a missionary zeal
in forcing other nations to desist from what was to them an abomi-
nable traffic; and the latter, the merchants and the manufacturers,
eager to sell their products to a wage-earning consuming public, were
equally sincere. There were, also, the people who had invested money
in the West Indies and who suffered from the competition of slave-
run sugar plantations.

All of these ignored, or failed to take into account, the fact that
Negro slavery was an integral part of the development of Brazil as a
source of wealth for Portugal and the Portuguese settlers. Much more
than in Spanish America, Negroes in Brazil had taken the place of
the Indians as the labor needed to cultivate the land and work the
mines. Both mines and sugar-growing were enterprises that devoured
the labor supply as fast as it became available. Brazil was so thoroughly a slavocracy that to abolish slavery would have been to pre-
cipitate as complete a social upheaval as an economic one.

No white man who aspired to any dignity worked for his living.
He might hold political appointments or in a desultory way practice
one of the learned professions. If he did not draw his income from
a plantation, he bought slaves and set them to work for him, as porters
or skilled workmen in the cities. So sensitive had Brazilians become on
this score that an English visitor in the early years of the nineteenth
century recorded the incident of a young Brazilian who was asked
whether he had a job and who left the room in a towering passion,
saying that in Brazil no respectable man worked; they had slaves for
that. It was not surprising that there was no common ground in this
subject for such Brazilians and an English public educated to view
slavery either with horror or as an economic anachronism.

Many Brazilians were uneasy about harboring this anachronism
in their country. The most distinguished of early Brazilian statesmen,
José Bonifacio de Andrada e Silva, Dom Pedro I's first minister and
the tutor of Dom Pedro II, was bitterly and uncompromisingly opposed to slavery. As the century went on, the growth of this sentiment among Brazilians became the principal reason for the decline
and final abolition of the traffic and the institution. But, in the mean-

time, the abolitionist sentiment was associated with the troublesome political elements of republicanism and separatism, particularly in the south of the country, and with the machinations of foreigners, particularly the English. The misunderstanding created over it between the Brazilian and the British governments caused irreparable damage to the friendship and especially to the commercial relations between the two countries.

Opposition to slavery was one of the things Irineu learned from Carruthers. The idea, in fact, became a fundamental principle of his economic and social thinking. Throughout his life he was to maintain that one of Brazil's greatest needs was a free laboring class. His contracts undertaken with the government for public works invariably included the phrase until then used only in contracts with Englishmen: the contractor binds himself not to use slave labor. He was always the exponent of immigration schemes to bring free white labor into the country. In common with a few other Brazilians of his day, he realized the terrible significance of importing thousands of African slaves into a wild, underpopulated country barely conquered by Europeans. He was under no illusions concerning the effect of the institution of slavery on the mass of white and mulatto people who were free but poor. Only a small percentage of the population—the landowning families—could be benefited economically by such a system. Even to them and certainly to the country as a whole, socially, physically, and morally, slavery could only be a curse.

Irineu's personal feelings on the subject were so strong that he helped runaway slaves to escape from their masters and supplied them with false papers as evidence of their freedom, allowing them to hide in the wild grounds of his Santa Teresa property until the way to liberty was clear. Gabriel Terra, at one time the president of the Republic of Uruguay and the son of a close friend and business associate of Irineu's, recalled in later years an incident that occurred when Irineu came to visit in the elder Terra's house. One of the servants there was a Negro who had been freed by Irineu and who now ran forward to kiss his hand.

"I remember very well," said Terra, "the quickness with which he avoided this humiliating and debasing gesture, catching the man in

his arms to give him the embrace of one equal to another, so that
the man broke down and wept on his shoulder."

It was about this time—the year 1839—that he decided to bring his
mother away from the dangers of life on the border. She was again
a widow, having lost the husband for whose sake she had been willing
to dispose of both her children. The motives and the reasons behind
these early family changes may best be understood in the light of the
conditions and opinions of the times. A young woman left a widow in
the violent, unstable country of the southern border would naturally
seek another husband, for protection, if for no other reason. The man
Dona Mariana selected apparently objected to taking on a family.
She lost no time, therefore, in marrying off her twelve-year-old
daughter—it was not an unusually early age in that primitive period
and country—and in sending Irineu off to Rio with her brother the
ship captain. For Irineu her choice had turned out a lucky thing.
Down in the prairies of the south, where his life would probably have
mirrored his father's, his gifts would have been lost in the obscure
and violent life of the ranch.

His sister, Dona Guilhermina de Sousa Machado, was widowed
early, too, nor was she entirely forgiving toward her mother, for
family tradition declares that Irineu had often to play the part of
referee between them in the constant little irascible quarrels that
arose in the household. For Irineu, shortly after sending for his
mother, sent for his sister and her daughter, ten-year-old Maria
Joaquina. With such a family on his hands, he found the lodge on the
mountain impracticable. He moved to a big, colonial house down near
the waterfront in the vicinity of Gloria Church, a house now replaced
by a school, within a stone's throw from the Catete Palace, which now
houses the executive offices of the President of Brazil.

He was growing busier, too, because he had other new ideas. He
had decided to go to England to visit his old patron and friend. Three
years had gone by since Carruthers had retired to his new house, Eden
Grove, near Carlisle, and this seemed a suitable opportunity to see
the world. It is a little difficult now to imagine what that first trip

abroad must have meant to the energetic young Brazilian merchant. Coming out of Brazil must have meant coming out of a sleepy, intellectually but barely aroused world, where life was in the main still primitive, amenities few. Going abroad was a journey ahead in time as well as across space.

In Rio he had been used to a society that did not believe in allowing the women of the family abroad except when heavily guarded; that depended for its livelihood and comfort on a multitude of black slaves; that lived in stone colonial houses, likely to be damp and musty and sparsely furnished; that dressed with great ceremony and, at the same time, with great negligence; that was inured to filthy streets, poor pavements, no sewers, and poor street lighting. He was used also to a fine, warm climate, spontaneity of emotion in the people around him, and the tantalizing sense of a vast country beyond the town, untouched, abundant in lumber, metals, food—a paradise of plenty locked away out of reach by the lack of any means of transportation.

In England he stepped into a brisker, harsher atmosphere. Here was the bustle of trade, and manufacturing was looked upon with a degree of approval amounting to religious fervor. Here steam engines did the work of many men and carried about the land as common necessities things that were luxuries for the few in the New World. Here great slums had grown thickly in crowded towns. Here the lack of a day's work meant starvation for a family. He must have seen, too, the evidences of the rise of a social conscience generated by the Industrial Revolution—the Factory Acts, the protests against child labor, the work of reformers reminding their fellow men that the creation of great industries devoured the health and souls of many thousands of human beings.

The greatest contrast lay in the social implications of the contrasting facets of the two economic systems. Brazil was the land of a small group of educated people dependent upon the labor of a vast crowd of illiterates, slave and free. Within that small group ideas fermented, ideas of political freedom, independence. But the world of ideas was closed to the general mass. A man who did not have a family important in the political circles of the day had no group of congenial, well-informed, well-educated men with whom he could mingle on terms of equality. Self-improvement for Irineu had had to be a solitary task, or at least a task in which he was aided only by foreigners.

In England he found the antithesis of Brazil. England was a country with a great middle class that had acquired the habit of reading, of formal education and of social advancement. A man might be a merchant whose father had been a laborer and whose son would be a scholar, a member of Parliament, a lawyer, or a doctor. The preëminence of the landed proprietor had not been so absolute in England as in the Iberian Peninsula, at least since Norman times. The merchant, especially, had always been a figure of social and economic power. The highest rank of the peerage and a member of the county families might deprecate any connection with "trade," but there were comparatively few important figures of English social and political life and of English letters and the learned professions who did not own a grandfather who had made his money in commerce or, more recently, in industry.

More recently in industry. Irineu had not gone abroad to adopt ideas and methods already passing out of date. He did not neglect to observe that industry promised fortunes and power much greater than those possible in commerce. In the ship that took him to England he had fallen in with a young Englishman, John Charles Morgan, who had come to Brazil with the idea of promoting steam railways. Morgan's brother owned an iron foundry in Bristol, and this fact was not lost on Irineu. Leaving the ship at Falmouth, he went to Bristol and visited this establishment. No man knew better than he the shortcomings of his own country in this matter of manufactures, of the mechanization of labor and transport. He was aware of the importance of heavy industry, or at least of iron-working; in his own phrase, it was the "mother of all the others."

By the time he reached Carlisle, where Carruthers lived in prosperous retirement, he was full of new schemes. At first he had difficulty in winning over the old man to these adventures. Probably Carruthers thought he had tried enough experiments in his long commercial career. But in the end Irineu succeeded. He knew how to be persuasive, especially with his fond old patron. They agreed to found a new firm in Manchester, to be known as Carruthers, De Castro and Company. De Castro was José Henrique Reydell de Castro (or Joseph Henry Reydell de Castro, as he signed his name to English documents), a Portuguese who had been the partner of Carruthers' brother in Portugal and who was the son of the chief physician to Dom João VI, Miguel Caetano de Castro. Irineu later called him his boyhood friend, of whom he could demand sacrifices as of a brother, maintaining the equality of friendship by rescuing him from beggary when De Castro once was bankrupt.

Carruthers, De Castro and Company of Manchester thus began its long and brilliant career as Irineu's financial agent in many of his great industrial undertakings in Brazil.

The year Irineu spent traveling abroad, 1840, was one in which Brazil reached another political milestone. For nine years after the abdication of Dom Pedro I, the country had struggled along, narrowly escaping disintegration and fragmentation under the Regency. It had learned, in this uneasy state, the first steps in self-government and in local government. It had taken also a few timid measures to acquire a more modern economy, particularly under its regent, Feijó. But separatism and republicanism flourished, especially in the southern part of the country, made restless by the constant civil warfare across the border in the countries of the River Plate. From 1835 onwards for ten years the War of the Farrapos raged in the province of Rio Grande do Sul, where the monarchy was not popular and where economic interests were more closely bound to Montevideo to the south than to Rio to the north. The solution, for those who wished to preserve the empire seemed to be to cut short the boy emperor's minority and declare him of age to ascend the throne.

Dom Pedro II was at this time only fourteen years old and by law did not reach the age of majority until he was eighteen. But his governors and ministers, seeing the country on the point of disintegration, proposed a desperate measure: they began to campaign to have him declared of age immediately. It was not a unanimously popular idea, but in spite of the opposition of some conservatives, the idea caught on. Debates in the Chamber of Deputies aroused the populace, who, on several occasions, invaded the Chamber and the Senate, cheering the Emperor. Finally, on July 22, 1840, a special delegation from the Chamber called on the royal stripling at the Palace of São Christovão (St. Christopher), on the outskirts of the city, and asked him for his decision. Would he be Emperor now or later? According to tradition, he replied, "*Quero já*" ("I want it now"). There were three days of celebration with fireworks, street shows, church ceremonies, and he was crowned a year later, on July 18, 1841.

Thus Irineu returned from England to find Brazil with an Emperor and General Lima e Silva (later, as the Duke of Caxias, the only Duke of the Empire), doing his best to pacify what was left of the armed rebellions in the country. The Brazil of Dom Pedro II was on the road to success.

In his personal affairs, Irineu was slowly reaching a decision. He was now approaching thirty, a personable young man, with dark-brown hair, dark, dreamy eyes, and a fair complexion, cheerful, energetic, pleasant. Characteristically, he thought out his course of action well in advance, but once his decision was made, he carried it through without hesitation. Life had taught him self-confidence early. He did not neglect its lessons, and whether he had to do with political affairs, business, or family matters, he chose his own path regardless of tradition or other people's opinions.

As an importer of foreign goods he was aware of a growing danger to his business in the current political and international events; such an ominous danger, in fact, that he was contemplating the abandonment of one well-established line of business to take up another far more speculative, far more hazardous in its nature. He had made a shrewd evaluation of the current situation in Anglo-Brazilian commercial relations, in which the terms of the 1828 treaty formed a bone of contention. From 1841 on, a new tariff was under consideration. In August, 1844, this new tariff, under the name of the Alves Branco reform, was adopted by the Brazilian government, the purpose of which was to make radical changes in the privileged position of English imports into Brazil. It was to take effect as soon as the treaty of 1828 should expire and leave Brazil free to revise her scale of customs duties. The new tariff named 2,919 articles on which duties of 20, 40, and 60 percent were to be placed. It was a protectionist tariff, intended to stimulate the creation of industries within the country and to invite foreign capital for that purpose. Irineu was not slow to see the advantage in changing from trading to manufacturing. The ideas that had been in his head since his visit to England crystallized. In 1846, he wound up the affairs of the commercial house of Carruthers and Company, and with its liquidation the whole first chapter of his career was closed. He had come a long way from the boy whose early training had been to work all the daylight hours in a poky little shop, to sleep at night on the counter, to guard his master's capital in a cash box. He had developed his economic thinking along the lines Carruthers had taught him. An assiduous reader of John Stuart Mill, he had adopted economic and sociological concepts that amounted to, as far as Brazil was concerned, a new theory of the relationship between man and money. He was emancipated from the cautious, time-honored Portuguese ideal of a hoard of gold to represent wealth. He had learned the English idea that sound credit could be used in the place of money in business expansion.

In his old age he was led to dramatize this change in his affairs, when he told the creditors of his bankrupt firm:

"On this occasion a lively struggle took place in my soul between the egoism that is more or less natural to the human heart and the generous ideas that carried me on to other destinies. I can say boldly and with a clear conscience before God that the idea of seeing a great fortune in my possession was a secondary matter to me."

It was a secondary matter to him because the making of money was something he had already learned to do with considerable ease. At thirty-three he had more money than most men about him gained in a lifetime. He had had the opportunity to go abroad and compare the backwardness of his own new country with the thriving surge of life in England. His imagination had been fired by the idea of experimenting with the vast unrealized possibilities of Brazil. This was the "other destinies" that lured him on into the role of industrialist.

On the voyage back from the Old World he must have given much thought to what he would do when he got home. The creation of the firm of Carruthers, De Castro and Company before he left England is a sure indication that the decision to leave commerce for industry had already been taken in his own mind. That decision in turn is evidence of the fact that he had rejected the idea of abandoning the world of business to enter that of the traditional aristocracy of Brazil. Otherwise, he would have liquidated his affairs, invested his money in a *fazenda* (that is, a sugar plantation) and a patent of nobility, assuming the idle, static life of a man of social position. Politics was the only field of activity open to a gentleman of the early empire. He was undoubtedly aware that his political and social outlook was entirely unacceptable among the ruling class of Brazilians in the 1840's. The way of life of the *fazendeiro*, alternating long periods of absolute passivity in the country with visits of great ceremony and social display in Rio would have seemed slow death to a man of his physical vigor and habits of energetic work.

If he had contemplated this traditional procedure of the Portuguese merchant about to step into Brazilian society, he would not have neglected the opportunity to marry well—politically and socially well. He would, by a prudent marriage, have repaired his own lack of an important family connection among the oligarchies that owned the greater part of Brazil. He had, on coming back from England, a strong position to make such a bargain. He was a very eligible bachelor, with an independent fortune to take the place of social standing. He was a well-made, temperate, energetic man, with much charm of manner, a modestly carried self-confidence that attracted most people. But this he did not choose to do. His was the instinct to dispense, not to receive; his the temperament to create, not to inherit.

The marriage he chose, indeed, cut him off from such possible political and social advantages. His wife could not help him with a father, brothers, uncles, nephews, cousins in strategic places in governmental affairs. Her origins were as obscure as his own: they were his own.

During the time he had been in England, observing new things and acquiring new ideas, Maria Joaquina, his sister's little girl, had been going regularly to school. One of the first things he had done when he brought his sister and her child to Rio had been to find a good school for Maria Joaquina, where she might acquire the education and poise of a young lady, might lose the awkward rusticity of a girl from the cattle country. He himself had taken her to school the first day and thereafter had watched with growing satisfaction as she changed from a little country girl to a slim, pretty, agreeable young Miss. When he came back from England he brought with him a gold ring to give the girl he would choose for a wife. He gave it now to his niece.

Maria Joaquina was a little startled by the gift. She remembered that he had once said that when he came to choose a wife he would indicate his choice only by giving a gold ring. There is also family tradition that there was another girl who had believed herself to be his probable choice. Whatever the circumstances, they are now unknown, for he kept his own counsel. To Maria Joaquina, her first surprise over, it was a welcome choice. She was a cheerful, healthy girl with a quiet good humor. No doubt this energetic, still youthful uncle, with the manners and habits of an Englishman, was the most attractive man of her limited acquaintance.

For Irineu it was in a way an inevitable choice. In marrying his own niece he had the example of the kings and queens of Portugal and of many of his countrymen in a country where the supply of white women was still limited. He wanted a wife he could understand and one who could understand him, one to whom his idiosyncrasies were not those of a foreigner. He had learned habits of thought and attitudes toward women that made him ill at ease with a Brazilian woman brought up in the usual fashion of the day. He was probably daunted at the prospect of marrying a stranger, perhaps sight unseen, through arrangement with her male relatives. He would probably have received an immature girl, less than fifteen years of age (Maria Joaquina was more than sixteen when they married, an advanced age for a bride in the Brazil of that day), raised on a plantation, ignorant, helplessly dependent on the attendance of slave women, trained to have no thoughts of her own and to show an outward submissiveness that might hide any individuality of character.

He was not of a jealous temperament, and in his marriage, as in all his personal relationships, he sought someone in whom he could place implicit trust. Unlike, for example, Councilor of Empire Perdigão Malheiro, a power in the Rio of the 1840's and 1850's, he had no wish to lock up his wife whenever he left his house, spreading corn meal on the floor in the front hall to make sure that no unknown visitors came in while he was gone. Nor did he want to emulate other Brazilian husbands who placed their wives in convents for safekeeping while they were absent from Rio. Evidently he got what he wanted in Maria Joaquina, for there are no legends of gay adventures, no extramarital romantic episodes recorded of him. English fashion, he called her "May."

Maria Joaquina bore him eighteen children, seven of whom escaped the diseases so destructive to children in mid-nineteenth century Brazil, to grow up and marry. With a courage not usual in Brazilian women of her day, she traveled with him everywhere, for, in her own phrase, "a man oughtn't to go about alone." Not as forthright in speech as her mother, not as sharp in wit and not as impulsive as her grandmother, she had tenacity and a faithful heart, as Irineu was to prove in a marriage that lasted forty-eight years and survived financial success and financial disaster equally well. She learned to be hostess at banquets and brilliant receptions given by a man who was sometimes the financial king of his country and sometimes the unsuccessful speculator keeping up a good front. She learned to be his representative in social affairs when business or policy kept him in his office. She learned to accept with patience and a good-tempered exasperation his constant and extreme preoccupation with business affairs, to wait in her carriage ready to drive to the theater while he scribbled away hastily in his private room urgent letters to catch the next packet for Europe, to remind him constantly of the ordinary matters of daily life that escaped his absentminded attention.

From the day of her marriage, November 4, 1841, she had no reason to complain of a dull life for the next forty years.

PART TWO

THE FRUITS
OF INDUSTRY

CHAPTER V

THE
INDUSTRIALIST

JOHN LUCCOCK, that untiring and painstaking English commentator on every practical detail of the lives of the people of Rio, whom he first visited in 1808, one day went walking in the Passeio Público, the Public Gardens. At the time of the arrival of the royal family from Portugal, this was the only spot in the city where the public might freely go for entertainment. It was, he found, a small, level space laid out in a rigidly formal pattern and carelessly kept. Its main avenues led from a handsome gate, designed by Mestre Valentim, to a broad terrace nearly a hundred feet long, paved with granite of variegated colors and furnished with seats. From here the sea could be seen over a parapet set with plants growing in pots and over another the garden (for the landfill that now separates the sea wall from the gardens by several hundred yards is a creation of the twentieth century). At each end of the terrace was a small square summer house, highly painted and gilded. Inside, these little houses were octagonal, with four windows and a pair of folding doors, and were furnished with gilt chairs. The domes were covered with paintings, in one of which appeared the products of Brazil—indigo, cotton, sugar, mandioca—and the methods of processing them for the market. In the other were scenes of Rio and its history, scenes of whales being caught in the bay in olden times and of the naval battles fought against invaders.

In front of the terrace was an artificial grotto covered with ferns and other plants, among which were entwined two bronze alligators eight feet long. Water poured from their mouths into a stone basin and from this into two more, level with the ground, one on each side of the avenue, and behind this were long stone seats, shaded by fine large trees and sheltered by passion flowers growing on a lattice. At either end of the esplanade was a broad flight of steps. A small flying, laughing cupid at the top of one flight held in his hand a tortoise, through whose body the water flowed into a granite basin below, furnished with a ladle. Over his head was the motto: Even while playing I am useful. It was a charming fancy in a city in which the water supply was always a major problem.

Luccock did not end his researches into the water supply with this. Its source was on the Corcovado Mountain, he found, and it was brought down by an aqueduct by way of the Santa Teresa Hill and drained into a number of public fountains. The aqueduct had been built in the middle of the eighteenth century by slave labor. At the bottom of the Corcovado was a covered reservoir into which the water flowing from the mountain was collected. The aqueduct itself was a monumental work. It consisted of two sets of arches, placed one upon the other, shaded all the way down by dense woods, so that the water was still cool and sparkling when it reached the fountain in the Largo da Carioca (Carioca Square). Tradition said that from the name of this stream the natives of the city of Rio de Janeiro received their nickname of Cariocas—originally the Indian name of a species of ducks which inhabited the nearby marshes and then the name of the Indians of the locality. The stretch of the aqueduct down from the Santa Teresa Hill was a favorite promenade for the citizens. Later it became a bridge to carry a line of electric streetcars up to the breezy heights of the suburb on the mountain.

This first fountain, so supplied and situated in front of the Convent of St. Anthony, was a semicircular affair, reached by a flight of five steps, and the water poured constantly into its basins from eleven brass pipes. The surplus overflowed into a washing tank, where the black women were forever washing clothes. Two or three policemen were always about with whips in their hands to keep order in the unruly throng of slaves sent to fetch water. Horses and mules were also watered there, and the square had a whipping post and some stalls where edibles were sold to the very poor.

The most elaborate of the city fountains was that in the Largo do Paço (Palace Square). Here the water flowed from three pipes into a large stone basin shaped like a conch shell and from there into a small trough around the bottom, which fed other pipes from which slaves drew water. Near the army barracks was another fountain, with large troughs for washing clothes, but the supply of water was scanty and the fountain was little used. There was one at the head of the Rua das Marrecas in what was then the suburb of Lapa which had two statues in bronze, one of Diana the huntress and the other of Acteon. The ships in the harbor were provisioned with water from the Bico dos Marinheiros, where the water flowed from the Rio Comprido into the bay.

Such a water supply could not be sufficient for a city suddenly growing with the influx of the twelve thousand Portuguese who followed the court and the many thousands more who came each succeeding year, to say nothing of the army of emigrants from all over Europe, attracted by the new trading possibilities. Dom João acted to better the situation. Two more sources of water were found in the waterfalls in the forest on Tijuca Mountain, eight or ten miles outside the city. In 1809 the first stream was canalized into wooden pipes, and after nine years' work another fountain was built to receive the water in the Campo de Sant'Ana, the parade ground for the royal troops. This fountain was inaugurated with great celebrations on June 24, 1818, when Dom João and his family went to see the water flow for the first time from the twenty brass spouts.

Even so the city needed water. It was, indeed, a never-ending problem.

By a whim of the goddess Fortune, Brazil has been endowed with every mineral resource except an adequate supply of both coal and iron. In the industrial age of the nineteenth century, in the reign of the steam engine, this lack was an almost insuperable barrier to industrial development. Nor did the economic viewpoint of the kings of Portugal concerning their colony in the New World in any way tend to make allowance for it. Iron had been worked, in a small way, in the captaincy of São Vicente as early as 1597, but the industry disappeared completely through the intervention of the Portuguese crown, which prohibited its expansion. Dom João's ancestors were not alive to the fact that wealth in the modern world was not a matter of unending supplies of gold and silver but of the fabrication of objects out of baser metals. All the labor supply there was must go to the further exploitation of the mines of precious metals. João himself, always so surprisingly perspicacious for so weak-willed a man, saw the fallacy in this and encouraged a little iron-working when he arrived in Brazil. It was, however, a very small affair, representing merely a breath from the European world, where the role of machines in the lives of men was changing the economic patterns of nations.

Senhor Irineu, back from his first trip to England, saw an opportunity but he was cautious in his approach to the problem. He realized that he was not in the position of a typical English manufacturer of machinery and tools, who expected to find his market, either in England or abroad, among a numerous middle class accustomed to having at its disposal carriages, cutlery, and a thousand objects manufactured with the aid of steam engines. There was a ready sale for steam engines and boilers for sugar mills and coffee plantations and there were great landowners willing and able to buy such things. But the economy of Brazil was agricultural and slavocratic, where the demand for machines was low and the demand for slave labor high. If he founded an iron foundry in Brazil, therefore, he could only expect success if he had the government as an eager customer.

His first action was to come to an understanding with the Minister of Empire for a guaranteed contract for the improvement of the water supply in Rio. He proposed to supply iron pipes for canalizing the waters of the Maracanã River to bring more water into the city. He did so, providing pipes so well made that thirty years later, when repairs were necessary to the system, they were found to be in perfect condition.

He had found and acquired a small iron-working establishment at Ponta d'Areia, across the bay from the docks of the harbor of Rio, in the suburbs of the town of Niteroi, the capital of the province of Rio de Janeiro. He bought it in 1846 and developed it so quickly that at the end of his first year of ownership it represented four times the amount of capital originally involved. The drain on his resources, however, was such that he was forced to ask for a loan from the government of about three hundred *contos* (U.S. $150,000 or £30,000, which was granted to him and which was to be repaid in eleven annual installments at the usual government rate of interest. In 1856 the Brazilian *conto de reis* was worth U.S. $500 or somewhat more than a hundred pounds sterling. One *conto* was subdivided into one thousand *milreis;* the *milreis* was the equivalent of the modern Brazilian *cruzeiro.*)

The success of that first contract started the new foundry off to a flourishing career. It gained fame in its second undertaking, the building of steamboats and sailing vessels which were invaluable during the troubles in the River Plate in the 1850's and in the Paraguayan war in the 1860's. A year after he bought the Ponta d'Areia works he employed there three hundred workmen under the direction of an English engineer. The factory grew quickly. At the peak of its prosperity it employed a thousand workmen. Within a short time the capital sunk in the establishment amounted to more than $600,000, at a time when the budget for the Brazilian government was about $13,500,000, when the population of the country was somewhat more than six million, and when the only Brazilian bank (the Banco do Comércio) had a capital of $1,250,000. It produced boilers, stills, steam-driven machines of all kinds, cranes, sugar mills, and walking beams for paddle-wheel steamers, besides more piping for the city's water supply. On the evidence of some of its products exhibited there, it won a silver medal at the great exposition held in London in 1862.

Unfortunately its prosperity did not last long. In 1857 a disastrous fire wrecked half of the buildings at the plant, destroying many valuable molds and designs and obliging Senhor Irineu to get another loan. Its heyday passed with the new tariff reform in 1860. In that year, the government, in the so-called Ferraz tariff, reversed the protectionist policy it had followed since the adoption of the Alves Branco tariff in 1845 (which had been a principal incentive to Senhor Irineu to leave commerce for industry) and admitted into the country all sorts of manufactured articles that formerly had been excluded. By 1862 the iron foundry had only 384 employees. After the fire Senhor Irineu had tried to revive the establishment but (in his own opinion, because of the malice and envy of certain persons of political importance) he failed and was eventually out of pocket a half million U.S. dollars. From then on Ponta d'Areia vegetated.

Rio de Janeiro, as the seat of the Court, was crowded into the small space between the Rua Direita and the Campo de Sant'Ana, a comparatively minor section of the modern city. Here the police, the municipal government, the Emperor's city palace, the principal commercial houses, the diplomatic corps, the foreign colonies, the schools, and the theaters were all crowded together. Only this privileged area had any illumination at night. In fact, up until the time of the Viceroy Count Rezende, the only public illumination was provided by the oil lamps or wax candles lighted by pious persons before the niches of saints set up at the street corners. Like the Londoner of medieval times, the solid citizen who went abroad after dark was preceded by a servant bearing a torch to light his way. Otherwise, the streets were in the deepest darkness, dangerous to the passerby because of swampy places and footpads. Count Rezende provided fish-oil lamps, for which action the government was congratulated as showing a progressive and foresighted spirit. When Irineu became a clerk in Carruthers' firm, the city was still lighted by these three or four hundred oil lamps, cared for by slaves, who, in order to attend promptly to any accident that might put the lamps out, slept on the paving near each standard.

The idea of the profit to be made by providing the city with a modern system of street-lighting occurred to various people. On October 23, 1828, Dom Pedro I's Minister of Internal Affairs signed a decree which granted a franchise to one Antonio da Costa, citizen of the empire and merchant in the London market, to light Rio by means of gas. He was to furnish fifteen hundred lamp standards (for which the government agreed to pay sixty contos annually), was to have a monopoly for twenty-two years, and was to receive an additional forty milreis for each new standard set up. His idea was to form a company with English and Brazilian shareholders, but since he failed to organize his company within the two months specified by the decree, his franchise lapsed. On May 9, 1834, the Englishmen Charles Gregg and William Glegg Glover were given a franchise to light the city and suburbs with gas, which also failed to become a reality.

Although London had had gas lighting since 1813 and other great cities of the world were also more modernly provided, the Cariocas hesitated to invest in such schemes. They did not believe in such novelties. In their view, one could not have light without oil or grease to burn. Therefore, a law of 1840 merely provided for another hundred new fish-oil lamps. However, in 1843 the duty of supplying illumination was given to the Minister of Justice, who at the moment happened to be Eusébio de Queiroz, a forward-looking man to whom the idea of modern street-lighting was not a fanciful dream. He announced in 1846 that the government was prepared to receive bids for a contract for a new lighting system. Only one offer was made, by an Englishman.

Several more years passed and then Senhor Irineu was looking for more work for his new iron foundry at Ponta d'Areia. He realized that the ministry in power in 1851 included men especially friendly to him: besides Eusébio de Queiroz, there was José da Costa Carvalho (the Marquess of Mont'Alegre), who had been a regent during Dom Pedro II's minority and was now Minister of Empire and President of the Council of State; and Paulino Soares de Souza (Viscount Uruguai), the Minister of Foreign Affairs, with whom he already had had much to do in another connection. In later years, in describing his actions, he was quite candid about his demands:

I approached men in the government of the country for the purpose of demanding work for the establishment [Ponta d'Areia], considering that such protection was due it, especially since the government needed such services as those I offered. . . . When I declared, in conversation, to one of the ministers that I had made a study some months before of the question of illuminating the city by gas, I was informed that a proposal was being debated in the Council of Ministers and that they were just on the point of signing its terms.

He thought the matter over and offered a contract providing for a cost considerably under that estimated by the Englishman. He made a shrewd bargain, for, in spite of the lower price, he made money from his contract. In 1866, when he handed his franchise over to an English company, it was valued at £600,000. It was an enormous transaction for the Brazil of that period. He had contracted to extend his lighting system, and in 1858 more than doubled the capital sunk in the enterprise. As a shareholder in the new company he received from his fellow shareholders three times the face value of the original shares. Besides this, he received 6,000 shares for the cession of all rights and privileges that had belonged to him as manager and in compensation for the expense of organizing the new company. Altogether he made a profit of more than $1,200,000.

He had taken the risk, however, and he had taken it alone, without a partner. It was all his own money that had provided the initial outlay in lighting up all the center of the city, on March 25, 1854. In constructing the physical property of the system he had encountered enormous difficulties. 1850 was the year of the first great yellow-fever epidemic, the disease brought in by a sailing vessel from Havana which was to remain thereafter in Rio as a seasonal scourge, until the role of the *aïdes aegypti* mosquito in its dissemination was discovered many years later. It took a large toll of the English skilled workmen Senhor Irineu had imported to build the gas works. Of eleven machinists who arrived in 1853, ten died of the fever within three months. The price of English labor rose accordingly. More Englishmen came, in spite of the threat of death, some of them drawing wages larger than the salaries of the Brazilian ministers of state.

In spite of all these difficulties, Senhor Irineu did not seek to extend the time limit of the contract. He did not even ask for bonuses to compensate for these unforeseen hazards, even when torrential rains added to his troubles, ruining some of the work already begun. In

1855 came an epidemic of cholera, killing off thousands of Negro workmen and driving up the price of the lime necessary to purify the gas, since lime was a product almost exclusively manufactured by Negroes. So, if Senhor Irineu made a profit of approximately $1,-200,000, he made it by conquering obstacles that would have discouraged a less determined man.

The Cariocas were entranced with the results of all this labor. Why had they waited so long for this enchantment? In 1855-1856, an American traveler, J. C. Fletcher, could report:

> The streets of few cities are better lighted than those of Rio de Janeiro. The gasworks on the Aterrado sends its illuminating streams to remote suburbs as well as through the many and intricate thoroughfares of the Cidade Velha [Old City] and the Cidade Nova [New City]. They have not the convenient fiction which city governments often palm off upon themselves in the United States—viz.: that the moon shines half the year; for in Rio, whether Cynthia is in the full, or whether shorn of her beams by unforeseen storms, the lamps continue to shed their brilliant light.

As soon as they were convinced that the gas tanks would not explode and that the investment was a profitable one, the Cariocas flocked around Senhor Irineu with money to invest in extending the system. All over Brazil, even in the smaller towns, there was a sudden interest in the creation of gas-illumination companies.

Few people who lived far from the Court at Rio ever dreamed of the possibility of visiting it. The immensity of the country and the dangers and fatigues of the journey there by horseback, burro, ox cart, or even in the comparative ease of coastwise vessels, made such pilgrimages unthinkable for all but the hardy few, with real business or political necessity to drive them to it. Even communication between the heart of the city and its nearest suburbs was difficult, being entirely a matter of private carriages, horses, or ox carts.

Public transportation within the city was almost nonexistent. Any scheme to introduce a system of conveyances needed a banker. Senhor Irineu was already, in 1856, the logical source for the money necessary to start any such enterprise.

His first experiments in that field did not encourage him unduly.

It was his friend, an English doctor, Thomas Cochrane, who interested him in the scheme of building a railroad up Mount Tijuca, the highest and most beautiful peak within the city limits. Cochrane had organized a company to undertake the construction of a railroad and had received from the government a franchise and a grant of £30,000, with which he perseveringly tried to bring the railway into existence. He did not succeed and his franchise lapsed, but with the £30,000 he opened an account in Senhor Irineu's banking house and began his attempts to interest Irineu himself.

But Irineu, with a better grasp of the difficulties of raising money for such enterprises, hesitated. The doctor, to keep his shareholders interested, had acquired parcels of land along the right of way on Tijuca.

"I declared then to Dr. Cochrane," said Irineu, many years later, "that he could not count on me for anything; that I would only take a few shares, because I would not have it said that I would prevent my name from appearing in any useful enterprise."

In the end he was persuaded, in friendship's name, to buy a few parcels of land, for almost nine contos, a sum he immediately thought was gone for good; that is, a loss of $4,500. Cochrane carried on the enterprise on his own initiative, and the financial disaster that would inevitably result was looming. Still Irineu turned a deaf ear to his entreaties for aid.

But then Irineu made one of the long journeys he was in the custom of making in the interests of his banking house in Montevideo, and when he returned he could no longer resist the temptation to try something new. While he had been gone, a large loan had been floated for the Tijuca Road, on the undertaking of three directors of the company, one of whom, at least, had excellent credit. Irineu hesitated no longer but plunged in. The financial disaster came nevertheless, and the shareholders, in a general meeting, resolved to turn the enterprise over to Senhor Irineu's bank in payment of the debt.

Irineu accepted the settlement. At first he tried to obtain contributions from the three directors, but to no avail. One was unable to honor his signature. Another said he would not sacrifice his own fortune to pay a debt that was not his but the company's. And the third,

Irineu shrewdly suspected, refused to come through because, although he had the reputation of being a man of great means, he did not have the wherewithal to meet even a third share of the liability. In the end, during the 1860's, Senhor Irineu finally liquidated the company as unprofitable, since it had cost his banking house something like seven hundred contos or about $350,000.

This experience did not make him very receptive to the idea soon afterward put forward by another friend of his, Councilor Cândido Batista de Oliveira, who wanted a franchise for a tramway line to the Botanical Gardens. This line, which would connect the center of the city with the prosperous suburb of Botafogo, situated on the broad curve of beach under the shadow of the Sugarloaf itself, proved to be a gold mine for the shareholders. At first the idea of laying out more capital in tramways did not appeal to Irineu. However, Oliveira, who was a former cabinet member, a director of the Bank of Brazil, and a senator, had sunk a considerable sum of money in the enterprise, money which seemed hopelessly lost. Again Senhor Irineu yielded to the temptation to attempt a financial recoupment. He took as a partner a former attaché of the United States legation and began a campaign to find capital in the United States. The line, known as the Botanical Gardens Railway Company, became a success, one of the most profitable investments in Brazil and the first in which United States capital formed a large part. Its success had two results. One was to encourage the idea of profitable investment for United States capital in Brazil, which was to culminate thirty years later in the great flow of United States and Canadian investments in light and power and street-railway companies. The other was to prompt Brazilians with capital to invest to place it in city transport companies in foreign cities.

Illuminating the city with gas and launching the first tramway line, though the two most important and successful of Senhor Irineu's civic improvements, did not exhaust his activities. In the region north of the city a swamp had existed in the time of Dom João VI. That monarch had had in mind a project to drain the marsh, which was a focus for infection and disagreeable smells, a breeding place for mosquitoes. But nothing came of the project, except the construction of a carriageway and a bridge over the deepest part, to provide easier access to the Quinta da Boa Vista, the suburban royal palace of St. Christopher.

In 1853, when the yellow fever had come to stay, its presence was somehow associated with marshes and bad air, though the agency of the yellow-fever mosquito was still unsuspected. The city alderman, Haddock Lobo, in that year raised the question of draining the swamp. His suggestion at once interested Senhor Irineu, whose gas works were situated in the midst of this marshy place. He undertook the construction of the Mangue Canal, a deep ditch, lined on either side by an avenue and bordered with palm trees to disguise its less agreeable features. This ditch cost one thousand, three hundred and seventy-five contos, or almost $700,000, and in its original form did not go all the way to drain into the bay. But it was the starting point of the plan later developed, at the beginning of the twentieth century, by Lauro Muller and Paulo de Frontin, to modernize the water front of Rio.

Thus Senhor Irineu's interests were many and varied. They ranged from such humble but profitable enterprises as the creation of a company to manufacture stearine candles to such ambitious but unprofitable schemes as the provision of a drydock for the harbor at Rio. He speculated in gold mines, steam towing companies, and leather tanneries; his interests centered not merely in one part of the country but everywhere in Brazil and its neighbor to the south, Uruguay.

His railway-building and his banking enterprises require chapters to themselves. But it is obvious even from so brief a catalogue that his greatest characteristic as an industrialist was the very catholicity of his interests. Wherever his eye lit he saw something that perhaps deserved bold, sometimes audacious efforts to develop. The financial adventures he undertook were no more extravagant than the imagination he used to envisage them.

Not a small part of the problem confronting him in every such venture was the great gap in outlook between himself and the society in which he lived. He would have had no success at all if he had not

firmly grasped, at the very beginning of his career, certain fundamental facts about his world. He realized, certainly after his first trip
to England, that he was dealing in Brazil with a country thoroughly
inured to the paternalistic form of government, a country in which
individual effort in enterprises touching upon a large source of revenue had been consistently repressed. Portugal had never been a land
where the individual, even the merchant, acted without expecting
the intrusion of the government's interest into his business. Brazil
had suffered an even more thorough education in this acceptance of
government tutelage. The great riches of the colony had been first
and primarily the special property of the crown of Portugal. The
mines, the great sugar crops, were sources of revenue for the Portuguese king, who strove to maintain control over the landowners.

Into the cloistered, derivative society of the Second Reign Senhor
Irineu brought ideas that he had learned first from Carruthers and
then by observation of what was being done through the development of industry in England, the United States, and France. He was
thoroughly imbued with the economic principle of the maximum of
freedom for private enterprise and initiative in the creation of wealth.
Being by temperament also a generous and kindly man, he added to
this belief the further idealization that in the economic betterment of
the individual lay the best hope for the betterment of mankind generally. In England and the United States he would have found many
to sympathize with his views and applaud his actions. In Brazil he
encountered either indifference or hostility.

In 1878, as a man already aging and beset by insurmountable financial difficulties, feeling the weight of years of strenuous effort to
bring modern ideas of the creation of wealth by investment of money
in industry to a nation reluctant to learn, he remarked:

It is claimed that in Brazil everything waits on the government and that
individual initiative does not exist. And how can the case be otherwise, if
the action of capital is blocked, as soon as it is gathered up for any purpose
of public or private utility (in which freedom of contract must be the principal regulator) by restrictive laws, and as if these were not enough, by
undue intervention on the part of the government in the character of
guardian? And what shall we say concerning credit, that great lever of

civilization, which creates ninety-five percent of the transactions upon which the economic life of modern companies is founded? Credit is either handed over to the regime of privilege or it does not exist outside of the limits of the individual's resources, where its action is necessarily weak. Especially is this true in a new country which has not had time to convert into realizable capital more than a minimum part of its natural resources. Among us, credit can not take a step forward without encountering these preventive laws, which suffocate liberty of action.

The fact of the matter is, therefore, that such a reproof, that everything waits on the government, is met with the response that this is the necessary consequence of the legal regime to which the country has been bound over by those who govern it.

These words contain the synthesis of the problem with which he was confronted throughout his business career. They are the key to the story of his successes, his failures, his extraordinary achievements, and his final bankruptcy. With remarkable clearsightedness he saw, in the heat of the struggle and in the cold light of retrospect equally, the great gap between his own ideas and aspirations and the prejudices and preconceptions of the society in which he lived. That same clarity was not granted to his associates and contemporaries, and in that fact, more than in any other, lies the explanation of the failure of his own countrymen either to understand him or to accord to him a just appreciation for the contributions he made to Brazil.

CHAPTER VI

BARON MAUÁ
OF THE
RAILROADS

THE BRAGANÇAS, on being transplanted to Brazil, showed very little enterprise in building royal palaces. Mad old Queen Maria I and her son Dom João, on arrival were lodged in the conventual buildings near the waterfront, which had been used as a jail and as the royal mint. These were uncomfortable and unsuitable quarters for the royal emigrants, even though hastily modified into a semblance of a royal palace. When the old Queen died and Dom João went back to Portugal, his son Dom Pedro I made further modifications to make it habitable.

Dom Pedro II, however, never lived in this makeshift palace. He would stop there overnight when some state function required his presence late at night in the center of the city. But he much preferred the Quinta da Boa Vista, otherwise known as the palace in the St. Christopher district, where he had been brought up by his tutors and guardians. The Quinta was a big country house with a large park, built in 1803 by Elias Antônio Lopes, a merchant of the city, who gave it to Dom João in 1808 as a summer residence. While his mother lived, Dom João had spent his days at the Quinta, but had always returned to sleep in the old palace near the waterfront. The Quinta then was well out in the country, on ground lying a little higher than the center of the city, at the foot of Mount Tijuca. As soon as the old Queen died, Dom João moved out there as his permanent residence, though it was too small for him, his widowed sister-in-law and his two sons and eldest daughter. His queen and her other daughters preferred to live in Botafogo, a suburb along the ocean side.

Dom Pedro I had had his own favorite summer palace, the old *fazenda* or plantation of Santa Cruz, much further out in the country to the west. Originally Santa Cruz had belonged to the Jesuits, who drained the surrounding marshes and built canals and dams to make it more healthful. It had come into the possession of the crown after the confiscation of the properties of the Jesuits during the administration of the Marquess of Pombal as Prime Minister of Portugal. Dom Pedro I favored it because there he could go native, free from the trappings of royalty, which irked him. It provided, however, no change of air, for the climate was little different from that of Rio itself. Dom Pedro II did not care for Santa Cruz, and he acquired a horror of the place when his first son and heir died there of fever.

In search of a more agreeable residence for the hottest part of the year, Dom Pedro II's thoughts turned to the *fazenda* of Córrego Sêco, up in the Serra da Estrella, the range of high mountains that lie to the north of Guanabara Bay. He had inherited it from his father as his own private property. There the air was fresh, limpid, free from the heavy murk that sometimes lay over Rio. For several years, however, his plans were dormant. He had tradition against him in thus going so far to seek his summer home, tradition and the difficulties of climbing a steep mountain in carriages and on horseback.

In the meantime, the site became involved in the first formally undertaken experiment in European colonization in the Empire. Frederico Koeler, a German by birth, was an engineer in the Emperor's army. In 1837 he was in charge of the construction of a highway that would eventually link the Serra da Estrella with the province of Paraíba do Sul and which passed by the *fazenda* of Córrego Sêco. In that year, the vessel *Justine*, bound for Sydney, Australia, with two hundred and thirty-eight German immigrants, put into the port of

Rio, because the passengers had revolted against the treatment they were receiving from the captain, who retaliated by having them placed under arrest. Koeler, who wanted to prove the superiority of free immigrant labor over slave labor, asked for permission to use the services of these men in his road-building. He succeeded, and the government of the province of Rio de Janeiro passed a decree on May 10, 1843, providing for the establishment of colonies of immigrants. An imperial decree of March 16, 1843, set forth the terms of an agreement between Koeler and the architect in charge of the royal palaces, Paulo Barbosa da Silva, which created such a colony on the site of the *fazenda* of Córrego Sêco, henceforward called Petrópolis, Peter's City, in the Emperor's honor.

It was, however, the beginning of the great yellow-fever epidemics that stimulated the growth of the mountain city. It did not take long for the well-to-do, who could afford to think of escape from the scourge, to notice that the fever clung to marshy, swampy places and that it spread more readily after four o'clock in the afternoon. Those who could fled to the mountains, and since the Emperor and the royal family were at Petrópolis, the diplomatic corps, the government officials, and the fashionable world went there, too. The town grew magically, with a fine main street, shops, hotels. In November of 1853, Mariano José Pinto, an official of the imperial household, wrote to Paulo Barbosa, who was in Europe, to give an account of the city Barbosa had worked so assiduously to create. Buildings worth more than forty contos ($20,000) had been built, and among the others in the process of construction were two schools for the children of the well-to-do, two hotels, a house each for the French Minister, the Minister from the Republic of Uruguay, Andrés Lamas, and the Brazilian businessman Irineu Evangelista de Sousa. The streets of the little mountain city were like well-kept country lanes, down which flowed canalized streams crossed by ornamental rustic bridges. Its houses were small palaces surrounded by flower-filled, shady gardens. Here the air was fresh, the temper of life calm, the beauty tranquil. And the way up to this little artificial paradise had been made so much easier by the building of the first railroad in Brazil. Its creator was that same enterprising businessman, Senhor Irineu.

Felisberto Caldeira Brant Pontes, the Marquess of Barbacena, had kept his eyes open when he went abroad in the late 1820's to find a second wife for his royal master, Dom Pedro I. When he returned to Brazil he had brought with him the idea of a railroad to be built between Rio and the province of Minas Gerais, in the interests of realizing some of the potential wealth pent up in that interior region. His idea awakened sympathetic attention, somewhat later, in the regent, Father Feijó, whose grasp of the economic necessities of the country was perhaps stronger than that of most of his contemporaries and successors in office. A law providing for such a line was passed, signed by the Regent on October 31, 1835.

An Englishman was the first to try to use the privileges granted by the law. He was the same Thomas Cochrane who had first interested Senhor Irineu in the line up Tijuca Mountain. But his efforts to form a company to build a line linking Rio de Janeiro with São Paulo, in the south, failed, for neither in England nor in Brazil could he find partners to share the financial risk. The franchise he obtained in 1839 lapsed. Thus the matter remained for several more years.

Dom Pedro II also had a minister of empire who saw the value of railroads. Luiz Pereira de Couto Ferraz, Viscount Bom Retiro, occupied a unique position in the Second Reign. He had been brought up as Dom Pedro's boyhood companion, for the Emperor had no brothers, and throughout their lives they stood in a special relationship to each other. Dom Pedro II had been orphaned early and had been left to the care of strangers—well-meaning and conscientious, but strangers nevertheless. He developed, therefore, a marked preference for those who had been his intimates in his youth, who were well-acquainted with his habits and opinions.

This steady, ungregarious, loyal man, Bom Retiro, educated with Dom Pedro in childhood, filled the place of an affectionate brother in the Emperor's private life. Unlike the Emperor, Bom Retiro, though conservative in his opinions, was an innovator and a practical man. He was not a social man. He hated crowds, society, and life in society. His very title gave his contemporaries cause for amusement; he seemed indeed a man always in search of a *bom retiro*, a pleasant retreat, away from interruptions and vexations. He puzzled his contemporaries, for though he held political office, he had an invincible fear of speaking in public. He hated to be talked to as much as he hated to talk, and he was no party man.

But he was an indefatigable worker and he was always in a hurry. This furious energy he preferred to exercise far away from the distractions of city life, in his picturesque lodge high in the forest on Mount Tijuca, and sometimes even out on the bay in a sloop borrowed from the Navy Yard. The thousands of recommendations and suggestions that he showered upon the Emperor's ministers of state were made chiefly without official position. He never experimented with the power he undoubtedly could have wielded. This was a deliberate sacrifice, for his brief term of office as Minister of Empire was the high point of his life.

But he knew the Emperor. He understood his weaknesses and his fetishes. One of these was the horror of showing favor, or appearing to show favor, to a personal friend in public office. Bom Retiro knew that as holder of a public office he would no longer be the Emperor's confidant and intimate adviser. He could not walk in and out of the palace of St. Christopher as if it was his own home. He was a discreet man and a loyal friend, with much the same sympathies, the same tastes, the same likes and dislikes among people as the Emperor. However, where the Emperor erred on the side of inertia and conservatism, Bom Retiro was the friend of progress, always with an eye out for the practical developments in other countries that might benefit Brazil. It was he who persuaded the Emperor of the usefulness of railroads.

His interest in the subject had led him (as president of the province of Rio de Janeiro) to sign a concession, dated April 27, 1852, granting to Irineu Evangelista de Sousa the right to build a line from the little port of Mauá, at the head of the bay and within the territorial limits of the province, to Raiz da Serra, at the foot of the mountain on which Petrópolis is situated. This franchise was confirmed by a provincial law of September 23, 1852, which granted a monopoly through a zone some five leagues across.

Senhor Irineu had been thinking of railroads since his early days in the house on Santa Teresa, when he had filled in his idle moments reading magazines published in England and the United States concerning the building of railways. The Charles Morgan with whom he had crossed the ocean for the first time was a young Englishman who had been visiting South America with railroad construction in mind. The franchise in hand, Senhor Irineu was ready to go ahead. He had already provided himself with plans and blueprints, made under his orders by an English engineer, Robert Milligan. Now he formed a company, with a board of directors made up of his personal friends. He intended to raise two thousand contos, or about a million dollars, but he succeeded in finding only two-thirds of this sum, so he subscribed the rest himself. His final list of shareholders was impressive. Besides Isaac Carruthers, the representative of Carruthers, De Castro and Company, it included: Honorio Hermeto Carneiro Leão (the Marquess of Paraná), a former regent during Dom Pedro II's minority and still one of the most powerful men in the government; José Antonio Pimenta Bueno (Viscount São Vicente), the Emperor's private legal counselor; and Teófilo Otoni, the leader of the extreme republican wing of the Liberal party. It was an undertaking that began with the Emperor's personal interest. Dom Pedro himself turned the first ceremonial clod in breaking ground for the new line, using for the purpose a silver-mounted shovel and a wheel-barrow made of dark jacarandá wood.

In September, 1853, the *Jornal do Comércio*, Rio's most important newspaper, carried an account of the first experimental trip made on the line:

> Yesterday an experiment was made with the locomotive steam engine on the rails of the finished portion of the road from Mauá to the Estrela mountains. Our Weekly Correspondent sent us last night the following account of this trip: I and some other curiosity seekers, among whom were the ministers of England and Austria, risked our lives in a trial of the first steam engine carriage that ever traveled over the first railway in Brazil. We crossed the bay in a vessel which was propelled by Fulton's invention, and in two hours (the steamer was low-powered) we arrived at Mauá. The first part only of the pier for disembarking being laid, we climbed up by the aid of ropes, and threaded our way over a succession of loose and insecure planks to the shore, at the risk of taking a mudbath. A few paces distant we saw a single, graceful-looking locomotive, with the certificate

of the year of its birth and the name of its worthy papa engraved on the center wheels. The legend, in yellow metal, was as follows: Wm. Fairbairn & Sons, 1853, Manchester. The proper carriage was not yet attached. They had substituted for it a rough wagon, used for the conveyance of materials, and without further delay we squatted at the bottom of this impromptu vehicle. Suddenly a prolonged and roaring shriek, a whistle with the power of fifty sopranos, screamed through the air, deafening the hearer and causing us to raise our hands to our ears. It was the signal for departure; the warning to those who might be on the line to guard against a mortal blow; an announcement made by a tube attached to the locomotive itself. Swifter than an arrow, than the flight of a swallow, the locomotive threaded the rails, swung about, ran, flew, devoured space, and, passing through the fields, barren wastes, and frightened animals, it stopped at last, breathless, at the point where the road does not yet afford a safe passage. The space traversed was a mile and three quarters, and the time occupied in the transit was four minutes. What a brilliant future for Brazil do we see in the wheels of that locomotive! Happy those among us who may have long lives. They will travel by great cities, great farms, remembering that once these were swamps and forests. Oh! if man's existence were not so short; if at least we could return to this world as invisible shadows, wandering in our native country, how small we should find ourselves, comparing our past, that is, our present of today, with the progress to be made by the coming generation. But human beings are like workmen who help each other in building an edifice; each age deposits its stone towards completion of the great work. Our first stone has been laid on the plain of Mauá.

Several months later, on April 30, 1854, the first locomotive made a trip of fifteen kilometers in twenty-three minutes. The locomotive's name was symbolic: *A Baroneza*, the Baroness. For it was named for Maria Joaquina, whose husband was now no longer simply Senhor Irineu, but Baron Mauá.

Dom Pedro II inherited from his father and grandfather a convenient method of rewarding valuable services to the crown: the conferring of titles. Dom João VI's criterion for such gifts was purely monetary. The visiting Frenchman, Auguste Saint Hilaire had once unkindly remarked that in Portugal it took five hundred years to make a nobleman but in Brazil only five hundred contos. The system of Dom Pedro II was based on quite as shrewd a calculation. The titles he conferred were, in much the greater proportion, granted to *fazendeiros*, well-to-do plantation owners whose power in their home regions was unquestioned, the class upon which the security of his throne depended.

A New World character was given this peerage by the fact that the titles were not hereditary but only for use during the lifetime of the men (or occasionally women) upon whom they were conferred, although sometimes the Emperor gave titles to several generations of the same family. Now and then he added to his list of honors the names of men who, though neither *fazendeiros* nor military heroes nor men of state, had made some indisputable contribution to the grandeur of Brazil. It was undoubtedly Viscount Bom Retiro who suggested to him that the man who had succeeded in building the first railroad, the all-important link between Rio and Petrópolis, deserved a title.

Therefore, on the same day that the new road was inaugurated, Irineu Evangelista de Sousa became Baron Mauá. The Emperor had chosen the title himself, the Indian name of the little port at the head of the bay from which the railroad started. Francisco Octaviano Almeida Rosa has left a description of that first imperial ride in the new train. In summary, this is what he reported:

The tall, blond Emperor and the short plump Empress and all their court had gathered in Mauá. They were surrounded by the higher officials of the province of Rio de Janeiro, the president of the Council of State, the Ministers of Empire, Navy, and War and their wives, with many more distinguished visitors. The hot sun of a noonday in April beat down through the perpetual haze of the low-lying marshy land that lay around the headwaters of Guanabara Bay. Far in the distance, toward the north, could be seen the dull blue ridge of the Serra da Estrella, the mountain range on the scarp of which Petrópolis was perched.

In spite of the warmth of the season (the cooler weather of the subtropical winter had not yet arrived) the gentlemen wore heavy black broadcloth, high collars and satin cravats, and tall hats, unless they were officers in the armed forces, in which case they were encased in heavy uniforms stiff with the elaborate braiding of the period. Their wives, too, were victims of fashion, for they were dressed in the latest French style, with voluminous skirts, high button shoes, trailing shawls, with no thought of compromise with a tropical climate. There was a hubbub of excited talk over this fascinating new toy of the nineteenth century, this string of gleaming new varnished wooden coaches drawn along a track by a shiny, noisy monster.

The whistle blew for the departure, and the company embarked to the strains of a military band and amid bursts of applause from the crowd come to greet the Emperor. He and the Empress had a special royal coach, placed in the middle of the train, furnished with armchairs. It took a scant twenty-three minutes—from twenty-seven minutes past one o'clock to one-fifty—to reach the end of the completed portion of the track. The stop was at a place called Fragoso, where the official party alighted to follow Their Majesties to the house of Lieutenant Colonel Albino, president of the municipal chamber of the township of Estrella, within whose jurisdiction lay the town of Mauá. At twenty-seven minutes past two the party reëmbarked, to make the journey back in twenty minutes.

The Emperor, when he stepped from the coach, was greeted by rounds of enthusiastic applause. He was yet very popular, this only American monarch. The applause was redoubled when Viscount Bom Retiro, as Minister of Empire, walked forward with Senhor Irineu, who wished to present his formal thanks to the Emperor for his new title, Baron Mauá. The patent was signed the same day, April 30, 1854, and countersigned by Bom Retiro. With it went the right to a coat-of-arms, displaying a design of the locomotive, surrounded by gas streetlamps; and a set of ceremonial china, made in the great Derby potteries in England, white with a broad band of reddish orange.

Thereafter the trip from Rio to Petrópolis was a matter of six hours by steamer, rail, and wagon road. Fletcher, an American visitor, described the trip thus:

An agreeable steamboat transit amid the picturesque islands brings you to Mauá, the terminus of the first railroad formed in Brazil, and for which the Empire is indebted to the enterprise of that enlightened and patriotic Brazilian, Evangelista Ireneo de Souza, who, on the opening of this railway was created the Baron of Mauá by the Emperor. The road is about ten miles long and leads to the foot of the mountains, where carriages, each drawn by four mules, receive the travellers. The ascent is by an excellent road, which was built by the government at an enormous expense, and reminds one of the Simplon route. In some parts the side of the mountain is so steep that three windings are compressed into a space small enough to allow your being heard as you speak to the persons in the carriage going in the opposite direction. When you reach the summit, before descending into the valley, in which stands the town, a magnificent prospect opens before you. All the bay and city of Rio, the plains of Mauá, across which lies the diminutive railroad, are mapped out below. The palace of the Emperor stands in the centre of the town, and when finished and surrounded by cultivated grounds, will present a beautiful appearance. Here the Baron of Mauá has a mansion pleasantly situated at the meeting of two mountain brooks. Petropolis is annually becoming of greater importance. Its salubrious and delightful climate will make it a large and fashionable resort for the Capital of the Empire, and perhaps the day is not distant when it will become the second city of the province. It stands at the entrance to the fertile province of Minas Gerais, and should some plan be devised for constructing a railway up the mountains, its growth will be most rapid. If the Baron of Mauá would pay a visit to the United States and examine the Pennsylvania Railways or the Baltimore and Ohio Railroad, he may be encouraged to persevere. The mountain barrier once passed, a portion of the rich interior regions of Brazil would then be brought within a short distance of the seaboard.

But the line had its financial difficulties, and the new Baron of Mauá, who at the time held a seat in the Chamber of Deputies as representative from his native province of Rio Grande do Sul, asked the government for a guarantee of interest for a period of ten years. In later years he described the scene himself:

The discussion of the subject in the Chamber of Deputies was short and happy. One deputy whose name escapes me spoke against the petition and attacked the concession, on the pretext that the country could not be charged with this expense. I rose with some heat and made the Chamber feel the weakness of this attack, asking if it was proper to deny a little aid to the first railroad built in Brazil at a moment when an artist (the

singer Tamberlick) was being paid eighty-four contos so that we might
hear his fine notes for four months!

The apostrophe was not lost, no one said another word, and the vote
showed a majority in favor of the guarantee, three of the ministers, Nabuco, Paranhos (later the Viscount Rio Branco) and Pedreira (Viscount
Bom Retiro) voting for it.

I remember going that same afternoon to visit Viscount Paraná, who said
to me, in the tone of friendly reproof that he sometimes used with his
friends: "Then you had the power to divide the ministry with your petition?" "No, Your Excellency," I replied; "I said nothing of the sort to
your colleagues; it was the idea that triumphed!" "And do you believe it
will in the Senate?" "I do not know. It is clear that it will not, if Your Excellency is opposed to it. I, however, have done my duty, and that is
always a satisfaction."

Viscount Paraná (Honório Hermeto Carneiro Leão) was at the
time on his deathbed, though no one suspected the fact. He was also
the most powerful political figure of the empire, in a good measure
simply because of his gifts as a politician and his instinct to manage
other men. In many ways he was a contrast to the Emperor's other
favored counselors, being a man from the province of Minas Gerais,
neither bookish nor intellectual. He had been one of Baron Mauá's
earliest political friends. His allusion to difficulties in the Senate
awaiting the petition for a guarantee of interest for the Petrópolis
line was well-founded.

For another of the Emperor's ministers, Joaquim José Rodrigues
Torres, Viscount Itaboraí, a senator, was conservative and opposed
to financial experimentation. Itaboraí was consistently Mauá's enemy
in all attempts to obtain government aid. His idea and Mauá's idea of
what constituted wealth and progress were diametrically opposed to
each other. Itaboraí was one of the Emperor's favorite counselors. He
was undoubtedly the power behind many of the government-sup-
ported schemes that competed with Mauá's enterprises, as, for example, the railroad under construction between Rio and São Paulo
(to be known as the Dom Pedro II Railway) one stretch of which,
across the lowlands at the head of the bay, would take away from
Mauá's line the freight traffic coming from the province of Minas
Gerais.

This maneuver, so obviously intended to undermine his interests, infuriated Mauá. At first he was so angry that he wrote to his partners in Europe, asking for authority to tear up the rails of his own line. However, in a cooler moment he handed over the management of the line to other officials and went abroad. When he returned from England, he found that the line, because of the increasing traffic between way stations on the run from Rio to Petrópolis, was paying its own way and was increasing in prosperity.

In Europe he had looked into the methods used by European engineers to solve the problem of lifting railroads over mountains. When he arrived home, he commissioned Francisco Pereira Passos, a very young man but already enjoying a considerable professional reputation (he was later to make himself internationally famous as the builder of modern Rio) to study the question of a railroad up the mountain to Petrópolis. Mauá sought a loan of six hundred contos ($300,000) from the government of the province of Rio de Janeiro for the purpose, and to get around the objections of the imperial government, guaranteed the whole sum himself. But he did not have the real support of the imperial government, and he became discouraged as the years went on. In 1871, when the financial difficulties that culminated in his final bankruptcy were increasing, he turned over to several friends his interest in the Petrópolis line, today called the Leopoldina Railway, including new plans made by Pereira Passos.

But in the meantime it had made possible the most characteristic setting for the Second Reign. Like the court of Napoleon III at Saint Cloud and Compiègne, the Brazilian court at Petrópolis adopted an elaborate informality. Throughout the last thirty-odd years of Dom Pedro II's reign, it held a special place in the life of the empire. Visitors would comment on its European distinction, its luxurious air, its mingling of aristocratic elegance with bucolic simplicity, its atmosphere of half-intimacy between the imperial family and the members of the court circle.

It was a society that reflected the same triumph of bourgeois manners that was so completely embodied in the French Second Empire. The arrival of the train from Rio was a high social moment of the day, when the railway station was the rendezvous of fashion and elegance. Many of the ladies came, riding sidesaddle on spirited horses and wearing hats with trailing feathers, to meet their friends arriving from Rio. The more elderly or the more sedate came in carriages, in silks and satins, in an expensive simplicity. The Princess Imperial, heiress to the throne, drove her own carriage out in the fresh early morning, with a lady-in-waiting beside her and a lackey riding along-side. Her French husband, the Count d'Eu, rode out for exercise on a thoroughbred horse, accompanied by a liveried servant and bowed amicably to the passersby. The Emperor and Empress rode about in an open carriage with six horses. There were no dirty streets, no reek-ing slums.

Today the old ferries across the bay to the port of Mauá have been abandoned and the original rail line from there to the foot of the mountain is no longer used for the trip to Petrópolis. The traveler leaves Rio and crosses the flatlands by train, skirting the bay to the foot of the mountain, where a cogwheel train (the solution of the difficulty of climbing up the face of a mountain scarp two thousand feet high—a cogwheel modeled on those already in use in the Alps and constructed in 1882) lifts him up the somber gray mountain, through dense woods and outcroppings of weathered gray granite. The memory of the enlightened Baron is only preserved in the name of the railway station from which the train leaves Rio—the Baron Mauá Railway Station.

Throughout his life, railroads for Brazil remained to Mauá among the most inspiring and attractive of enterprises. The second railroad to be built was the inland road from Recife, the capital of the north-ern province of Pernambuco. Its initial financing, the sum of £300,000 ($1,500,000) was raised in London by his partner, De Castro, chiefly on the prestige his firm enjoyed in English financial circles. It had the blessing of the Brazilian government but it ran into difficulties result-ing from poor management and from the fact that, said Mauá to his creditors in 1878, the calculations of the engineers had been based more upon what was written in books than upon what had actually been done in building railroads. In the end the Brazilian government, after twice supplying aid, took over the franchise.

The story of the building of the Santos-Jundiaí Railway, now called the São Paulo Railway, was much more complicated. In 1836 the government of the province of São Paulo had granted a franchise for a railroad to a German, Frederico Fomm, the managing partner of a firm of commission merchants in the port of Santos in the province of São Paulo. Twenty years later Fomm's concession was still unused, for the problems of gathering capital to lift a railroad over the mountain range of the Cubatão had defeated the dreams of wealth to be made in providing rail transport for the increasingly prosperous cofiee-growing interior of the province. Now, in the 1850's, the idea itself was even more tempting, for the age of sugar was giving way to the age of coffee, and the center of wealth in the empire was shifting from the sugar-growing northern provinces to the coffee-growing province of São Paulo.

When Mauá took up the idea, there were not wanting those who saw him as the shrewd entrepreneur taking advantage of Fomm's innocent heirs. It was Viscount Mont'Alegre (José da Costa Carvalho), once a regent during Dom Pedro II's minority and then a minister and a senator, who obtained the grant of the concession from the government and Fomm's plans from his widow.

With this important matter arranged, Mauá set to work in Brazil and London to finance the new line. His activities, however, were not restricted to drumming up the money. He set his engineer, Robert Milligan, to work to break ground in the Serra do Cubatão, and he commissioned other engineers to make plans and sketches, which cost him £25,000 ($200,000). It was these studies and his work as promoter that he sold to the company finally established, for £45,000 ($225,000). Of this sum, £12,000 went to Fomm's descendants and firm. Half of it went to the house of Rothschild, the empire's bankers in London, who had demanded that sum as an earnest for their help in raising the money in London. This, Baron Penedo, the Brazilian minister in London, had said, was a necessary condition for the success of the subscription.

The idea of building this railroad required considerable ingenuity for its realization, since the Cubatão mountain range was especially steep and dangerous. Things went smoothly at first. The contractors and builders made handsome salaries and used them to buy coffee plantations in the province of São Paulo. But more difficult times came. The provincial government started the building of a highway parallel with the new rail line, up the mountain. No clear reason seems to have existed for this sudden fancy on the part of the local authorities, unless it indicated a complete lack of confidence in the success of the railroad, or perhaps a political move to spread wages in an election year. The practical result was a labor shortage and a consequent increase in wages.

With profits diminishing and vanishing into losses, the management of the railroad ran into difficulties. With its shares below par, its credit fell so much that the London bankers refused additional advances. The president of the company at last told the Brazilian Minister of the Treasury that if the company did not get an immediate loan of £100,000 ($500,000), he would be forced to go on the Stock Exchange and declare the company bankrupt. Mauá campaigned on behalf of the company in London and made advances out of his own resources. Its difficulties contributed their share to the collapse of his banking house. In the wrangles over its affairs throughout the 1860's and 1870's, first in the Brazilian courts and then in England, he was never repaid, except in the bitterness engendered by what he considered ingratitude and bad faith. But the railroad survived, to be today one of the most profitable and most heavily traveled in Brazil.

Mauá was the banker for the Baía railroad, in the north of the country, and even at the time of his greatest financial difficulties, in 1871, he was working at the problem of raising funds for a railway into the great interior province of Mato Grosso. His old friend Thomas Cochrane, a Swedish engineer named Palm, and two Brazilian engineers, Antônio and André Rebouças, were concerned in the scheme to provide a rail link between Curitíba, the capital of the southern province of Paraná, with the town of Miranda, in the interior.

The Rebouças brothers had gone to him with their idea and he had received them with his usual kindliness and his old willingness to encourage a good idea. André Rebouças, idealistic and sensitive to the rebuffs too often received from businessmen and politicians, appreciated the sympathetic simplicity of this man, who even when financial misfortune threatened to overwhelm him, could respond with eagerness to the suggestions of an unknown and unimportant engineer. André in his diary called Mauá "undoubtedly the most intelligent and most patriotic of capitalists with whom I have dealt. If it was not for his financial embarrassments and his absence in the River Plate, I would never deal with any other."

His last effort concerned the Rio Verde Railroad, to connect Rio de Janeiro with the province of Minas Gerais. The franchise for the line had been obtained by a friend who invited Mauá to come in as a partner. At first he accepted but, sinking more and more deeply into the morass of bankruptcy, he was forced to withdraw.

The only major railroad with which he was not intimately associated was the Dom Pedro II Railroad, now called the Central Railroad of Brazil. Some of the Emperor's advisers sought jealously to exclude Mauá nor did the Emperor's official bankers, Rothschilds of London, wish him to have any interest in the enterprise. Nevertheless, Mauá is credited, at the beginning of the negotiations to raise capital for the railroad in London and during difficulties arising during its construction, with having smoothed the way for the Brazilian government. No small part of his final disaffection for the Emperor's mode of government arose from this studied exclusion from one of the great industrial developments in nineteenth-century Brazil.

CHAPTER VII

THE MAN
OF AFFAIRS

IN THE LATE 1850's and early 1860's, as a man in his forties, Mauá was at his prime, physically vigorous, spiritually adventurous, and mentally keen. He was a man of average height, with brown hair, penetrating dark eyes under straight eyebrows, a long nose, and a firmly closed mouth. His very attitude in standing for his portrait distinguished him from the typical Brazilian man of his day, the inheritor and perpetuator of traditional gestures. He stood straight, energy apparent in every line of his figure, as if he had only paused for a moment to interrupt his all-absorbing affairs, with a trace of preoccupation still in his expressive yet reserved glance, a man whose attitude toward life was in doing, not in being. He was no longer the young experimenter. According to his own statement, his annual income when he was thirty years old amounted to fifty contos or $25,000; when he was thirty-six it had grown to $1,500,000. He was a made man, the owner of large industries, with a reputation of dealing in international affairs.

In private life he was a family man of simple tastes. His house filled steadily with an increasing family, boys and girls, many of whom, in the wasteful hygienic ignorance of the day, succumbed to childhood diseases, but who were, during their sometimes brief lives, his dearest care and chief interest. He had no inclination to build a mansion, like many of his contemporaries, and, after his working day, filled with the preoccupations of a man of affairs, he had little energy for social activity. His most pretentious dwelling, into which he moved from the house in the Rua do Catete, where he had married, was the little palace close to the Quinta da Boa Vista, once the property of the Marchioness of Santos, the redoubtable mistress of Dom Pedro I. It had come into his possession from a bankrupt debtor, and he had accepted it to avoid a forced sale. His sister Guilhermina, the vigorous chatelaine of his house, disliked this choice of dwelling exceedingly, as she disliked his title of Mauá. To her mind, no good could come from such associations and such a pagan name.

He was a devoted father, though he had not much time to give his children. He never forgot to bring sweetmeats home to them in the evening, and he never went on his frequent long journeys without taking his wife and some of the older children with him. The younger —there were always so many of them—stayed in Rio with their grand-mothers. Their numbers did not diminish the affection he had for each individual child, and he suffered acutely when he lost one of them. To lose a son or a daughter, he told his friend and partner in Montevideo, Ricardo José Ribeiro, was like losing a piece of his own soul. There was a certain refinement of cruelty in the fate that per-mitted him to arrive back in Rio from a long journey, to find the body of a two-year-old daughter laid out on the diningroom table. His quick sympathies were never asleep, and in 1855 he had to bear the loss of his eldest, thirteen-year-old Lísia Ricardina, the namesake and godchild of his old patron, Richard Carruthers. In January, 1861, he described his children to Carruthers:

> I accept with all my heart the felicitations which you send me in refer-ence to the happiness which it has pleased God to bless me with in my family circle. Indeed in this respect it were ingratitude on my part to wish for more. I am surrounded by the most affectionate cares of a wife, a mother, and our only sister, who all strive to guess what I want. The six children are also a source of indescribable happiness. It is curious to observe

the extraordinary diversity of characters among them. Ireneo, the eldest, is a flighty headed boy, always running and jumping and who cannot be prevailed to remain in the same place for ten minutes. He is by no means void of ability. Henrique, the next in age, is a very intelligent boy, full of ideas, and who is liked by everybody who sees him. Arthur, the next, is a reflective boy, always serious, but withal amiable, affectionate, and very fond of his parents. He learns everything that is taught *quicker* than his older brothers. All these three are at Petropolis in one of the best colleges we have. Then come the big-headed Ricardo, who is a most amusing little fellow, full of mind and of an excellent temper; with kind words he does all he is told to do. If I am not mistaken, this boy, if God allows him to be a *man*, will be a *master* in his profession, whatever it may be. Little Maricota is a sweet girl, but unfortunately nearsighted to an alarming extent. She must put objects very close to her eyes to see them. The baby, Lizia, four-teen months old, is our angel. She is a perfect replica of the one God took from us, a loss to which we are not yet reconciled. Surely to look at the little thing would make any man happy! I have enough to compensate and render life as agreeable as can be hoped for in this world of cares, and I am sure you will be delighted to know it, as I pride myself in believing that you take an interest in all that is important to me, as I do indeed in everything that concerns your good. I never for a moment cease to con-sider you my second father.

When he was in Rio and came home of an evening, he saw his children first and then joined his wife and mother in their sitting-room, where he dozed on the sofa while they sewed and talked. Or if he was much preoccupied with financial affairs, he would walk up and down the room, thinking aloud in English. After dinner at five o'clock, for half an hour he would sit in a chair overlooking the garden and throw bits of bread to the swans and geese. His working day ended late, in the office he kept next to his bedroom, where he sat and wrote letters for half the night. He began a new day sharp at nine o'clock, reaching his downtown office before the clerks, and often in the press of business he forgot to eat. Especially on days when the steam packets left for Europe, when he had long letters, full of detailed instructions and advice, to prepare for his partners, MacGregor in London and De Castro in Manchester, he stayed at his desk, the porter bringing him food from the nearest hotel.

His memory was prodigious, for he could carry in his head the balance sheets and business details of all his enterprises, which at one time numbered twenty or more. His manner with his employees was part of his art of managing his affairs. He never shouted at them, even when the work was badly done, but instead questioned and advised, and when he gave orders, gave them in a low voice. If he was dealing with a man expert in some technical field, like metallurgy and shipbuilding, in which he had only his own practical genius to guide him, he never presumed to give orders. In a subject in which he was really an expert, like accountancy, he always had a reasonable explanation and the patience to present it in persuading those who worked under him to do as he said. But in spite of these soft manners, there was never any doubt when he had made up his mind. He paid good wages and was liberal with bonuses. The old business habits he had learned with Carruthers remained with him, with the concept that a well-paid employee was worth the money, in the loyalty and willingness thus obtained. Thus he once distributed two hundred contos ($100,000) to the employees of the Petrópolis railroad. On another occasion he ordered £10,000 ($50,000), which an English company was going to pay him for his services as its promoter, to be paid to the company's lawyer. The lawyer earned the money, he said; "there was no need for any effort of mine."

In times of public disaster he was extraordinarily generous. When Rio was scourged by yellow fever and cholera, he had not only contributed money but made himself a member of a committee to find houses in which the sick might be treated when the existing hospital space became inadequate. When there was a cholera epidemic in the River Plate following the Paraguayan war, he was as a matter of course treasurer for the relief fund. When the great droughts came to the north of Brazil, bringing famine and disease in their wake, he contributed sums as great or even greater than those donated by the Emperor himself.

A delicate, cheerful courtesy was a part of his nature. Intrigue, bad faith, personal attack, could make him angry and even violent and abusive, but mistakes and a lack of understanding never awoke anything but a tolerant patience. Unlike the typical public man of the Brazil of his day, raised in the enervating climate of slavery, he was not touchy, arrogant, autocratic. He was vain of one thing only: his own ability to solve financial and economic problems.

The letter he wrote in January, 1861, to Carruthers was typical of him in the heyday of his physical and mental powers. He wrote in English, an English so obviously the language of his private thoughts, the language in which he could most naturally clothe the expression of his ambitions:

Dear Mr. Carruthers: Being aware that my correspondence with De Castro is constantly laid before you and from him getting also, regularly, accounts of your health, I have not thought it advisable to send a duplicate of what I write to him. At the commencement of a new year I cannot, however, allow the first Packet to leave without directly expressing my heartfelt pleasure at the continuance of your health and well-being at the lovely spot you picked for your residence, where I conceive you enjoy as much happiness as can be hoped for in this earthly habitation. It is indeed singular that, with minds equally disposed to enjoy quiet and home happiness, and all that is good in me arising from the lessons inspired into my mind thirty years ago by you, we should have adopted such widely different means of life to arrive at the same end. The facts, however, can be explained with greater ease than would appear at first sight, for, amongst the lessons imbided in my mind by the friendly or rather father-like advice given me by you at that early period of my life, the love of one's country was a theme very frequently touched upon in our conversations, and the seed existing, it could hardly fail to grow up and engross my ideas with the hope of being useful to my country, at all events in the sphere of life which fate has destined for me. Believe me, the idea of doing good, both to my country, and as extensively as my means would allow, privately, to those who need it, has been the groundwork of my apparent ambition, and I cannot help thinking that this honesty of purpose has merited the approval of Providence, on reflecting that more than once I have been saved by almost miraculous interference. I refer to the support obtained at the close of 1857 from a perfect stranger, who advanced two hundred thousand pounds at a critical period, which saved my firm from liquidation. And as regards my pocket, the past year has been a brilliant one and every succeeding one henceforward will show increased profits as the vast accumulation of capital in my establishments at a low rate of interest must become of great profit; and confidence is daily strengthening on the part of the public. As regards my mercantile position, a number of envious wretches have repeatedly tried to do me harm. Last year they redoubled their efforts to succeed at a moment when the Banking house met with hard times. My calmness and firm bearing brought the plot to the ground. Now they appear to have given up as a bad job such attempts, and the establishment is getting stronger than ever with the public. By the end of the present year its position *will leave nothing to wish for.* Early next year, God willing, I shall have no impediment to realise my long protracted voyage to Europe, leaving everything on this side in perfect order, and after eighteen months' residence abroad, I hope on my return to have silenced forever the gratuitous enemies I have had. The Government and the Conservative party, so called, lost the elections entirely—this party from an anxiety to govern *too much,* meddling with all the dealings of trade and have alienated all tradesmen from them, their main support before. On the other hand, the Liberals have entirely changed their ideas, being now men of order, aspiring to get into power only by legitimate constitutional means, and as they promise to meddle but little with the working of industry and trade, their attainment of power is hail'd with hope. In fact, dear Mr. Carruthers, I fully expect that my troubles are over.

Carruthers, from his years of residence in an earlier Brazil, must have had a clearer understanding of the problems faced by his erstwhile protégé than many of the other European men of affairs with whom he dealt. It was true that the empire of Dom Pedro II had moved away from the society of the earlier reigns. Dom João and Dom Pedro I, like their ancestors before them, had relied heavily on the merchants and traders to maintain their governments, and the merchants therefore had a well-respected status. The world of Dom Pedro II, however, was not hospitable and sympathetic to a man with the taint of trade about him. It was, as Lídia Besouchet has pointed out, a "bookish, overstuffed, superficial culture," with an almost fanatical worship of foreign literature and political models imported from a Europe in the full upsurge of industrialization.

It was the Emperor himself who fixed the pattern and set the tone of that circumscribed world. And the Emperor was the product of historical accident and a faulty education. His father, in abdicating the throne of Brazil to go to Europe to secure that of Portugal for his eldest daughter, had assured Brazil of a romantic, legendary history unlike that of any of its neighbors in the New World. It was personified in his small son, who at five years of age was the nominal ruler of an immense territory, a handful of European settlers, an army of African slaves, and roving bands of wild Indians. In the centuries before, Brazil had been the land of many legends, but none were more exotic, more carefully nourished, and longer sustained than that of the Second Reign.

Dom Pedro II was physically like his mother, blond, vigorous, tall —six foot two or three inches in height. He was like her, too, in his extreme fondness for dabbling in scientific studies. Dona Leopoldina had been blond and bookish, but unlike her son she neglected her personal appearance. Lord Strangford's chaplain, Richard Walsh, described her as going about in heavy spurred riding boots, a dilapidated riding coat, and a man's hat. But she brought the first scientists to Rio, founded a private library that was the wonder of the natives, was a faithful and loving wife, and gave her old father-in-law more sympathy than he received from any other member of his inharmonious family.

Dom Pedro I was ignorant, violent, and dissolute. He, too, was an accomplished horseman, but one who preferred the stables and the company of the grooms, with whom he had grown up. He was intelligent enough, however, to realize that the neglect he had experienced as a child was not the proper upbringing for the second emperor of Brazil. He was an affectionate father to all his children, royal or illegitimate, and even after he had left Brazil he kept up an active correspondence, questioning their tutors about their health and themselves about their lessons. Undoubtedly he better than anyone realized the emotional blankness in the lives of the three small royal children left among strangers, without adult relatives capable of giving them loving kindness. By this understanding he earned the affectionate and lasting devotion of his straitlaced son.

Before he left, he appointed his former minister, the man whom he had once exiled for plain speaking, José Bonifacio de Andrada e Silva, as tutor for the royal princelings. He thus assured them an incorruptible preceptor and a conscientious chamberlain. José Bonifacio—otherwise the Patriarch of the Independence—would never shirk his job, wink his eyes at bad practices, nor forget that he was bringing up a future emperor. But warmth, cheeriness, and an understanding of child nature were not to be expected of him. These qualities were hardly more to be expected of the other conscientious people who catered to the young Dom Pedro II: Maria Catarina Equy, his Swiss nurse and governess; Dona Mariana Magalhães Coutinho, the "Dadama" of his childish speech; his schoolmasters; his spiritual preceptor, Brother Pedro de Santa Mariana—even after the strict supervision of the Patriarch of the Independence was replaced by the more casual tutelage of the Marquess of Itanhaem. The young Emperor was not allowed to skip his lessons. He was taught French, English, German, Latin, and Greek, drawing, history, geography, the "positive sciences," music, everything with the greatest care and none of it with the least freshness. The result was to produce three great faults in his education as a man: he remained a foreigner in Brazil; he never experienced a carefree childhood; and he never really learned to be king. This, certainly, was the opinion of the French minister Ney who was in Rio in 1844.

It was also the opinion of the preceding French diplomatic agent in Rio, Edouard Pontois. The Emperor's teachers, instead of being the best trained and the most able that money could obtain in Europe, versed in the educational and scientific reforms of the eighteenth century, were merely the best that could be induced to go to South America or who happened for some private reason to have wandered to Brazil and there tarried. It was enough to make one's heart contract, said Pontois in 1837 in a letter to Count Mole, to see into whose hands the Emperor's education had been delivered, what frivolous and ridiculous studies he was given, what narrow thoughts, unworthy of his rank, his spirit was nourished on. If things went on like this, he would be neither a man nor a king.

These were uncompromising strictures, and fortunately the young prince escaped the worst. The result of this education was an Emperor who, in the words of Alberto Rangel, had extraordinary moral qualities, was always urbane and attentive to the most humble of his subjects, maintained the highest possible standard in disinterested affection for his people, and was the severest judge of the public and private morality of the men who took part in his government. Rangel said:

But the error which the exotic figure of the ruler, with his faults and insufficiencies, represented, was an error essentially Brazilian. We adopted the son of the foreigner and we kept him as foreign as possible in the environment that received him. We had everything in our hands to prevent the frustrated and incomplete formation of the sovereign . . . but we forgot to Brazilianize the chief of the Brazilians.

The victim of this faulty education grew up into a tolerant, honest sovereign, with a respect for learning. But he disliked practical affairs, and of economics he understood only enough to grasp the fact that the real foundation of his throne was an agricultural, slaveholding society. His father and his grandfather, far less admirable characters than he, had nevertheless not hesitated to confront the realities of the Brazilian scene. Dom Pedro II, on the other hand, Vicente Licinio Cardoso has said, would have been admirable governing England:

He would have made of his court there an admirable stage for all the learned men of the world, gathering them together with all the goodness of his mind and the intelligence of his heart . . . but in Brazil he failed. He cultivated nobody. Even worse: he did not discover the best talents of his time, the *critic* and the *builder*, the "man of the north" and the "man of the south"—Travares Bastos, the political thinker, and Mauá, the man of action and the magnificent master of economic and financial problems. . . . If, instead of Sanskrit [Dom Pedro] had learned the value of the machine in the economy of modern peoples; if, in the place of keeping up a correspondence with egyptologists, he had taken care to hear the opinions of technicians who could have solved the basic fuel problems of Brazil; if, instead of professors of Tupí and Arabic, he had kept next to him men who could have explained to him the causes of the decadence of the Iberian peoples, the evolution of the Anglo-Saxons, the German resurgence, and the North Americans' admirable work of assimilation and organization, then—so I believe—the usefulness of his long reign would have been very different, for, long as it was in time, it was ephemeral in the real achievements which influence or decide the predominance of a people.

As the 1850's came to an end, Dom Pedro II's court became more bookish, sober, and ceremonious. He cultivated the arts in the true spirit of the New England transcendentalists, as a form of moral uplift. In 1843 he had married a princess of German origin, with no beauty nor quickness of mind, but with every domestic virtue, a sympathetic, motherly, gracious, unintellectual lady with no talent for dancing or managing state functions. So, like Queen Victoria's, his brief years of genuine youthfulness—for as an eligible bachelor he had been gay enough in a discreet way—vanished and were swallowed up in the preternaturally serious atmosphere of his court. The theater and especially the opera and the concert he could conscientiously encourage, for these were obviously cultural forces that would raise the intellectual level of his capital.

In this he succeeded. Italian opera companies came to Rio, and French actors and actresses. Even local talent was received. There was Dona Paulina Porto Alegre, for example, the daughter of one of the Emperor's ministers and wife of the composer Paul Faulhaber, who sang in Rio with the Philharmonic Orchestra. And there was Carlos Gomez, the mulatto, who was sent abroad by the Emperor to study music and rewarded his patron by writing Brazilian operas in the most approved Italian style. Rio had become a thoroughly cosmopolitan center, a profitable place for artists, teachers, scientists to visit. It was also the mecca of all Brazilians anxious to exchange the narrowness of life in the provinces for an acquaintance with the great world.

One of these Brazilians was Councilor Albino José Barbosa de Oliveira, whom the Emperor had named judge of a high court in Rio (the *Relação da Corte*). Councilor Albino came of a landholding family many of whose members had been lawyers. His great-grandfather had been a Portuguese who had settled in Baía sometime in the early eighteenth century. Like his father before him and his eldest son after him, Albino was educated at Coimbra University in Portugal. When he married he became a wealthy man, for his wife (whom, as was the custom of the day, he married sight unseen until the wedding day) was one of the three heirs to a fortune that included one hundred and forty slaves, coffee and sugar plantations, the value of which, including houses, furniture, jewels and silver, was estimated at more than two hundred contos ($100,000). His father-in-law, Francisco Inácio de Sousa Queiroz, was the scion of a family established in the genealogical rolls of the province of São Paulo and one of the wealthiest men in his part of the province.

Thus the Councilor, when he went to Rio, was far above the considerations of money, though he liked to make note of how much things cost him. He had a taste for the theater, especially for the opera, and he faithfully recorded in his memoirs the times when he heard the "heart-stirring" Italian singer, Candiani, and saw the performances of the French actress Eugénie Mege, who was shot by her husband, jealous of the attentions she received. Councilor Albino liked another French actress better, Artemise Duval. She was a little woman with black eyes and hair, very cute, and he danced with her at the ball at the royal palace in December, 1846.

When the Emperor gave a ball it was a very stately affair. Councilor Albino attended one on the night of April 25, 1852, the day of the funeral of two of his friends from the current yellow-fever epidemic and shortly after the deaths of two of his children in Campinas, in the province of São Paulo, where he had sent them to be safe from the fever. As a man rising in the imperial service, he could not afford to be absent when summoned. The ball was held at the then famous Casino Fluminense. He resolved to go but not to dance.

"I was sitting sadly in a corner," he said later in his memoirs, "when the Empress, seeing me, bowed her head. I rose at once and hurried over to the place where her majesty was and she had the goodness to ask after Isabelinha [his wife] and the girls, which made the conversation fall naturally on the recent fact of the death of my children in Campinas. She displayed a good deal of sympathy."

A few minutes afterward, one of the gentlemen of the court told him that he had been chosen as partner for her majesty in the next contradance, waltzes not being in favor.

"I was very pleased with such notice and at once told my brother about it, who also gave it the highest importance. . . . On the following day my parents were very happy to know that I had merited such a high honor from the Sovereigns."

He was perfectly reasonable, therefore, in looking for a steady rise in the royal favor. The only fly in the ointment was that he did not care for commercial court work, since his tastes and his talents did not lie in commercial subjects. As a lawyer, however, he knew that one of the most important events of the decade had been the adoption, on June 25, 1850, of the new Commercial Code, under the provisions of which a special Commercial Court had been created in 1855, its first session being held on July 1 of that year. The new code had been under preparation for twenty years. Once adopted, regulations had to be provided for its enforcement and a special committee was named to prepare these, a committee composed of Eusébio de Queiroz, José Clemente Pereira, Nabuco de Araújo, Carvalho Moreira (later Baron Penedo), Caetano Alberto Soares and, last but not least, the businessman, Irineu Evangelista de Sousa, lately made Baron Mauá. Councilor Albino, much against his own choice, was appointed judge on the new Commercial Court. He found commercial causes confusing, vexatious, and distasteful, but in the interests of his career he could not refuse the appointment.

In 1857 Mauá became mixed up in the affairs of A. J. Domingues Ferreira, who had sold him negotiable paper which had been put up as security for a debt. The day the notes fell due, Domingues Ferreira was declared a bankrupt. When Mauá presented himself as owner of the notes in the bankruptcy proceedings, he found his title to them disputed by Comendador Rodrigues de Moura. The Commercial Court, which had cognizance of the matter and which was made up of three regular law judges (including Councilor Albino) and two special masters (merchants appointed for the case) decided against Mauá and in favor of Moura.

Mauá was indignant. He had had the best of legal advice, for his lawyer had been Teixeira de Freitas, the legal genius who compiled the first draft of a Civil Code for Brazil. Besides, he accused Moura of bad faith and falsification. Characteristically, he did not mince his words when describing his adversary. The decisions of the Commercial Court, he declared, were neither just nor impartial, and in writing to his partner MacGregor and his friend Andrés Lamas, he called the judgment a robbery. In February, 1860, he wrote to his partner Ribeiro in Montevideo:

"The law judges were bought with a lot of money by Moura, and among the special masters, Samuel Mayrink is my personal enemy and a corrupt man. General opinion is revolted by such villains."

The Supreme Court granted a review of the case on the ground of "notorious injustice" and passed it on to the court in Baía (the *Relação de Baía*), which found in Mauá's favor.

The lawyer for the other side in this legal wrangle was José Tomas Nabuco de Araújo, who had been Minister of Justice in 1854 and in 1857 and, with Mauá, one of the draftsmen of the regulations for the Commercial Code. He was also a leading figure in the Liberal party. He was at the moment in a very awkward position, for he was trying to recoup his financial position by the private practice of law, for which purpose he had withdrawn from political office. But his position as a public man was altogether too well established for him to be disassociated in the public mind from government policies and political events. As Minister of Justice he had promoted the changes in the commercial law, especially those governing the creation of commercial courts. Drafts of these changes he had submitted to Mauá for his opinion as banker and merchant. Nabuco had also presided over the drafting of the new law governing mortgages and the law creating the Commercial Court.

But unfortunately Nabuco de Araújo was not a man of wealth. He came of a modest family that had emigrated from Portugal and settled in Baía in the eighteenth century. His father had risen in importance as an army officer and political man in Pará during the turbulence that lasted in that part of Brazil long after the independence. José Tomas himself had adopted politics as his career as soon as he had left law school and he had increased his opportunities by marrying the daughter of a family related to the Cavalcantis, who from time out of mind had been all-powerful in the province of Pernambuco. His wife, however, unlike Councilor Albino's, was not a great heiress. Politics was an expensive career for a poor man. As one of Dom Pedro's ministers of state his salary was modest, and when he left the ministry in 1857 he was in debt.

His house was the meeting place for the deputies from the northern provinces, and the gatherings there reflected the characteristic notions of these representatives of the old, sugar-growing Brazil. As his son, Joaquim Nabuco, described them later, this Pernambucan gentry had an invincible aversion to money and a touchy sense of honor in matters of hospitality. These were men who were ready to live for years on a plantation in the backwoods or to rusticate on their mortgaged sugar factories, where they remained through the good nature of their creditors, so long as they could save the decorum of their position. They preferred being in debt to making money. Debt, in their eyes, could be honorable, whereas there was nothing chivalric about making money. Unlike the men from the south, they had no acquisitive instincts, none of the competitive sense of commerce. What they did not understand was that there was nothing so commercial as debt. This very weakness, perhaps, made them all the more acceptable to the Emperor, for in public affairs they were the soul of honesty, incapable of making a profit at the expense of the country or out of any public transaction in which they had a part.

Nabuco de Araújo, however, had a family to support, and he had no taste for retiring and vegetating in poverty. Instead, he withdrew temporarily from politics and opened a law office in Rio. He at once acquired a lucrative practice, and in 1858 he became attorney for Antônio José de Moura. He was in a vulnerable position, and Mauá, angry at what he considered a denial of justice, attacked him in the Chamber of Deputies. As deputy for Rio Grande do Sul, Mauá introduced a bill, on June 3, 1860, for a law providing that bond must be posted by the successful party in the lower court, until the final decision in the case was handed down by the court of appeals. In the course of his argument in favor of the bill, he said:

Unfortunately, Mr. President . . . we see among us eminent men, most unhappily drawn by immoderate ambition to enrich themselves quickly, to descend from the councils of the crown to go and open a lawyer's office. . . . By the old laws of the Portuguese monarchy, *in the time of absolutism*, powerful men were forbidden to practice advocacy. And in that there is the idea of public morality. The man, for example, who, in the exercise of high office as the Minister of Justice, organizes a tribunal, names the judges, and is in a position to be called again at any moment to the Ministry, necessarily exercises a great influence, with grave danger to the sound administration of justice. . . . And if that man, soon after exercising power and ready to return to such exercise from one moment to the next, sells not only his services as legal counsel, but his influence (for nothing else can be understood by the settlement of commercial causes by the payment of many tens of contos, as was, it is notorious, done in this case), where will there be, I ask, the necessary protection for the rights of those who litigate?

Nabuco de Araújo was stung into self-defense. He was a senator and he introduced in the Senate a bill for a law providing that parties to litigation or any other person interested in a suit, be prohibited from publishing in the newspapers comments on decisions handed down by the courts, so long as such decisions were subject to appeal or review, under pain of six months' imprisonment. The bill was obviously directed against Mauá, who he believed had inspired the publication in newspapers of attacks on him. He called the Senate's attention to the fact that Baron Mauá had referred to "eminent men, who, with a desire to get rich quick, opened lawyers' offices, after having been ministers of state." He defended himself, pointing out that he had sought advocacy, not to enrich himself, but to earn money to pay off his debts—debts incurred during the honorable discharge of his official duties.

As for his influence:

"My influence! My influence, because I created the Commercial Court and named its judges! There is a good deal of error in that argument. The Commercial Court was converted into a tribunal of second instance, not by an act of the executive, but by a law; also I did not name the judges who composed it." He repelled the "atrocious insult" that he had sold his influence. His profit from the case was his fee as a lawyer and a honorarium from his clients, and he had earned that as advocate. Nor was the sum of twenty contos too much for a case so complicated, so controversial, and involving so much work.

Gentlemen, there is nothing more improbable, more ridiculous, than the contrast that the noble representative of the house of Mauá, MacGregor and Company wants to establish, representing himself as weak and me as

powerful. I powerful, gentlemen, because I had been minister, when there
are so many former ministers who also practice law and have more advantageous circumstances, circumstances of greater influence that I have!
Furthermore, Baron Mauá weak! Baron Mauá, with numerous partners
to support him, interested in the same case and in the same affairs; Baron
Mauá, aided by so many powerful friends and former ministers; Baron
Mauá, disposing of much money, money which is like the Medusa's head
and petrifies everything in our material age!

Mauá might deprecate his own strength. Everyone knew him to be
the most powerful man of money in Brazil. Nabuco de Araújo might
deprecate his own political influence. Everyone knew him to be one
of the most important men of the Second Reign. Probably because to
the one, as a businessman, such battles were a commonplace, and to
the other, an experienced politician, they were incidents of public
life, the rupture did not last. Mauá in the end forgave Nabuco and
Nabuco was not adverse to being forgiven. Before Nabuco died, they
were reconciled and Mauá attended his old adversary's funeral.

But though Mauá could forgive the lawyer for the other side, he
did not forgive the court nor the judges. In 1878, in his statement to
his creditors, he listed "some unjust decisions of the courts of my
country," of which this was the first, as one of the major causes of his
bankruptcy.

Councilor Albino did not take the matter so casually. He saw his
reputation as a judge left under a cloud. He was resentful against "that
rascal, that knave," Mauá, and against the Minister of Justice, Sayão
Lobato (later Viscount Niteroi), whose "miserable servility" made
him the Emperor's ready tool. There were rumors, too, that the government would force the judges implicated in the case to retire. Councilor Albino continues in his memoirs:

It was then September, 1861, and on the 15th the General Assembly
would recess. On the eve of this day, at night, I was with my wife in the
São Pedro Theater, watching a comic representation of Othello by Vasques
[Francisco Correia Vasques, a very popular actor], laughing very much,
and with the intention of leaving at ten o'clock to take part in the birthday
celebration of Cousin Urbana Perdigão.... Before this took place, Eusébio

de Queiroz arrived, called me out of the box and in the corridor informed me that I had been dismissed from the Commercial Court. . . . He asked me to keep it secret . . . for what reason I do not know since in the morning all the newspapers carried the news. I spent the night on foot, walking backward and forward, with Isabelinha seated on the bed, and I did not lack tears, because this outrage was very great and the blow immense, since the government had placed my honor as a judge, which I had safeguarded for thirty years, in doubt. My conscience sustained me at the time, my fortune in the future. But seeing my probity so directly attacked by the Emperor, just the person to whom I had always been so devoted, so faithful, so grateful, because he had always been favorable to my ambitions and especially so in the matter of my father's pension—besides which, he knew me personally, and once I had even heard mass in the imperial pew with him and the Empress, I having gone with Isabelinha to the Paço in the company of the Marquess of Valença—my reason was threatened. I am certain that everything came from him [the Emperor], the rascal Sayão, the Minister of Justice, being only the hangman.

But in spite of his despair, he kept up a good appearance:

The 22d came, the birthday of Yaya Macedo, and we had previously arranged, since this day fell on a Sunday, for a picnic on a steam launch, hired for the occasion, which we carried out. I contributed a turkey and some cold meat. . . . The day was very cheerful. I never left the company of the ladies. We disembarked on the Ilha d'Agua, where we had lunch and danced under the mango trees; afterward, sailing about the bay, we went to Paquetá; and a little later we went to the Quinta do Cajú, where we had dinner very frugally and without ceremony. At night we went to the house of Comendador Luiz Tavares Guerra, where we danced and played, and I didn't feel tired. Afterward we came to the Palace Square, where we disembarked and separated. I was considerably distracted, and the day would have been complete if at every moment there had not come to crush me the memory of the horrible outrage which Dona Ana Delfina sought so energetically to dissipate.

In December, 1861, on Eusébio's advice, he called on the Emperor to take leave before going to São Paulo. He led the conversation around to the question of his dismissal, and when the Emperor declared that he was not convinced of the justice of the accusation of venality against the Commercial Court, the Councilor, in tears, offered to prove the quality of his public career with official documents. The Emperor said he might do so. When the Councilor told Nabuco de Araújo of this conversation, Nabuco said he must be very proud, for the Emperor did not treat everyone like that. Nabuco persuaded him to put off gaing to São Paulo and to go to Petrópolis instead with his official documents, the Emperor being in residence there. When Albino saw the Emperor again, Dom Pedro was noncommittal, questioned him about his opinion of his fellow judges, and raised no objection when the Councilor announced that he would resort to the newspapers to state his case.

He did so, preparing what he himself described as "the finest papers that ever came from my hand." He showed the statement to Nabuco, who admired it, and then he had it published in the *Jornal do Comércio*. When it appeared, he was stopped by a lot of friends when he strolled in the Rua do Ouvidor, the chief gathering place of the elite of Rio, and "everybody to whom I showed it or recited it has praised it and even a year later my cousin Ruy Barbosa carried it off to copy it in his own hand, which could not fail to flatter me very much."

It was really a demand on Sayão Lobato to explain the reasons why he had removed the judges from the Commercial Court. In a debate in the Chamber of Deputies on May 20, 1862, Sayão Lobato refused to give reasons, except for a general statement that it was for the public good and that he had not intended to bring any individual judge's character into question. The next day the Councilor went to the Chamber and challenged the Ministry, with no effect. In point of fact, the episode did little permanent damage to his career, for the next July he was named to the Court of Justice, though he was convinced that the Emperor continued to look upon him with disfavor.

However accurate he might be in that statement, Albino was not correct in supposing that all this took place because the Emperor favored Mauá. To the Emperor Mauá was a suspect person, dangerous because he was powerful and not thoroughly subordinate to the dictates of the Emperor's government. On no occasion did the Emperor show his dislike more clearly than in the Christie affair, which came to the fore as the last scenes of the Councilor's discomfiture were closing.

The crux of Brazilian foreign affairs during the Second Reign was the long-standing, embittering dispute with England over the slave trade. On August 8, 1845, the British Parliament had passed the Aberdeen Act, which provided that all cases involving vessels captured by the British navy as slavers should be tried by the British admiralty or vice-admiralty courts, instead of by a joint Anglo-Brazilian mixed commission, as had been provided for by the treaty of 1828. The effect in Brazil of the act was immense, for besides the indignation aroused by the slight to Brazilian sovereignty there was the feeling that there was not much that Brazil could do against the British navy. No one felt the situation more sharply than Dom Pedro. In anything to do with the complicated problem of slavery in Brazil he was especially sensitive, for morally he thought the institution indefensible, yet politically he hesitated to touch a matter of such vast importance to the economic basis of his empire.

The chief justification for the execution of the Aberdeen Act, in British eyes, was the failure of the Brazilian authorities to take effective steps to put an end to the contraband importation of slaves into Brazil. The 1840's were uneasy years, for the unsettled conditions within Brazil made it impossible for the imperial government to act energetically. The volume of importations of slaves steadily increased, until in 1850 the British government ordered its cruisers to enter Brazilian harbors and seize vessels outfitted as slavers.

Even though the general situation improved when the power of the imperial government grew stronger, the indignation aroused by the Aberdeen Act left a residue of resentment that soured any situation in which Brazilian and British officials came into conflict. Matters grew worse in 1860 when William Christie was sent to Rio as British Minister, for Christie was unsympathetic to the Brazilians, impatient, undiplomatic, and shortsighted. His truculent attitude and want of tact magnified every small incident that arose—and the situation was such that many were bound to arise—until it was beyond compromise.

In 1861 the trouble culminated in a commonplace incident, the arrest of disorderly sailors from a British vessel anchored at the time in the harbor of Rio. The sailors had been sightseeing on Mount Tijuca. The Brazilians said they had been drunk and had attacked a sentry. The sailors said they had been arrested without cause and thrown into jail. Christie, without due investigation, demanded blood, and his superior in London, Sir John Russell, accepting his version of the episode, demanded punishment of the sentry and of the ensign in charge of the post, censure of the chief of police of Rio and the local prison authorities for their treatment of British subjects, and an apology from the imperial government. Furthermore, he wanted damages in the case of the *Prince of Wales*, a British vessel that in June, 1861, had been wrecked off a lonely part of the coast of Rio Grande do Sul, some of its crew murdered, and its cargo looted by the local inhabitants.

The Brazilian Minister of Foreign Affairs at the moment was the Marquess of Abrantes, Miguel Calmon du Pin e Almeida. Calmon was one of the men Dom Pedro II had inherited from the time of the Regency. He was the son of a wealthy sugarmill owner of Baía, and his habits of luxury were those of his class; when he went to the University of Coimbra in Portugal for his education, for instance, he took with him two slaves, a present from his mother. Furthermore, he had married the daughter of the head of the wealthy banking firm of Baía Irmãos. He had been abroad in 1844 on a diplomatic mission and he had discussed international affairs with Lord Aberdeen in person. Perhaps in this background is some explanation of his behavior in an incident which the Emperor and the crowd in the street took seriously. For, when his secretary came to tell him that Christie had delivered an ultimatum, that vessels of the British navy were in the harbor with guns trained on the city, he did not interrupt his game of ombre, which he was playing with friends there in his great house in Botafogo. In fact, he turned the announcement off with a joke.

But in the meantime the Minister of the Navy, Admiral Lamaré, had gone to the palace to tell the Emperor a complicated story about Baron Mauá, who, it was said, was acting as intermediary between the imperial government and the British legation. It was the first intimation that the Emperor had had of such a thing, and he was angry. He did not tolerate such volunteers, acting without his advance approval. The situation was explosive. The British ships were blockading the port and holding in the harbor five Brazilian coastal vessels. The city was in a panic, afraid of a bombardment and indignant at its own helplessness.

The Emperor in his diary recorded the scene when he called Calmon—Marquess Abrantes—onto the carpet for an explanation. Abrantes made his explanation. Mauá, he said, had approached both him and the Marquess of Olinda, and Abrantes had replied that, if "he would assure him in writing of Christie's acceptance of such mediation, he would present the idea to his colleagues and to me," wrote the Emperor, "showing me Mauá's letter on the subject." The Emperor turned the idea down. It would look peculiar for a banker, with the closest possible ties with England, to mediate in such a matter. Abrantes excused himself. He had, he said, judged it his duty to accept the intervention. The Emperor reprimanded him: "You would have done your duty if you had consulted your colleagues and me before you gave Mauá any reply."

There was no harmony in the Cabinet, and the Emperor knew it. Viscount Sinimbú, for instance, at the time Minister of Agriculture, especially did not approve of Abrantes and threatened to withdraw from the Ministry if Mauá's intervention were accepted. The Emperor sadly observed: "God will that rather we should fight with the English, than that we should fight among ourselves!"

The Emperor's energetic manner made Christie see his mistake and the British vessels were withdrawn, but the situation itself remained at an impasse. In February, 1863, Carvalho Moreira, Baron Penedo, the Brazilian Minister in London, paid the damages demanded for the *Prince of Wales*, but he accompanied the payment with a protest against the incident in the port of Rio and a demand for damages in return. The British government refused the demand, and in June, 1863, Brazil broke off diplomatic relations. They were not resumed until the middle of 1865, when the Emperor, visiting the River Plate after the commencement of the Paraguayan War, received the British Minister to Buenos Aires, William Thornton. The British government still refused to pay damages but was willing to apologize, so the incident was closed.

Mauá thought the whole affair had been badly managed. On January 6, 1863, he wrote to his friend Andrés Lamas in Montevideo:

"We have here a grave complication with the British legation. There has fallen to me the thorny task of convincing Mr. Christie of his lack of reason and happily he admitted more than anyone expected." On February 6, 1863, he added:

In truth, we here run a *great risk* of the *sovereign people* getting into the street in order to make their will known to the government! In the question with Mr. Christie, things do not run as well as the public press indicates, because unhappily our government gave evidence of its usual knack for making mistakes, allowing an honorable arrangement to lie neglected, an arrangement which could have been carried out and which would have prevented the display of insolence of which we have been the victim. We shall converse on this subject there [Montevideo], for I intend to go by the French boat of the 24th of this month.

Unfortunately, whatever else he had to say to Lamas has been lost to posterity.

CHAPTER VIII

OPENING UP
THE AMAZON

THE BLUE WATERS of the ocean had changed to a muddy brown. Everywhere streaks appeared of different colors, and the surface was troubled by whirlpools and tumbling water. Quantities of driftwood, tropical fruits and plants were tossing about, and huge fishhawks, gulls and terns hovered over the turbulent currents. To the right the island of Marajó came into sight, and to the left long, low land lay on the horizon. As the banks of the great river drew nearer, tall trees, as thick as a hedge, shot up their arrow-like stems. Broad palm leaves waved with every breath of air. A thousand shades of green were enameled with flowers, in red, white, gold. The loud tones of the toucans, the shrill cries of parrots sounded as the traveler's welcome, mingling with the twittering of hundreds of martins. Here and there little patches of clearings and haystack-shaped huts indicated the home of some ease-loving Indian. Some of these huts consisted merely of a few poles, covered with palm thatch, but occasionally a delicious little retreat would peep out through the almost concealing shrubbery, surrounded by a grass plot and overshadowed by the huge leaves of the banana or the feathery tufts of the cocoa tree.

Huge canoes, hollowed from single trees and with mat sails, crept along the shore, bound to market and loaded with all kinds of produce for the city. The city itself showed fine buildings of three or four stories high, facing the water, all yellow in color and roofed with red tiles. A vast cathedral and churches, covered with the mold of age, shot up their tall spires, their walls and roofs affording sustenance and support to the venerable mosses and shrubs of good size. Garden walls were overhung with creeping vines, like ancient ruins.

These are the words in which a visitor of 1847, William Edwards, described his first glimpse of the city of Belém in the province of Pará, at the mouth of the Amazon. Up the great river and its tributaries, the Tocantins, the Rio Negro, the Madeira, the Solimões, lay a land of unrivaled fertility.

"This," said Lieutenant of the Navy Herndon to the United States Congress in 1853,

is the country of rice, of sarsaparilla, of India-rubber, balsam copaiba, gum copal, animal and vegetable wax, cocoa, Brazilian nutmeg, Tonka beans, ginger, black pepper, arrow root, tapioca, annatto, indigo, sapuaia, and Brazil nuts; dyes of the gayest colors, drugs of rare virtue, variegated cabinet woods of the finest grain and susceptible of the finest polish. The forests are filled with game, and the river stocked with turtle and fish. Here dwell the anta or wild cow, the peixeboi, or fish-ox, the sloth, the anteater, the beautiful black tiger, the mysterious electric eel, the boa constrictor, the anaconda, the deadly coral snake, the voracious alligator, monkeys in endless variety, birds of the most brilliant plumage, and insects of the strangest forms and gayest.

And the only means of penetrating this earthly paradise was by primitive canoes and river craft that took days to make the trip between the few riverside settlements. What was needed was steam navigation.

"Then would the mighty river no longer roll its sullen waters through miles of unbroken solitude; no longer would the deep forests that line its banks afford but a shelter for the serpent, the tiger, and the Indian; but, furrowed by a thousand keels, it would bear upon its waters the mighty wealth that civilization and science would call from the depths of those dark forests."

In more prosaic language, the fact was that the province of Amazonas had remained for many years isolated from the rest of Brazil and the world. The only communication it had with the outer world was by means of sailing vessels that went up the river from Belém to the town formerly called the Barra do Rio Negro and now known as Manáus. Old prejudices and antiquated laws had guarded the entrance to the river like the dragons of fable, barring the gateway to this new garden of the Hesperides. In 1826, a steamboat from the United States had tried to carry a cargo of merchandise to Peru by way of the Amazon, but did not succeed. Other attempts were made in the same year and in the years between 1837 and 1840, but they had all failed.

When Dom João VI opened the ports of Brazil to the commerce of the world in 1808, the Amazon River remained closed, and it continued to be closed after the establishment of the empire. The reason for this inhospitality was nothing more nor less than fear on the part of the imperial government, a fear of what the enterprise of foreigners might lead to. The Amazon was far away from Rio and the center of things Brazilian. It was mysterious, almost unknown, certainly too big a proposition to be handled by Brazilians, whose hold on all their huge country was precarious and restricted chiefly to the seacoast. And so long as Brazilians were unable to exploit the great river basin, it was better, in the eyes of the imperial government, to bar the intruder and leave the jungle in its solitude.

Brazilians and Portuguese had indeed attempted to develop the Amazon valley but their attempts were unsuccessful, for their projects did not meet with the wholehearted approval of either the imperial or the provincial government. As Arthur Cezar Ferreira Reis has pointed out, the policy of the Portuguese crown, in the days of the colony, was to permit only as much use to be made of these natural inland waterways as was convenient for government purposes. Any development of trade and navigation that injured or threatened the interests of the crown was suppressed. A good deal of this old attitude lingered after independence among the more conservative men of the imperial government, fearful of the strength such a region might attain if permitted unlimited freedom of growth.

It was not only the imperial government that was to blame. In 1826, when the Brazilian diplomatic agent in the United States, José Silvestre Rebello, with the support of the imperial government, attempted to form a "New York Society" for the navigation of the Amazon by steam vessels, his efforts were nullified by the local provincial government in Amazonia, headed by José Felix Pereira de Burgos, later Baron Itapicuru-Mirim. The reason adduced for this attitude was the danger that would threaten the existence of small river craft and the livelihood of those dependent upon these vessels if the steamboats were allowed to come in. During the Regency, a number of other attempts were made, without success. Either the capital required was not available, or the vessels could not be obtained.

But unfortunately for the peace of mind of those who favored the status quo, the foreigners who were the most actively interested in the development of the Amazon basin were the Americans, and they had been stirred up by an energetic, enthusiastic, tenacious man, whose indignation at this retrograde policy knew no bounds. Matthew Fontaine Maury was not one to qualify his enthusiasms, and this matter of free navigation of the Amazon was one of the major enthusiasms of his life. It was a busy life, for he was the first head of the United States Naval Observatory and Hydrographic Office. It had been his work in setting up a system of reports on winds and currents from ship captains supplied with especially prepared log books that prompted the convocation of the international conference in Brussels in 1853 whose purpose was to provide for a pooling by all nations of information about navigation and meteorology.

Maury was only distracted from a wrathful contemplation of the problem of the Amazon by the Civil War, during which he was the dynamic head of the coast, harbor, and river defenses of the Confederacy, and invented an electric torpedo. After the Civil War he went to Mexico as commissioner of immigration in the government of the Emperor Maximilian, and attempted to found a colony in Mexico of his fellow Virginians, a scheme that collapsed with Maximilian's regime. But it was undoubtedly his propaganda that inspired other groups of discontented Confederates to seek a new home in the Amazon basin after the surrender of Lee's army.

His newspaper attacks on the policy of the Brazilian empire in keeping the Amazon shut up had a highly disturbing effect in Rio. Dom Pedro II, said Maury, was the Rosas of the Amazon, shutting in five nations which held the headwaters and closing out the commerce of the rest of the world. This was nothing short of a sin, since, "All must admit that the valley of the Amazon is not only a great country, but it is a glorious wilderness and waste, which, under the improvement and progress of the age, would soon be made to 'blossom as the rose.' We have, therefore, but to loose upon it the engines of commerce—the steamer, the emigrant, the printing press, the ax, and the plough—and it will teem with life."

There was nothing in these remarks to reassure an already alarmed government in Rio. In fact, Maury stirred up a tempest in South America—not only in Brazil, but in Peru and the other nations who owned the headwaters of the Amazon. His articles had repercussions in Europe and in the United States as well. His somewhat flamboyant style of approach was useful in awakening even in Brazil considerable popular sympathy, especially among those who could publish their views in the newspapers. It also aroused an equally violent defense of the official attitude. The Brazilian government, fearful of an invasion by foreign traders, held its ground, suspicious of what the correspondent of the Brazilian newspaper, the *Observador*, in May, 1852, described picturesquely as "this nation of pirates, who like all those of their race, wish to displace all the people of America who are not Anglo-Saxon."

In self-defense, the imperial government adopted a law on September 6, 1850, which authorized the establishment of a steam-navigation service on the Amazon and its tributaries. In 1851, The United States Navy Department instructed Lieutenants William Lewis Herndon, a kinsman of Maury's, and Lardner Gibbon to explore the Amazon:

> The government desires to be put in possession of certain information relating to the valley of the river Amazon, in which term is included the entire basin or watershed, drained by that river and its tributaries.
> This desire extends not only to the present condition of the valley, with regard to the navigability of its streams; to the number and condition,

both industrial and social, of its inhabitants, their trade and products; its climate, soil, and productions; but also to its capacities for cultivation, and to the character and extent of its undeveloped commercial resources, whether of the field, the forest, the river, or the mine.

You will, for the purpose of obtaining such information, proceed across the Cordillera, and explore the Amazon from its source to its mouth.

The imperial government gave its consent to the passage of the expedition through Brazilian territory. But at the same time, the Brazilian diplomatic agent, Duarte da Ponte Ribeiro, was sent to Peru and Bolivia to make treaties excluding citizens of the United States from the right to navigate the Amazon. Later another diplomatic agent was sent to Ecuador, New Granada (as the modern Colombia was then called), and Venezuela for the same purpose. For some time Ribeiro and the American minister, J. Randolph Clay, carried on a lively competition in Peru and Bolivia. On October 23, 1851, Ribeiro signed a treaty at Lima, one provision of which declared that the navigation of the Amazon should belong exclusively to the states owning its banks, and another which required Peru to give a subsidy of twenty thousand dollars annually to a Brazilian steam-navigation company to be organized for service on the Amazon and its tributaries. The treaty was ratified in spite of Clay's protests.

The man invited, in the name of the Emperor, to form a company was Irineu Evangelista de Sousa, who in August, 1852, incorporated the Amazon Navigation and Trade Company. In telling his own story of its founding, he began with the statement:

"This was one of the great enterprises I created."

And he continued:

In that age when no one believed in free enterprise, it was announced by the government that it was authorized to contract for such navigation, by means of a subsidy and monopoly. No one came forward, notwithstanding the fact that the daily papers repeated the announcement during the course of some months! As a personal and devoted friend of one of the ministers [Viscount Mont'Alegre, at the time Minister of Empire] in office during this period of skepticism, I was urged to undertake the civilizing mission which was necessarily involved in this operation, and I accepted a contract according to which modest favors were granted to me, enlarged, however, by a monopoly of navigation on the Amazon and its tributaries for thirty years, providing thus a minimum, necessary service, since the capital that was to be employed was to be used in confronting the *unknown*.

When Clay heard of the contract, he reminded the Peruvian Minister of Foreign Affairs that the treaty concluded between Peru and the United States in July, 1851, contained a clause giving the United States most-favored-nation treatment. But the contract stood. On April 15, 1853, the President of Peru signed a decree making Loreto and Nauta ports of entry and extending the privileges given to Brazil to all other nations enjoying a most-favored-nation status. To this the Brazilian minister, Cavalcanti, registered a protest, so that in January, 1854, Peru again restricted the right to navigate the Amazon to Brazilians and Peruvians. In the treaty on river navigation signed by Peru and Brazil in 1858 these provisions were reiterated. In 1863 Peru terminated the treaty made with the United States in 1851.

Meanwhile, Bolivia, on January 27, 1853, opened its ports to world trade and confirmed the privileges so granted in a treaty made with the United States five years later. New Granada (Colombia) had made a treaty with Brazil closing her ports to all but Brazilians. Ecuador, in a treaty with the United States signed November 26, 1853, declared navigation on the rivers within her boundaries open to the world. But neither Brazil nor the United States gained a decisive victory with Venezuela.

These were all skirmishes on the sidelines. Direct negotiations between Brazil and the United States began April 4, 1853, when the Brazilian minister in Washington, Carvalho Moreira (Baron Penedo) made a formal inquiry of the United States government concerning rumors of merchant vessels traveling up and down the Amazon. The United States Secretary of State replied that the only vessels he knew anything about were those of the Herndon and Gibbon expedition and that these were there with the express approval of the Brazilian government. But Carvalho Moreira, always suspicious of new infiltrations and nervous because of the persistent rumors that flowed around him, called on the Secretary whenever a particularly violent newspaper attack on the Emperor's government appeared.

In August, 1853, Trousdale, the new United States minister in Rio, was given instructions "to secure for the citizens of the United States the free use of the Amazon." He went to work with a will and made a formal claim, supported by a brief based on international law. The Brazilian officials did not admit the claim. Instead they asked for a formal statement of the views of the United States government, to which, when they received it, they did not reply for a considerable time. In the end, they declared that there was no basis for comparison between the Amazon and the Mississippi (as the Americans had contended), and that furthermore there were only savages in the Amazon valley, who had no use for trade with the outside world.

Maury could not contain his indignation when he heard of the contract granted to Senhor Irineu. He said:

> This contract was entered into the 30th of August [1852] and is one of the most odious monopolies that were ever inflicted upon free trade, or that now retard the progress of any country. A stringent monopoly of steamboat trade and travel on the Amazon for thirty years! The preamble of this contract states, that in order to enable this Souza to form a company for the establishment of steam navigation upon the Amazon, the exclusive right for thirty years to the steamboat trade, travel, and navigation, up and down the river have been granted to him upon certain conditions.

Maury's pamphlet, *The Amazon and the Atlantic Shores of South America,* which he published in 1853, pointed out that the Americans were

> nearer to the Amazon or rather to the mouth of it, than any other nation, not even excepting Brazil herself, if we count the distance in time, and measure from Rio de Janeiro and from New York or New Orleans as the centers of the two countries. And therefore, it may well be imagined that this miserable policy by which Brazil has kept shut up, and is continuing to keep shut up, from Man's—from Christian, civilized, enlightened man's—use the fairest portion of God's earth, will be considered by the American people as a nusiance, not to say an outrage.

Maury's attacks had their effect in Brazil itself. A current of public opinion was gathering force which the imperial government found difficult to ignore. Its most eloquent exponent—and the most formidable Brazilian defender of Maury's views—was Aureliano Cândido

Tavares Bastos. Tavares Bastos was a born reformer with a literary gift that commanded the attention of his generation of political men. As "The Hermit" (*O Solitário*) he wrote a series of "Letters" which were published in the newspaper *O Correio Mercantil* and in which he took the government to task for the policy of "Chinese" exclusion maintained by "our Mandarins" of the Conservative party. Certainly, said Tavares Bastos, the government cannot think that it can perpetuate this policy; it must go some day. He pointed out that the policy of the Brazilian government was especially anomalous since it was the reverse of the stand taken by the empire a few years before against Rosas, the Argentine dictator, on the matter of opening up that other great river system of South America, the River Plate, to world commerce. Besides, he continued, if the imperial government insisted on ignoring the economic well-being of the people of the Amazon basin, it would find those people disaffected, ready to follow the foreigner, unimpressed by the provisions of treaties made between Spain and Portugal generations ago.

Tavares Bastos also took Mauá to task:

> I do not intend to deny that the Companhia do Amazonas was born of a patriotic idea, nor to throw aspersions on the real merit of the distinguished citizen whose activity and intelligence we must thank for making a reality the thought behind the law of 1850. But Baron Mauá, a Brazilian and a progressive man, certainly recognizes the fact that to stop up the Amazon is to impose on our own rich provinces of the equatorial regions and on the neighboring republics, the monopoly of the flourishing and powerful company founded in 1852.

More than the monopoly, the subsidy put the company beyond all effective competition.

"At present the valley of the Amazon is for that company what Hindustan was to the East India Company: it navigates it, exploits it, buys, sells, governs."

Mauá went ahead with his company. He defended his monopoly on the grounds that in order to find capital for an enterprise that was necessarily extremely speculative he had to offer special guarantees to the would-be investors. Especially was this the fact since much of the capital had to be raised in England. The Brazilian public, including the Portuguese merchants established in Belém, subscribed less than half the initial sum necessary. Further than this, he realized what many of his contemporaries did not, that the imperial government did not intend to permit free development of the Amazon valley, that its purpose in providing for a single, government-subsidized steamship company was to maintain rigid control over the great waterway.

Three regular lines of steam vessels soon began to operate, one from Belém, at the mouth of the Pará River, to Manáus, a thousand miles into the jungle; one from Manáus to Tabatinga; and a third from Belém to Cametá. At the same time, other lines were established with a subsidy from the government of the province of Pará, running from Belém, at the ocean, up the rivers to Chaves Itacuam and Soure. The result was a five-fold increase in the income of the imperial government and of the provincial government of Amazonas within eight years; a three-fold increase in that of the provincial government of Pará. And in the meantime the Amazon Steam Navigation Company paid a dividend of twelve percent. Fifty years after the initiation of this steamer service the province of Amazonas had an income eight hundred times greater than that of 1853.

On October 2, 1854, Mauá's original contract was altered by an imperial decree which obliged his company to establish twelve colonies of six hundred persons each on the banks of the Amazon and its tributaries. The government intended this as a first step in increasing the population of the area with individuals whose allegiance was to the empire, as a protective measure against the possible infiltration of unfriendly foreigners. It was a reflection of the growing concern over the power of the rising public opinion for a change in the status of the valley. Mauá himself was directly attacked, for the fact of his monopoly and his subsidy did not sit well with the more liberal elements among the Brazilian public, now acutely sensitive to the bad light in which their government appeared.

In time some competition was permitted and developed. A Portuguese merchant, Alexandre de Paula de Brito Amorim, with the support of the government of the province of Amazonas, incorporated the Companhia Fluvial do Alto Fluminense, with offices in Manáus and Belém and a capital of eight hundred contos, for which, after a hard fight, he succeeded in obtaining a monthly subsidy from the imperial government. In 1867, João Augusto Correia succeeded in founding the Companhia Fluvial Paraense.

The years went on, the United States suffered through the Civil War, and Brazil became embroiled in the long drawn-out struggle with Paraguay. Tavares Bastos had made many converts, and so thoroughly did he prepare the way that when the moment was ripe the Emperor's government could no longer hold out against the new current of thought. The incident that precipitated the matter was the coming to Brazil of Louis Agassiz and the Harvard Scientific Expedition.

It was the sort of thing that particularly appealed to Dom Pedro II—a visiting scientist in search of the secrets of the natural history of Brazil. Pedro had a steamer placed at Agassiz's disposal, in which he could visit the Amazon and its affluents, and the governors of the several provinces through which the expedition would pass vied with each other to gain the royal favor by making the way smooth for the visitor. The paraphernalia of the expedition were waived through the customs without delay.

On the evening of June 25, 1866, the American chargé d'affaires, Charles Lidgerwood, gave a dinner for Agassiz in Rio. Brazilian officials and distinguished men came to hear the naturalist describe the wonders of the Amazon. They were pleased and flattered by his complimentary remarks about their Emperor-Scientist, for Agassiz was tactful and ingratiating. Indeed, they found no objection to his apparently incidental remark that the first means necessary for the development of that marvelous region was the opening of the river to navigation. The effect of this seven-hour session of sociability was clearly in evidence at the close, when the old Marquess of Olinda, at the time Minister of Empire, expressed regret that Agassiz could not remain long enough to be bearer of the terms of a decree which he felt soon would be passed by his majesty's government, opening the Amazon to all nations. When the dinner was at last finished, the Marquess escorted his guest to the Navy Yard, where an imperial barge was waiting to carry him to the mail steamer bound for New York.

Five months after Agassiz's departure, the Brazilian Council of

State came to an agreement on the terms of the decree. Signed on December 7, 1866, it provided that after September 7, 1867, the Amazon should be free to the merchant vessels of all nations. It also provided for the opening, in part, of the main tributaries of the Amazon. When Peru followed the Brazilian example on December 7, 1868, the great river and its important tributaries were free throughout their courses.

Mauá was prepared for the change. When the Brazilian government announced its intention of abandoning its exclusive policy in the Amazon valley and of subsidizing a company, national or foreign, which would carry on trade between the Amazon and the United States, he put in a bid. He pointed out that such direct service was hardly possible at that time if profits were to be made, and so suggested a service that would link Belém with the Royal Mail and the French transatlantic steamers which maintained regular schedules between Europe and the United States. To this end he founded in London in 1870 the English Amazonas Steam Navigation Company, with an initial capital of £600,000. In 1872 the old Companhia do Amazonas disappeared, and in 1874 its two rivals, the Companhia Fluvial do Alto Amazonas and the Companhia Fluvial Paraense, were merged with the English company. The new company was a powerful and wealthy enterprise, paying dividends of between 10 and 12 percent.

But its contract expired on November 1, 1877, and when Mauá sought a renewal, a new burst of heated discussion was stirred up, in the parliament and in the press, concerning the excessive favors it was claimed that the government made to him. He felt the full weight of this new attack, for at the time he was inextricably involved in the final disasters that led to his bankruptcy.

In its heyday, however, his company had given the Amazon river region a standard of service that could have been envied in many more populous regions of the world. In April, 1858, he had seven steamers in operation, and two new vessels were expected. One of them was the *Bay City*, built in New York for the trade between San

Francisco, in California, and the east coast of the United States, but it was so badly twisted in a storm trying to double Cape Horn that it put back into Rio for repairs and was bought by Mauá's company from the underwriters. Some of the others were built at Mauá's iron-works at Ponta d'Areia. All of them had more business than they could handle. Every town on the rivers provided wood for their engines. To the inhabitants of the valley they were a means of getting produce down to market on the coast. They created a market, too, for imports; for these shy forest dwellers quickly learned new tastes. In the upper reaches of the valley, they created a new trade, for from the Peruvian towns on the eastern slopes of the Andes came a flow of goods to meet the steamers at Nauta.

The sight of a steamer and its effect on the inhabitants of the remote regions of the Upper Amazon have been described by an American engineer named Nesbitt:

As we would be passing a sand-bar on the upper rivers in Peru, where a steamboat had never before been heard of, and while all the fishermen and fish-driers would be standing in amazement, gazing at the "monster of the vasty deep"—not knowing whether it was a spirit from the *diabo* or some new saint sent by the Immaculate Virgin—I would touch the steam-whistle, which would give such an unearthly screech that men, women, children, dogs, and monkeys would take to their heels and run for dear life, and would never stop to allow me to make the *amende honorable*.

At the opposite extreme of sophistication, these steamers made an equally striking impression on seasoned travelers by the luxury of their appointments. Louis Agassiz's New England wife, who while in Brazil rarely forgot the comforts to which she was accustomed in the northern United States, did not fail to comment on the pleasures of traveling in Baron Mauá's river boats. Agassiz, on his return home, wrote the Emperor a letter. It was impossible, Agassiz told Dom Pedro, to have been better treated as travelers than he and his party had been on the Amazon steamers. Although to Mrs. Agassiz the day seemed "yet far distant when a numerous population will cover the banks of the Amazon, when the steamers will ply between its ports as between those of the Mississippi, and when all nations will share in the rich products of its valley," the company was piling up nice profits. During the first five years of its service, between 1853 and 1857, its receipts amounted to $250,000. In the second five years, between 1857 and 1862, it made $400,000, and in the third, between 1862 and 1867, $1,000,000.

CHAPTER IX

THE BANKER

WHEN DOM JOÃO VI left Portugal to take refuge in Brazil, he was well aware of the importance of money. He was himself the inheritor of an empire that had been founded on international trade and which had evolved into a powerful business concern. Portugal's dominions were a vast business monopoly for its reigning house. But it was a concern that was far gone in financial troubles, a house whose mortgages were accumulating faster than its receipts, which had lacked competent managers for so long that it had irremediably lost its recuperative power. Dom João was land-poor, and what he needed was ready cash. Shrewder than many of his family, he realized the usefulness of banks and bankers, and when he sailed from Lisbon in 1807 he did not neglect to take along with him all the money available to him in Portugal.

There were a number of men, in the decadence of the Iberian empires, who realized, in some degree, the ruin that faced them, and some of them sought solutions in the economic theories of Adam Smith. Among the Portuguese one of the most alert of these was Rodrigo de Sousa Coutinho (later Count Linhares), and it was he who first had the idea for a Bank of Brazil. Nothing illustrates more clearly the primitive ignorance of the Brazil in which he lived than the difficulties he and Dom João encountered in founding their bank. Ready money had been carefully excluded from Brazil in colonial times, and paper money was a new thing to the Brazilians. Banking transactions, therefore, were little understood, and shares in the new bank sold slowly. According to John Armitage, an Englishman who wrote a history of Brazil contemporary with these events, it was only after Dom João had made it known that he could confer a *comenda de cavalheiro* (the rank of gentleman) on all principal shareholders that he was able to obtain sufficient capital to start operations. Nevertheless he was not able to raise the nominal capital of one thousand two hundred contos, and up until 1812 only 126 shares valued at a conto each had been subscribed.

This first Bank of Brazil—the first bank in South America—was a commercial bank with an unlimited power to issue notes. Its notes were dependent on the stability of the English pound, and at first it enjoyed a certain prosperity. But the capacity of the country to absorb its paper money was soon exhausted. In the first place, the Brazilians were unused to the idea, and in the second, the population of the country, spread sparsely along the coast, was not sufficient to provide a large market. The fact that Dom João treated the bank as his private supplier of ready money did not tend to inspire confidence in the shareholders. When he returned to Portugal in 1821, he took with him the gold, the silver, and even the deposits made in the last month by local charitable institutions. Thereafter the country had only paper money and copper coins, one-third of the latter being falsified by private speculators, for it was a period in which counterfeiters, particularly in the north of the country, flourished. Finally in 1827 the government took over the issuing of paper money, and in 1829 the General Assembly decided to liquidate the bank. It was an ignominious end. Its history had so discouraging an effect on the minds of possible investors that, when in 1833 (two years after Dom Pedro I had abdicated and left Brazil in the hands of the Regency), an attempt was made to found a second bank, only 171 shares were subscribed, and the scheme failed.

This lack of confidence was slow to dissipate. Only in December,

1838, was the Banco Comercial do Rio de Janeiro founded, as a bank of deposit and discount, with the power of issuing money, which it never used. Other banks were founded in the country: one in Baía in 1845, with a capital of a thousand contos; one in Maranhão in 1846, with a capital of four hundred contos; and one in Pará in 1847, with a capital of four hundred also; all of them in the north where the economic and financial strength of the new empire still resided.

One of the things that the boy Irineu had learned in Carruthers' firm was the idea of financial credit as a basis for industrial expansion. The most important practical result of his first trip to England in 1840 was the founding, in Manchester, of the firm of Carruthers, De Castro and Company. For many years this firm was the medium through which capital was raised in England to float many of his early enterprises.

Irineu's banking career was based on Carruthers' international connections, for Carruthers had his own net of international credit: his firm in London, a branch of the Manchester house; Carruthers, Sousa and Company of Buenos Aires; Carruthers, Dixon and Company of New York. Carruthers' name in the London money market was invaluable to Irineu when capital was needed to launch new companies. As the old man retired more and more from an active part in these businesses, it was Joseph Henry Reydell De Castro (linked with Irineu by boyhood friendship as well as business partnership), who took over the direction of these affairs in England.

This network of financial connections grew so quickly that by 1850 Irineu decided to establish his own banking firm in Rio, intimately associated with the Manchester house. In July, 1851, he founded the second Bank of Brazil (often called the Banco do Brasil de Mauá), which had a capital of ten thousand contos ($5,000,000). It did not have the power to issue notes, but in heated debates over its charter in the Chamber of Deputies it had won the right to issue drafts and bills of exchange. These drafts and bills were for a term of five days with a value of not less than 200 milreis ($100 or £25), and their total at any time could not be more than one-third of the bank's actual funds.

Irineu did not hesitate once he had the head office going. In 1853 he established branches in São Paulo and in Rio Grande do Sul. In 1851, the bank's deposits had been valued at 214 contos and by March, 1854, at 950 contos. In 1851, it had held discounted bills for more than one thousand contos; in 1854, for more than nine thousand. Only one other bank could equal it in volume of business, the Banco do Comércio. This fact in itself determined the fate of the Mauá bank and precipitated Irineu's first conflict with the Emperor and with those who advised him on the financial policy of the empire. Under the constant pressure from businessmen, the Emperor's government finally approved the creation of the third bank of Brazil, to be formed by the forced merger of the Banco do Comércio with Mauá's Banco do Brasil.

The 1830's and 1840's in England was the period of the struggle between the Bank of England and the private English banks on the one hand and the new public joint-stock banks on the other to dominate the market for credit for new industries. The structure of credit itself was much shaken during this period by various political and economic events both in Europe and the United States and the resulting instability caused a number of serious bank failures. The question then arose whether the power to issue notes, which was a usual one for banks at that time, was the cause of this unreliability of banking concerns. Bank loans were as a rule made in the notes of the bank giving credit. The private banks in London had fallen into the habit of using Bank of England notes, but the banks elsewhere in England made great use of their note-issuing power, which in some cases meant the expansion of loans in notes against insufficient cash reserves. This controversy has been simplified as the conflict between the currency principle, that is, the principle that no new paper money should be issued unless backed by specie, and the banking principle, that is, that as trade expanded so should commercial paper.

Clearly, on his return from his first English visit Irineu had adopted the banking principle and his first bank was organized and operated in accordance with it. Since he could not issue notes, he used his drafts and bills for the same purpose. However, in the meantime, the currency principle had triumphed in England, and after the Bank

Charter Act of 1844 no new banks of issue could be created there. This fact had its effect on the Emperor's advisers.

The chief of these, who was Minister of the Treasury in 1853, Joaquim José Rodrigues Torres, Viscount Itaboraí, was deeply conservative. He was a man whose political life dated from the days of the Regency, and he was therefore a man who carried considerable weight with the Emperor, whose favorite financial adviser he was until his death in 1872. He believed that money was specie, and that paper money was nothing more than a snare and a delusion. It took considerable persuasion to convince him that any bank should have the right to issue paper money and he certainly did not believe that such a bank should be a private concern.

In the end he was probably persuaded to agree to the creation of the new Bank of Brazil through the efforts of the Prime Minister, Honório Hermeto Carneiro Leão, Viscount (later Marquess) Paraná, a former regent and at the time the most powerful man in the country. Therefore, the Emperor, in his speech from the throne delivered in the Chamber of Deputies on May 3, 1853, recommended the immediate creation of a note-issuing bank, "since such an institution was indispensable to the economic organization" of the empire.

The law was promulgated on July 5, 1853, and the bank's charter was approved on August 31. Eighty thousand shares were distributed to the shareholders of the two banks which had been forced to merge into the new bank, the Banco do Comércio and Mauá's Banco do Brasil; forty thousand were reserved for the provinces, where branches were established, and thirty thousand were reserved for public sale in Rio itself. More than three thousand eager buyers presented themselves for this last lot, offering 10 percent above the face value, and the Treasury made a profit of six hundred contos, which was used to improve the paving of the streets of Rio. The new bank finally began operations on August 10, 1854, under the direction of Viscount Paraná.

The fifty thousand shares that Mauá (for in 1854 he was Baron) and his shareholders received for their part in the forced merger did not reconcile him to the destruction of his house. At first he could not believe that the government really intended to drive his firm out of existence or rather, absorb it, but Viscount Itaboraí soon made it plain that such was the case. Convinced finally, he desisted from actively opposing the government's plan, "nourishing the hope," he said, "that I could coöperate with the great credit institution which was to be created to introduce a new era of development and progress into the economic and financial life of the country."

He took an active part in the organization of the new bank and was elected one of its directors. He soon saw, however, that the board of directors was to be purposely weighted against him by men hostile to him, and he refused the office in spite of the insistence of the Minister of the Treasury that he should serve.

He followed the development of the new bank closely, watching to see whether it would provide all the banking services that he thought should be provided by such a powerful and highly favored credit machine. Especially did he look for the establishment of branch offices in the twenty provincial capitals of the empire.

"This," he declared, "would have provided teaching and apprenticeship in the *use of credit* in a country which at that time scarcely understood any of this, except in the Capital, and even there credit operations were hampered. Certainly the vacillating steps taken in the use of credit in a few provincial capitals represented no understanding of finance whatsoever."

The Bank of Brazil, he contended, had the mission of teaching the use "of this most powerful instrument of modern civilization, in the creation of wealth everywhere in the length and breadth of our native land, in penetrating into the economic life of localities where the presence of sufficient means, already existing or to be created, would permit it to be employed with advantage."

The mechanism of credit, he believed, would "bring to life the inert capital, that is, the dormant capital, abounding in all the corners of Brazil, converting it thus into an instrument of production, into resources otherwise dispersed and not used in the creation of individual wealth and consequently national wealth."

This was not what happened.

My intimacy with the first president of the Bank, Councilor Lisboa

Serra [José Duarte Lisboa Serra] who unfortunately was lost to the service of his country in the springtime of life, gave me a knowledge of what
went on in the bosom of that Board of Directors. The Bank of Brazil was
confronted by itself as a great local discount bank—and as such required
to obtain the highest rate possible, the governing factor being the greater
or lesser confidence of the directors of the firms involved in these transactions. The creation of branch banks met with persistent resistance, since
financial operations were not understood. Nor was this to be wondered at,
even among the high administrative officials of the country. Although we
have had many Ministers of the Treasury, those who could properly be
called ministers of finance have been few. How could any comprehension
of such problems be expected in those placed on the board of directors of
Brazilian banks as the so-called shareholders' choice?

In the face of all I knew, I was almost discouraged!

Almost but not quite. Seeing his enemies all-powerful, he had tried
to compromise with them, the line of action of a practical man. But
a government-created monopoly, which rejected the principle of
competition, feared the coöperation of a man so able in its own line
of business. He waited long enough to make sure of two things: that
he had no chance in controlling to any degree the future of the new
bank; and that the managers of the new bank were both ignorant of
the modern methods of finance and bent on ignoring them. His
answer to the problem was to create a new banking house of his own.

He still ran into trouble, this time over the type of company that
he wanted to form. The commercial laws of Brazil, up until 1850,
had progressed little since the country had achieved its independence.
The old colonial legislation, out-of-date for years, remained in force,
patched and amended by a mass of decrees and interpretations that
left businessmen in considerable doubt about the legal position of their
affairs. In 1850 a new commercial code had been adopted, which went
into effect on January 1, 1851. It provided for the creation of *sociedades anônimas*, equivalent to corporations in American law and lim-
ited-liability companies in English law. Mauá was seriously dissatisfied
with this form of company, for the Brazilian law provided that the
government had the sweeping right to dissolve such a company without consultation with the shareholders.

Mauá's acquaintance with the commercial systems of other countries supplied him with a possible solution. In France since 1673 there had existed a type of company which went by the name of *société en commandite par actions*—a partnership with shares. Why, thought Mauá, should he not use the same form in Brazil, whose system of law was similar to that of France? Having drafted the charter and bylaws for a new company on these lines, he presented the project to Viscount Paraná.

He asked Paraná for his own opinion and that of the Minister of Justice, Nabuco de Araújo, not disguising the fact that in attempting to create such a company he sought to escape the governmental control to which *sociedades anônimas* were subject.

One week afterward, His Excellency said to me that he found my arrangement free from any objection, whether legal or of any other sort; and to prove to me his full approval, told me that, not being able, as minister, to be concerned in the banking house, his eldest son would subscribe fifty contos, his son-in-law thirty, and the father of the latter, fifty, and that he would not hesitate to recommend to all his friends that they should subscribe shares. Such was the confidence that my management inspired in him.

Pleased with approval thus qualified and positive, I immediately started the project going, opening the list of subscribers with six hundred contos, besides my assumption of unlimited liability. In two days the company's capital was all subscribed and the list of subscribers was closed with one hundred and eighty-two partner-shareholders.

He had every reason to believe that the Viscount's attitude indicated governmental approval for his scheme. But he was mistaken. Either Viscount Paraná was not as powerful as he seemed, or he had found reasons for changing his mind. It may well be that he was unable to oppose successfully the enemies of the new company, especially if one of these was Viscount Itaboraí, implacably opposed to the idea of a competitor for the new governmental bank which he had been persuaded to support. Mauá described events thus:

It was then that the [government's] decree of December 13, 1852 [which declared such companies null and void] made its inopportune appearance without previous announcement, other than brief conversations during the foregoing weeks by means of which I was made aware of the decided opposition of someone who enjoyed the highest position of influence in the councils of the government, to the division of capital into shares as in *sociedades em comandita por ações,* especially as concerned banking houses, which in his opinion needed the supervision of the government. I had always denied such a necessity, which was a deathblow to private initiative. I understood, however, that some law would shortly come into existence which would make the organization of such companies difficult. It never crossed my mind, however, that the company I had organized, its charter and bylaws having been registered with the Commercial Court, would encounter any obstacle to its operations, except through the legal intervention of the courts in cases provided for by the commercial law. I was mistaken, however, because this decree appeared which prohibited what the law did not prohibit, and furthermore, it was given retroactive effect by the government! A surprising decision which did damage to all the principles accepted as unassailable by the governments of civilized countries!

Nevertheless, the fact remained that Viscount Itaboraí could stand his ground: simply because the law did not prohibit such companies it could not necessarily be assumed that it permitted them. It was the Council of State (the Emperor's advisory council and the Oracle of Delphi of the empire) that handed down an opinion against the possibility of the creation of such companies and suggested the dissolution of those already created. The majority of the ministers of state who made up the Council concurred in the opinion, although the old Marquess of Olinda voted against it.

Mauá, seeing the situation as hopeless, accepted it and reorganized his company. He now created Mauá, MacGregor and Company, with an English partner and a branch in London, as a simple partnership. In spite of the insecurity of such a form of company, of which he remained acutely aware, the firm flourished. He had no difficulty in accumulating a large sum in capital, for, he said, "it was my intention to do what the Bank of Brazil refused to do."

In the meantime, while Mauá, MacGregor and Company (whose drafts and bills were worth more than the paper money issued by the Bank) enjoyed a solid prosperity, the official bank had become a factory to turn out paper money. It had encountered, too, the world crisis of 1857, precipitated by the troubles of the cotton market in the

United States and the threat of war in the Europe of Napoleon III.
The price of coffee, which had become Brazil's great staple export,
fluctuated violently in the consuming markets. The Bank of Brazil's
paper money was depreciated, specie was driven out of the country,
the exchange declined, and the cost of living shot up.

That crisis [said Mauá] soon made obvious how weak was the prop on
which the men of the specie-money school relied to prove their golden
dream of converting paper money into specie, something I had always
considered impracticable, except during rare periods. . . . Gold, which
for a while served the purpose of a circulating medium in competition with
paper money, was rapidly converted into merchandise, which had at once
to be exported to supply the deficit which the fall in the value of products
brought about.

In 1857 the Minister of the Treasury was a friend of his and a vigorous opponent of the theories of Viscount Itaboraí. This was Bernardo de Sousa Franco, later Viscount Sousa Franco, and, like his
chief rival, he had had a long political career. At nineteen he had been
imprisoned in Lisbon as a conspirator for the independence of Brazil.
When he came back from Portugal, his father, disgusted with his
political adventures, had put him into a commercial house as a clerk,
where he stayed for seven years. He had not remained in the business
world, however, but had gone to the Law Faculty in Recife, had taken
a degree in law and had entered politics. To Mauá he was "one of the
most brilliant minds that ever passed through the administration of
the country." The link between them was strong, for Sousa Franco,
when he was Minister of the Treasury between May 4, 1857, and
December 12, 1858, and a senator besides, found in Mauá a spokesman
for his financial theories, Mauá being at the same time a deputy in the
lower house of the parliament. Many of their views were similar.
Sousa Franco had a plan for the abolition of slavery within ten years,
for, like Mauá, he considered slavery a burden on the economic development of the country. It should, he believed, be got out of the way
as soon as possible, so that Brazil might set to work to recoup her
inevitable losses with free, white immigrant labor from Europe. His
opinions, on paper money, on abolition, on immigration, he vigor-

ously promoted in an active, pugnacious political career and in the pages of his newspaper, the *Correio da Tarde*.

The period in which Sousa Franco took office as Minister of the Treasury was the worst moment of the contemporary world crisis. The Bank of Brazil was in difficulties and his first action was to rescue it by calling on the house of Mauá for help, in maintaining the exchange rate at twenty-five English pence to the milreis (the exchange rate had fallen as low as twenty-two pence) and thus preventing the silver money from following the gold out of the country. At his request, Mauá, MacGregor and Company drew on its London branch, on March 12, 1858, for the sum of £400,000; in April it drew again for £200,000; in May, for £150,000; and in June, for another £60,000. (That is, for $2,000,000, $1,000,000, $750,000, and $300,000.)

Though these maneuvers were successful, they did not meet with the approval of Sousa Franco's political opponents. For his ideas on the best financial policy for the empire were diametrically opposed to those of both Viscount Itaboraí and Viscount Inhomerim (Francisco de Sales Torres Homem), another convinced opponent of paper money who was shortly to succeed Sousa Franco as Minister of the Treasury. To these conservative men and to others like them, Sousa Franco's policy of permitting the issuance of paper money by six banks was nothing short of a "financial carnival." It was madness, and they believed that it had been inspired by Sousa Franco's close friend, Baron Mauá. Sousa Franco's time in office was brief. Inevitably Itaboraí and Inhomerim won the day, for their views, the reflection of the slowly accumulating and familiar type of wealth represented by the *fazenda*, a plantation, and slaves, were more acceptable to the Emperor.

As Joaquim Nabuco has pointed out, in his life of his father Nabuco de Araújo: "The truth is that the old fortunes, all the conservative interests of the country were alarmed, terror-stricken by the audacious actions of the Treasury, which completely turned the exchange upside down, causing it to touch twenty-two, and lifted it again by the artificial means of authorized withdrawals or by exchange transactions which the Minister himself approved."

Maua's position in the midst of these hotly debated theories was the same that he maintained throughout his business life. Credit, he said again and again, was the basis of capital and the source of new wealth. For credit transactions banks were necessary, a knowledge of credit operations was necessary, and a sufficient supply of some sort of circulating medium was necessary. Years later, at the time of his bankruptcy, he published a mature statement of his views in a pamphlet entitled *The Circulating Medium* (*O meio circulante*). These views were based on a simple idea: one does not develop a vast wild country, full of natural resources but needing an immense amount of initial outlay, with gold that one carries about in one's pocket. To a modern world, inured to a paper-money economy, this idea is familiar and even banal. To his own age, in Brazil, it was revolutionary and suspect. For to him, a country's wealth did not consist in the specie it held in its banks; but in that country's power to produce.

On March 10, 1861, Mauá wrote to his partner De Castro in Manchester:

The market is working under a great pressure for money, since the screw is being tightened by the Bank of Brazil to an almost unbearable extent, they say, with a view of permitting a rise in the exchange to enable them to pay in gold without danger. The everyday experience is, however, showing the Directors, who are about the most stupid men we have in the trade, that the means they adopt are not the right ones, for in this respect Brazil is not in the least affected by the markets around it, as occurs everywhere in Europe. We have *no other* means to support the value of our currency except the *value of exports*. This has been proved over and over again.

The financial crisis did not abate. It grew worse. In the United States appeared the menace of the Civil War. Europe was in the throes of financial troubles. Brazilian coffee was unsteady. In 1860 there had been deluges of rain in São Paulo, so that the trains of mules could not bring the sacks of the precious bean to market. In 1861 there was a drought in Rio Grande do Sul and in Uruguay that affected the cattle and hide market. Further south still, in the Argentine Confederation, civil war threatened between the Confederated Provinces under the leadership of General José Justo Urquiza and the province of Buenos Aires.

In Mauá's commercial correspondence during the first half of 1861, anxiety over these disquieting factors appears again and again. Mac-Gregor—his partner and the manager of the London branch of Mauá, MacGregor and Company—was frightened and angry at the threat to the stability of the firm, aggravated, he thought, by Mauá's own daring methods of confronting danger. He was a far more cautious man, less confident of his own ability to find ways out of difficulties as they arose, nervous about the least irregularity in the arrival of remittances from the head office in Rio or the branch offices in the River Plate. The failure of one steam packet to bring the sum he expected threw him into a panic, and he wrote to Mauá with more frankness than discretion.

His letter pained Mauá, whose interest in his partners' personal affairs was as lively as that in their business transactions. MacGregor's health, he thought,

must indeed be shaken, and to an extent seriously depressing your mind, for to observe your writing (it would appear, *in earnest*) about having been prevented from taking the necessary steps to place your family comfortably, for fear of seeing them turned *into the street!!* in consequence of the fear of funds not being forwarded to meet the obligations of the firm, must indeed be painful to me. . . . The remarks made by you under such circumstances, I say, are calculated to establish the conviction in my mind, either that you are a sufferer in health, which causes me heartfelt pain, being sincerely your friend, or that you are so utterly disgusted with the business in consequence of the misfortunes we have had to contend against, that you are looking for a pretext to withdraw your responsibility from such an ill-managed concern, which keeps you in constant dread of seeing your name in the gazette and your family in the street! On pondering over such grave assertions, and being well satisfied that you are a kind-hearted man and therefore not likely to write in such terms to create annoyance and pain in an equally kindhearted man and *friend*, I became convinced that I have no right to exact from you the painful sacrifice you evidently make in continuing my partner.

Instead, he suggested that they close the London branch office, which they could do at any moment, and so "avert the danger which haunts your imagination and makes you so miserable." In his place a new London firm of Mauá and Company was to be created, with De Castro as managing partner.

De Castro, he told MacGregor

> was a man of great business knowledge, who had also got experience in the school of adversity on one occasion, his mind is the very soul of honor, and his intellectual powers inferior to few in his class.... If you prefer it and your health requires it ... he can take charge of the firm in London whilst you get abroad to refresh your health, and the change above referred to may be brought about later on, or not at all, just as you desire or wish, for nothing is further from my mind than any idea of inducing you to retire—my object is merely to leave you *perfect freedom*, having your well-being and happiness *to heart*, for I am one of those who is always ready to make any sacrifice for my friends but who never desires that my friends make any sacrifice to serve me.... With De Castro the case is different. He knows that I would strip myself of my last shirt to save him and I know he would unhesitatingly do the same for me. We are attached to each other from *boyhood*. We have *both* a right to expect that each of us will do what the other desires; consequently I do not look forward to any refusal from him, and you have therefore only to tell him what you wish to be done and I am sure that he will agree to everything for my sake.

But MacGregor had been hasty, and now he made it plain that he had no idea of leaving Mauá, MacGregor and Company. Mauá, in a letter that was a mixture of exhortation, friendly advice, and cheerful remonstrance, was glad he had decided to stay:

> Allow me to repeat my request and recommendation that you take the necessary steps conducing to health, comfort and welfare and happiness, for being a man who finds so much happiness as can be hoped for in this world of cares in the bosom of my family, I cannot but sympathise, deeply, with you, when you tell me you have been eight months away from your family without seeing them once! No wonder you felt annoyed and disgusted with the cares and weight of duties which involved the necessity of so unbearable a sacrifice! I cannot but imagine, however, that within thirty or fifty miles in the suburbs of London, where Railway trains may be seen moving in all directions, there will not be many a nice, well-situated

country place which you might hire or purchase, to place your family and go every day to enjoy a quiet homely rest after the labor and care of the day's work; pray do so by all means, and you will soon see the agreeable change in the state of your mind which this modification in your mode of living will work.

In addition to De Castro, he had at this time three partners: MacGregor, who managed the London branch; Ricardo José Ribeiro, in charge of the office in Montevideo; and a young Englishman named Leslie, manager of the office in Buenos Aires, to whom he frequently wrote letters full of the advice of an old hand to a beginner in the financial game. The head office in Rio was under his own direction. It was always De Castro to whom he opened his mind, complaining sometimes, in a tone of reasonable regret, about MacGregor's limitations, and to De Castro he always signed himself simply "Mauá," without the "Baron" with which all his other letters concluded. Seeing things from the Rio office and full of the exhilaration that came from the successful management of something in which he was thoroughly the master, he could not understand MacGregor's fears and recriminations, pointing out that "we have just been robbed by a most unjust sentence of the Courts," and that "we were caught with all sails set during the greatest commercial crisis on record."

"Instead of complaining," he went on, "I am, therefore, most thankful to Providence that nothing worse occurred. As regards the partners, none of us (thank God) are working for daily bread, and the experience acquired is a large capital for future business, and in two or three years, I am quite certain, we will bring up the average of our earnings from so much labor, anxiety, and care."

In spite of the prosperity of Mauá, MacGregor and Company in Rio, he was somewhat chagrined at the failure of the London branch to shine with the splendor due a firm bearing his name. He told MacGregor that "two partners are required in London; one remains in the counting house, while the other moves about and is seen wherever other bankers and respectable merchants are to be seen. I am convinced that the firm in London stands inconceivably below its due position in London."

It was De Castro he wanted for the second partner in the London

house. He wrote to De Castro at the same time that he wrote to Mac-
Gregor, on January 7, 1861, and told him that he was certain that if
the London firm was conducted with greater energy by a man who
made better use of his time, "the business doing with Brazil, the
Plate, and other European correspondence, embracing operations to
the extent of three hundred thousand pounds per month, ought
surely to raise the house to a proper standing in London in a very
short period, instead of its being slighted by people who are as distant
from us in character and means as darkness is to light."

He had reason to be touchy. Mauá, MacGregor and Company had
branches in Buenos Aires, Montevideo, the city of Rio Grande do
Sul, Pelotas, Porto Alegre, Santos, São Paulo, Campinas, and Pará.
For a firm only seven years old it was doing marvelously well. Mauá
had moved into the River Plate very early. There, in Uruguay and
Argentina, free from the incubus of slavery, there was more opportunity for the sort of banking system he wanted to create. The first
branches of Mauá and Company had been established in the River
Plate in the middle 1850's and they continued steadily to spread there
as well as in the southernmost part of Brazil, the province of Rio
Grande do Sul. For Mauá there was plenty of precedent for this:
his old patron Richard Carruthers had for years had branches of his
firm established down in these fertile and thriving regions.

His partner MacGregor had once voiced the opinion that Mauá
always looked too much on the bright side of things. It was an accusation he good-naturedly repelled with the reply that, "I generally
look to all points, altho' certainly I am not one of those who fly
sem ver segue [without looking where I am going]."

He was an optimist by nature and he looked to the future always
with the idea of new successes to add to those of the past or to compensate for past failures. But it was also true that he "looked to all
points." He was faced with two problems peculiar to his environment, in the empire of Brazil, problems large enough to try the
patience and exercise the ingenuity of the cleverest banker. Abroad
he had the problem of obtaining money for what he considered first-
rate securities from people who wished speculative profits. At home

he had the problem of managing public men, from the Emperor down, whose grasp of finance and whose theories of economic development were rudimentary and out of key with the times—and as he thought, with the necessities of the country. Banking, to him, was not a business by itself, carried on independently of other interests. It was the basis for his vast and varied industrial empire. He wanted capital for investment, and he raised it in banking transactions. The loans for railways were particularly involved and difficult to manage. The money had to be raised in London for such enterprises; there was not nearly enough capital to be found in Brazil, or at least it was unwilling to come forward. But English investors, putting money into South American railways, were speculating. They did not consider such enterprises sound long-term investments, and they naturally expected speculative profits. Seen from the other side of the Atlantic, Brazil was a place in which to make a fortune quickly. Mauá, on the other hand, his head full of the immense potential wealth of the New World, insisted that such investment could be first-rate and comparable to the best to be found anywhere else in the world. He was aware of the problems presented by slavery, governmental inertia and a sparse, thinly-spread population, but he was also aware of the dangers to sound credit that arose from too much of the get-rich-quick mentality among many of his shareholders.

In a letter to his partner MacGregor in February, 1861, he voiced a bit of dry advice, in talking about English investors in Brazilian railway companies:

I observe that shareholders of Brazilian railway companies continue dissatisfied. The delay in the payment of dividends arises from the fact of improper items being charged in the accounts. Let the employees of the companies abandon the system of trying to *impose* on the Brazilian government, of trying to charge to capital account! disbursements which cannot even be admitted in the maintenance of the Railway, and all will be right. If the employees of the Company like to give a dinner to Baron da Boa Vista and his friends, let them first pay out of their own pockets, and if they like to subscribe to *obras pias* [charities] let them do it out of their own pockets.

It was good advice, but it was not popular with shareholders who saw Brazil from far away as a wild country with backward laws, whose government officials needed encouragement for the carrying on of profitable enterprises. Mauá was never to reconcile his own attitude with that of his investors. He came too early in the history of foreign investment in South America, where money invested meant wild money which was expected to grow enormous profits to compensate the investors for the risks taken. Nor did he fail to realize that in many instances the actions of his government were not calculated to dispel this belief in the essential economic instability of the countries of the New World, which existed in the London market.

In fact, at times he was outspoken in the expression of his frustration and impatience with the inhospitable environment in which he worked. His financial success in the 1850's left him little to desire, but he found that money alone and the power it gave him was not sufficient to make for him a comfortable position in the empire. There was really no place, in Dom Pedro's Brazil, for such a combination of gifts and disadvantages as he represented. He summed the matter up in a letter he wrote to his old friend Carruthers on May 8, 1861:

I am happy to be able to inform you that all my business and public undertakings are at this moment in a flourishing condition, Ponta d'Areia alone excepted. Experience, aided by indefatigable exertions, have enabled me to correct and put to rights all the working parts of the machinery which now performs its duty in perfect order, so much so that I can now contemplate, with comfort, a visit to Europe next year, taking with me all my family, with a view of remaining there for at least eighteen months, as it is my intention to see all that may be worth seeing from Portugal to Constantinople, remaining half of the time in London to get thoroughly initiated in the doings of the great Metropolis. I am anxious in fact for the moment of leaving Rio, for, with my feelings and hot temper, I cannot contemplate the *misgovernment* which is going on in Brazil in our days, without opposing the nonsensical proceedings of the Executive, which has been gradually absorbing all power. To take an active part, in contending against such ideas, would oblige me to come out of my obscurity, which I cannot think of, and consequently to withdraw for a period from the scene of action is my best course. On my return I hope to see better ideas prevailing, and, not having done much in the past, I can readily excuse myself from taking a prominent part in the direction of the government in the new order of things.

He was referring here to his seat in the Chamber of Deputies, which provided him with a vantage point from which to confront the political situation but in which he had never been very active. He was not yet able to carry out his plan of going abroad, however. For several years he postponed his journey from one financial crisis to another.

His hope, in combatting his twin problems, was to create a banking system on the English model, based on the deposits of middle-class people. In Brazil the success of such a system was necessarily limited, for the middle-class was still negligible in size and influence. The *fazendeiro*, the plantation owner, who grew a single great crop —sugar or coffee—with slave labor, had little use for banks. His sons and grandsons, if they emigrated to the cities and took up the practice of law or politics, received their financial support from the *fazenda*. The small landowner, the small merchant, the skilled workman, did not flourish under a slave regime.

Mauá once, in 1860, described his banking ambitions to his partner, Ricardo José Ribeiro, the manager of his house in Montevideo:

> In place of the ranch-owner, the husbandman, the landowner, the law-yer, and all others keeping what they own unproductively in money in their houses, we must induce them to bring these sums, great and little, and deposit them in the Mauá firm and its branches. When the masses under-stand the immense advantage of drawing credit from their money, what great sums may accumulate in our branches, to be newly employed with advantage, aiding labor and industry, producing conditions of prosperity in different localities, and what benefits will result from this impetus and how much faster will march the creation of wealth in our country! In the United States there is a branch bank or agency in all localities where more than fifty houses are built. In England, despite the small size of the coun-try and due to the denser population, there are three thousand seven hun-dred banks, banking houses, and their agencies! which occupy themselves exclusively in concentrating the money capital for useful employment, and from this fact arises the amazing creation of wealth that thus operates to transform these countries day by day.

In Rio Grande do Sul, he instructed Ribeiro, he wanted his idea advertised by means of circulars and other published notices, so as, in time, to establish a branch or agency of Mauá and Company in every town or city in the province with a population of three thousand or more. And in each office there must always be two or three promising young men who would learn to work in the bank and would be suitable material for advancement when the opportunity presented itself.

These were extraordinary ideas for a Brazil in which, as he complained in another letter to Ribeiro, unhappily there did not "exist a public spirit sufficiently energetic, on the part of the governed to require the governors to march in accordance with public opinion," the latter therefore going on in their own ideas until the results convinced them of their mistake. Sometimes these results were nothing short of catastrophic, as in the "September Crisis" of 1864. So great were the effects of that panic that the Bank of Brazil lost its right to issue paper money, which henceforth became a function exclusively of the Treasury.

The September Crisis was in fact the Brazilian reflection of the world-wide financial upheaval of the decade of the 1860's. The three great international firms of Baring Brothers, Peabody and Company, and Brown, Shipley, were badly affected by the inexorably approaching Civil War in the United States. The Brazilian government also felt the repercussions of bad news abroad. To the south, across the border in the old Banda Oriental, the eastern zone of the old Spanish viceroyalty of Buenos Aires, trouble was brewing which would culminate in 1865 in the Paraguayan war. Nevertheless, for Brazil, the sudden financial crash of 1864 came without warning to the people who had put their money in banks. The editor of the *Anglo-Brazilian Times*, William Scully, was in Rio at the time and described the effect of the panic.

It was the most extraordinary monetary crisis, he said, which had occurred since the days of John Law and the South Sea Bubble. On the 10th of September, A. J. Souto and Company, which had ten thousand creditors, closed its doors.

On the failure becoming known, an indescribable panic took place. The streets were crowded with persons hurrying to withdraw their money from the hands of the private bankers with whom it was deposited, and speedily became blocked up in the neighborhood of these establishments by a dense crowd, some denouncing in unmeasured terms the rascality of all bankers, some weeping and lamenting, while others, who were fortunate enough to obtain their money, throwing themselves on their knees, held it up to heaven within their clasped hands, and abandoning themselves to the extravagance of their unlooked-for happiness, pressed it rapturously to their lips, time after time, before they could induce themselves to withdraw their treasure from their gaze.

At length so great became the confusion that the police were ordered out to patrol and guard the streets, to quell any anticipated disturbance of the public peace; which delicate undertaking they performed by riding furiously up and down the narrow and crowded streets, cutting and lashing indiscriminately at everyone in their way who was not agile enough to find shelter in some adjoining house, and severely injuring many of the unfortunates, who, whatever their extravagance of gesture and manner, had acted with a forbearance which would probably find no parallel in any other country under similarly trying circumstances.

The crash of the great firm of Souto and Company made such an impression on the whole country that travelers, visiting the far backwoods, reported hearing even parrots that had learned to say *"O Souto quebrou,"* Souto has gone broke. Tito Franco de Almeida, recording the life of Councilor Francisco José Furtado, described the same scene of panic in Rio: Souto's bankruptcy was a signal for runs on all banking houses, "workmen, widows, old men, invalids, public employees, soldiers, all hurried to save their money. At three o'clock in the afternoon, a great mass of people inundated the Rua Direita in front of the Commercial Exchange and the Rua da Alfândega, opposite the banks. Only at nine o'clock at night could the police make the multitude disperse."

A few days later, at seven o'clock in the morning people gathered in front of the banks. "The government was accused of indifference, irresolution, and weakness in not taking emergency measures. This augmented the run on the banks. Then the panic became frightful, because the Bank of Brazil itself began to be assailed, and the run to exchange notes for gold became so violent that it was necessary to protect the establishment with police."

Mauá, MacGregor and Company were not spared in this run, yet with other banks crashing around it, it weathered the storm. In fact, Mauá had a new scheme in mind, the merger of his banking house with the London and Brazilian Bank. In 1864 he broke off his affairs abruptly and sailed for Europe.

In London he was successful. Much to the surprise of the international money market, he arranged the merger, the new company to be known as the London, Brazilian and Mauá Bank. It was to be an international house, with branches in Portugal, Argentina, and Uruguay. Each of these countries approved its charter within a few days, but for effectiveness in Brazil approval of the Emperor's government was also needed. The Emperor's Council of State thought about the matter for two months. In the end the idea was rejected, the Council ignoring the fact that the new company would have given considerable prestige to the empire at a time when it badly needed such support in international affairs.

For Mauá had succeeded in linking his firm with one of the most solid banking houses of the period in a merger that would have consolidated all his banking enterprises in Argentina, Uruguay, and Brazil. Probably it was this very fact, expressive of the tremendous power that would thus be concentrated in his hands, that frightened the Emperor's government. He was already too ubiquitous in the tangled affairs of the River Plate.

PART THREE

MAUÁ
AND THE RIVER
PLATE

CHAPTER X

FOUNDING
AN EMPIRE

Iɴ COLONIAL DAYS, the Banda Oriental, or the Eastern Zone, of the old viceroyalty of Buenos Aires, lay just south of the Portuguese dominions. Today this region just north of the River Plate, bounded on the northwest by the Uruguay and Negro rivers, on the east by the Atlantic Ocean, and on the north by the Brazilian state of Rio Grande do Sul, is the Republic of Uruguay. Montevideo, its capital and one of the great cities of the southern continent, has thus for centuries been the key to the river system that even today is the principal means of transportation into the interior of southern Brazil. The Paraná river, which for twelve hundred miles divides the modern Brazilian states of Mato Grosso and Goiás from São Paulo and Paraná; the Paraguay river, which flows from the watershed of Mato Grosso; and the Uruguay river, which is the boundary between the modern Brazilian states of Santa Catarina and Rio Grande do Sul; all these rivers are tributaries of the River Plate, at the mouth of which lies Montevideo.

Inevitably, the region and the city were, in colonial days, a source of contention between the Spaniards and the Portuguese. In 1860, the Portuguese founded the town of Colônia do Sacramento up the river from Montevideo, as a secure place of deposit for the smuggling trade carried on by Portugal, England, France, and Holland with the Spanish dominions, otherwise tightly closed to all outside commercial intercourse. They intended it also as a settlement by which they could claim rights to all lands north of the river. The possession of Colônia was thereafter the object of warfare and treaties throughout the seventeenth and eighteenth centuries, until by the treaty of Amiens the Portuguese were forced to relinquish their claim to the whole region north of the River Plate.

Dom João VI and his queen Carlota Joaquin each had intentions to reacquire the Banda. Haughty, energetic, vindictive Carlota Joaquina made her claim as regent for her brother, Ferdinand VII, the King of Spain captured and imprisoned by Napoleon. She was a Bourbon, with a fanatical belief in the divine right of her dynasty to rule and its infinite superiority to her husband's, the Bragança. Her relations with Dom João were a continual battle, on her side carried out with bold intriguing and on his by endless cautious delay and equivocation. He was in deadly fear of his wife, with reason, and never underestimated the lengths to which she might go.

Dom João was successful in thwarting his queen's ambitions, but he was unable to forward his own so long as Lord Strangford, the British minister, remained in Rio. Strangford was the descendant on his father's side of Sir Philip Sidney and on his mother's of the Philipse family of New York, one of whose daughters had declined George Washington's proposal of marriage. His appointment to the Portuguese court was his first important post, and in it he made his reputation as a diplomat. With patience he lasted out Dom João's vacillations between remaining in Europe as a prisoner of the French and escaping to Brazil through the last open door in the British blockade of Napoleon's Europe. Finally he arrived in Rio some time after Dom João, on July 22, 1808, after a voyage of seventy-seven days. Concerning the Banda, he knew what his business was: it was to keep the peace and to keep Portugal out of the struggle between Spain and her colonies. He was unable to prevent Dom João from sending his troops into the Banda Oriental in 1811, on the pretext of protecting

his southernmost province of Rio Grande do Sul from the disturbance caused by the warfare between the insurgents in Buenos Aires
and the loyalist Spanish troops in Montevideo. But in 1812 Strangford
persuaded him to withdraw, for Buenos Aires and Montevideo had
signed an armistice.

Dom João's real chance came in 1815, when Viscount Strangford
left Rio for London. For the first time he had enough troops at his
disposal, now that the armies in Europe had been disbanded. In January, 1817, Dom João took advantage of the perennial troubles in the
Banda to send his General Lecor to invest Montevideo. Three years
later the Montevideans voted for the incorporation of the Banda into
Brazil as the Cisplatine Province. In international affairs on the European stage, these events had extensive repercussions, but in the Banda
itself peace reigned more or less undisturbed until 1825. When Dom
João left Brazil for Portugal and his son proclaimed himself emperor
of an independent Brazil, Montevideo was the last city within his
domains to be cleared of Portuguese troops. Though a loyalist faction
and an imperialist faction existed, their presence did little to arouse
the fighting spirit of the region.

But in April, 1825, the guerrilla chieftain Juan Antonio Lavalleja,
who had taken refuge in the province of Buenos Aires, raised a band
of devoted followers, the "Immortal Thirty-Three," composed of
exiles from the Banda thirsting for independence, and invaded the
countryside behind Montevideo. He was joined by Fructuoso Rivera,
who had once served Dom João as a commander in the rural regions.
For three years the war continued between the Brazilian forces and
those of the province of Buenos Aires. The war did not go well for
the Brazilians. The imperial forces were twice defeated in 1825. Dom
Pedro I, trying to recoup the situation, himself took the field in November, 1826, but was forced to abandon the campaign and return to
Rio. In 1827 his forces on land were defeated; one of his squadrons
was captured by the British Admiral Brown, who commanded the
Buenos Aires squadron; another was lost off the coast of Patagonia.

By that time, both sides were ready to call the war a draw. To the
accompaniment of the announcement by Lord Ponsonby, now the
British minister in Rio, threatening both sides with dire consequences

if they breached their agreements with England, ratifications were exchanged at Montevideo on October 4, 1828, to a treaty in which both Rio and Buenos Aires agreed that the Banda was now an independent nation. The constitution for the modern Republic of Uruguay was accepted by Brazil and Buenos Aires two years later and the troops of both sides were withdrawn.

The years that followed this achievement of independence were not peaceful. The Banda was still the border, the debatable ground where the old ambitions of Spaniards and Portuguese lived on. It was inevitably drawn into the struggles between the Argentine provinces, in the attempts of Buenos Aires to dominate its own hinterland and in the determination of that hinterland to resist the domination of the city. From the north it was constantly being invaded by fugitive *gaúchos* from the Brazilian province of Rio Grande do Sul, who, when impatient with the central government at Rio, fell into trouble and escaped across the border, to join in the struggles between the various factions that kept the Banda in a constant state of civil war. Family ties and clan alliances overlapped the border. There was little distinction between the mode of life in Rio Grande and that in the Banda; all the region was open, rolling plains, horse and cattle country, feuding country. Damage to Uruguayan property was inevitable in these forays, and in Montevideo Brazil was frequently seen as the monster who deliberately created this trouble, in order that she might have a pretext for once more possessing the Banda.

Not only did Montevideo fear this, but also Juan Manuel de Rosas, the Argentine dictator, whose dream, on the contrary, was of a South American Republic that would incorporate all the territory of the old Spanish viceroyalty of Buenos Aires. On April 1, 1843, his forces controlling the rest of the old Banda, he laid the city of Montevideo under a siege which his general, Manuel Oribe, maintained for nine years. It was, however, not only Brazil who objected to this liquidation of an independent Uruguay. The European powers, particularly England and France, also wanted an independent government at Montevideo, and they sent fleets to blockade the port.

In the meantime, both Rosas and the government in Montevideo sought to enlist the interest of the imperial government in Rio. For that purpose, they both sent agents to the Emperor's court. The Emperor's government was in an awkward position as the year 1850 arrived. The Emperor, fearful of the power and the spread of ideas of republicanism and separatism, was naturally inclined to favor the constituted authority of the faction supported by Rosas, who had shown himself successful not only in holding together the provinces of Argentina but also in keeping out foreign influence. But this natural inclination was balanced by another and more powerful fear —that Rosas' ambition would not stop short of the boundary of Rio Grande do Sul. There is a geographical cohesion in all the lands that cluster about the estuary of the River Plate. To Rosas the logic was overwhelming. He openly said so.

So long as the war between Rosas and the forces besieged in Montevideo was stalemated, the cautious Brazilians could afford to procrastinate. But if Montevideo, abandoned by the European powers, should capitulate, there would be no further barrier to Rosas' attempts to conquer Rio Grande do Sul by force to arms, aided perhaps by certain disaffected elements within the province which had not been sufficiently convinced by the vigorous measures undertaken by General Lima e Silva (later the Duke of Caxias) in his campaign of pacification five years earlier. Thus matters stood in 1850, when Dom Pedro had been ten years at the head of his government and was leaving behind the uncertainties of his days as a novice in statecraft.

The man who represented Montevideo at the Emperor's court was Andrés Lamas. He had been born in Montevideo on March 2, 1817. As a very young man he had plunged into the turbulent politics of his harassed city. He had first shown his extraordinary capacities as a statesman while he was chief of police of Montevideo, during the siege by Oribe's forces and under the guns of the foreign warships in the port. In spite of his youth, he had the gift of inspiring confidence among his compatriots, to such an extent, in fact, that he was chosen as their last hope in the difficult and delicate mission of winning the Emperor of Brazil's aid for the Colorado party, which was entrenched in the besieged city. (The Colorado, or, generally speaking, the Liberal party in Uruguayan politics, and the Blanco, or, generally speaking, the Conservative party, acquired their nicknames, meaning respectively red and white, from the colors of the ribbons worn by the followers of Fructuoso Rivera and Oribe in the civil strife that preceded the siege of Montevideo.) Among the men of his generation he stands out as patient, subtle, devoted to his cause, the consistent friend of Brazil, in whose aid he saw the best chance for his country's independence and well-being.

Pedro Lamas, when years later he came to set down on paper his slight and graceful memoirs of his father, told a very romantic story about a certain Brazilian businessman, Irineu Evangelista de Sousa.

In the year 1850, Andrés Lamas lived in a house on the Rua da Pedreira da Glória, in Rio, near the favorite royal church of the Gloria, perched high on its eminence overlooking the Flamengo beach. Lamas, though astute, discreet, and persuasive, had not yet succeeded in having himself accepted by Dom Pedro II as the emissary of an officially recognized government. His rival, General Guido, Rosas' man, also lived in Rio, threatening the Brazilian government with war if it dared to recognize the agent of the anti-Rosas forces. Lamas, however, had certain advantages. He was socially at home at the Emperor's court and he was personally agreeable to the Emperor. His children, when he took his family up to Petrópolis to avoid the danger of yellow fever during the hot weather, shared the same tutors with the royal children. His house in Rio was a rendezvous for Brazilian military men who favored his party. He had a ready pen and he made good use of the newspapers to persuade Brazilian public opinion of the justice of his party's views.

His house on the Rua de Pedreira da Glória was spacious but unpretentious. Being on a height, it was reached by a flight of granite steps, wide and straight. At every fifteenth or twentieth step out of the hundred or more, there was a landing with a rustic bench shaded by shrubs, a thoughtful precaution in that hot climate, so that visitors might pause and rest on the way up. At the top was a great terrace, shaded by tall trees and perfumed by the jasmine, roses, and carnations that grew everywhere. From it could be seen below the full sweep of the great bay, with its dark granite and green sentinels, the Sugar Loaf and the mountains on the farther side, its islands and its forts, and in the distance the city of Niteroi, or as it was then called, the Vila Real da Praia Grande, the capital of the province of Rio de Janeiro.

One morning a new visitor climbed the stairs and, reaching the terrace, paused and clapped his hands sharply to call the servant. When the servant came, he gave him his card. He wanted to see Senhor Lamas.

Lamas, in his private study, weighed the card in his hand as he read: Irineu Evangelista de Sousa. The name was not familiar to him. He did not recognize its owner, when the servant showed him into the study. Lamas saw before him a man in his late thirties, of middle height, clean-shaven, with an agreeable, intelligent face, alert eyes, and a wide, straight mouth, firmly closed. The visitor stated his business without preamble. He had come to offer financial aid, arms, powder, munitions, victuals, and a monthly subsidy to the government of Montevideo, all to be delivered directly to that government. Lamas, surprised and nonplussed, sensing treachery, said nothing. His visitor continued with explanations. He was a merchant who had faith in the triumph of the Montevidean government. He would furnish these things at the same price at which they were furnished to the Emperor's army.

Lamas' immediate reply to these overtures was a noncommital excuse. He was very busy at the moment. Perhaps they could discuss the offer the next day. The strange young man withdrew with the same amiable simplicity with which he had come. Probably he accurately guessed the reason for his host's reluctance to begin negotiations at once. In fact, Lamas did suspect treachery. He knew that from the first day of his arrival in Rio he had been assiduously watched by Rosas' spies. All his movements had been noted, all his visits reported to General Guido. More than once he had had reason to suspect people who came to see him under various pretexts. He had even to be watchful of the servants in his house and keep his official papers under lock and key.

This sudden dazzling offer of aid, then, was too good to be true. In spite of all his efforts, the Brazilian government had not committed itself to his support. Montevideo was at its last gasp. All hope of effective French or British aid had collapsed with the withdrawal of the fleets. Montevideo had become, to an age which saw Rosas as a tyrant and the enemy of free men, in Alexandre Dumas' words, "not a city, but a symbol; not a people, but a hope; the symbol of order, the hope of civilization." Yet it seemed doomed. Why should a stranger, completely unknown to the agent of that government, all at once and at the eleventh hour, come forward with this miraculous offer of salvation?

Lamas temporized. That very afternoon he went to see the Emperor at the Palace of São Christovão. The Emperor gave him his answer quickly—he knew all about Irineu Evangelista de Sousa. He was indeed a very wealthy businessman, a friend of Paulino Soares de Sousa (Viscount Uruguai), the Emperor's Minister of Foreign Affairs. It was safe for Lamas to continue negotiations.

Unfortunately for the purposes of drama, Pedro Lamas' account of his father's first encounter with Senhor Irineu was not accurate. No doubt Pedro repeated the account which had come to him, in later years, by tradition. It was indeed a historic meeting, for it was the beginning of a friendship that lasted throughout the lifetime of these two extraordinary men, a friendship that ripened from mere cordiality into sincere affection. But what actually took place before that first meeting is recorded in letters which Lamas wrote to his chief, Manuel Herrera y Obes, the Minister for Foreign Affairs of the besieged government in Montevideo. In February, 1850, Lamas had sent a memorandum to Paulino Soares de Sousa, the Brazilian Minister of Foreign Affairs, declaring that the government of the Republic of Uruguay had firmly decided not to continue the struggle further without formal promise of aid from Brazil. It needed munitions, and since Brazil apparently would not reach an immediate and decisive agreement with Montevideo, Lamas declared that he demanded that Soares de Sousa make some effort, for example, find some businessman who would advance these munitions, receiving in payment dated bills of exchange—rather long-term bills, to be sure—against the Montevideo government.

The response to this memorandum was an invitation from Soares de Sousa for Lamas to visit him that afternoon, March 20. When Lamas arrived at the Minister's, he was assured that there was a businessman who would undertake to provide the greater part of the articles of war that the city needed and money to pay the fleet and other expenses, as might be desired.

"Then," said Lamas, in his letter of March 21, 1850, to Herrera y Obes, "speaking with greater frankness, we agreed that I should write to you confidentially at once and that this merchant should deal with an intermediary of mine, in order to avoid suspicion, because the frequency with which I should have to visit certain places during these days when attention is centered on the affairs of the River Plate would naturally cause someone to be set to watch my movements." Lamas clearly understood the situation. He had assiduously educated the Brazilian public in sympathetic preference for the side of the Colorados. It was infinitely to Brazil's advantage to have a free, independent Uruguay between the borders of her southernmost province and the rapacity of the Argentine dictator. Now, in the midst of Rio's first great yellow-fever epidemic, the fate of Montevideo had to be settled. There was a general panic in Rio. The secretary of the United States Legation, Morgan, had died of the new scourge. The Emperor, in Petrópolis, had had an intermittent fever. Paulino Soares de Sousa, himself, the victim of a light attack, had fled with the rest of the Emperor's court and the diplomatic corps to the comparative safety of the mountain resort, leaving the Brazilian diplomatic agent in Montevideo, Pontes, without instructions.

"Guido and I have stayed firmly here," said Lamas, writing letters home in his empty house on the Rua da Pedreira da Gloria, his family gone to Petrópolis and his two servants dead of the fever. He stuck it out, as did Rosas' agent, in spite of the "suffocating atmosphere" created by the constantly increasing number of deaths. Soares de Sousa, still frightened, paid only two visits to the city after he recovered. But by July he was fully restored and ready to act. He sought out Senhor Irineu, then reputed to have the largest private fortune in Brazil.

Paulino Soares de Sousa was an experienced man of state. He had been born in Paris on October 4, 1807, where his father while still a student had married the daughter of a bookseller who had died on the guillotine as a Girondist. He had been brought up in Maranhão, in the north of Brazil, and educated at Coimbra in Portugal and at the Law Faculty of São Paulo. He had been president of the province of Rio de Janeiro, the political proving ground for many of the ministers of state of the empire, and Minister of Justice of the imperial government. He had become Minister of Foreign Affairs on October 8, 1849, to replace the Marquess of Olinda, and held that office until September 6, 1853.

To Senhor Irineu, Paulino was "a great political chief such as we have not had more than half a dozen since our separation from the mother country," who "understood the gravity of the situation and attempted to break the strength of those elements which were preparing to attack us. From the beginning of 1850 I had followed all the evolutions of the Brazilian policy in the River Plate, through the confidence placed in me (by which I was honored) by the ministers.

In the middle of that year I declared to Councilor Paulino that, since the attitude of the Argentine Legation each day became more marked, and Brazil was not prepared to accept the gauntlet, I undertook, so far as the government was concerned, to bring together, without making a great to-do about it, the forces necessary for the blow, so that we should not find ourselves involved in a long war, which would be disastrous for the finances of the empire. His Excellency told me that, since the government of Montevideo had been abandoned by France, as soon as the resources which could be supplied to them were exhausted, their collapse would be inevitable and Rosas' dominion would be complete in the Republic, Brazil thereby losing its base of operations in the war that was inevitably approaching; that it was necessary at all costs to support the city with financial resources, so long as Brazil was not prepared to go to war; and that the government hoped in time to give this indispensable aid, such as the supplies I had made available. The secret treaty with the representative of the government of the city at this court set the sum of this aid, which I faithfully undertook, without the smallest profit to myself. Indeed, on the contrary, since I saw that the resources furnished were not enough to carry out the purpose in view, and certain that the imperial government could not draw back, and knowing that I had a superfluity of resources at the moment, I undertook to give efficacious aid to the defense of the city, with sufficient resources and at an insignificant rate of interest—the minimum current in Montevideo—my idea being to help bring about the triumph of the Brazilian policy in the River Plate.

When Brazil was prepared to make war, it ordered its sea and land forces to act, and in a few weeks had broken the power of the tyrant, who with an iron hand had for twenty years dominated both banks of the Plate and had daringly threatened us.

The Brazilians did triumph. The siege of Montevideo was lifted, Oribe's army was vanquished, and on October 8, 1851, a treaty was signed between the Blanco and Colorado factions which brought the civil war to an end. Among the Uruguayans, said Lamas, there must be neither victors nor vanquished.

But the real war, which had become inevitable between Brazilian and Argentine interests, was not fought in Uruguay. To the Brazilian and Uruguayan forces were added those of the governor of the Argentine province of Entre Rios and Corrientes, Justo José Urquiza, the first Argentine *caudillo* to rebel successfully against Rosas. In January, 1852, a combined force of men invaded the territory of the Argentine Confederation. Only one serious engagement was fought, for the Argentines also were weary of fighting and of Rosas' absolutism. This was the battle of Monte Caseros, which took place near Buenos Aires on February 3, 1852. It was one of the decisive battles of South American history, for Rosas was defeated and fled to England under the protection of Robert Gore, the British minister. The British had no objection to protecting him so long as he did not wipe out the independence of Montevideo. Uruguay was at last able to set up a stable independent government.

As a reward for his efforts, Senhor Irineu became the banker of the Republic of Uruguay. His bank there was to be the cornerstone of his new career, of his vast industrial empire in the River Plate, of his reputation, good and bad, in the political history of the relations between Brazil and Uruguay during the next twenty-five years.

He was not the first who had thought of founding a bank in Montevideo. The financial history of the city had its origins in colonial times. Spain as a colonial power was no more willing than Portugal to allow free commercial intercourse between her dominions in the New World and other nations. The natural resources of Spanish America were exploited by means of monopolies, any investment of money and labor in industry was subject to crushing taxation, and the circulation of money was inhibited by restrictive laws, such as that which provided the death penalty for anyone caught sending money out of the realm.

The nearest thing to modern exchange transactions was the buying and selling of bills of exchange between the merchants of Montevideo and Cadiz, in Spain. Within the colony, credit transactions were primitive and not even recorded, except for the dealings of wealthy merchants, who carried on accommodation banking operations under the cloak of commercial dealings. Money was scarce, and in its place merchants bartered in kind or circulated handwritten memoranda of debt, a type of commercial paper that was even substituted for silver coin, which had lost a good deal of its value through frauds in its specified weight. The first "internal loans" with which the people in the River Plate were familiar were the "patriotic contributions" levied on them by the Spanish crown during the first years of the nineteenth century, to pay for defense against invasion.

Things improved for Montevideo in 1815, for then a Commercial Court was established, the public treasury was reorganized, and treaties were made with the United States and England permitting a relatively free trade. Exchange operations with Buenos Aires, Rio, and Europe developed, including the system of buying and selling bills of exchange. Uruguay received its first foreign loan, 5,000 pesos, from the British, to take care of urgent expenses. Even during the invasion by Dom João VI's troops, commercial activity increased in Montevideo, stimulated by the circulation of the paper money of the Bank of Brazil and of the coin issued by the Mint in Rio. The first bank to be established in the city was a branch of the National Bank of Buenos Aires, which came in on the heels of the army sent by the Buenos Aires government to reinforce Lavelleja and Rivera in their efforts to oust the Brazilians. The notes of the new bank had a short life, for they were used to pay the soldiers of the reinforcing army, who, not being used to paper money, used them to make cigarettes.

Shortly after the siege of Montevideo was lifted and peace established in the Banda, the government of Uruguay began negotiations,

in October, 1851, with Fernando Menck for the creation of a bank,
a grant that was intended to recompense Menck for a loan he had
made to the newly reëstablished republic. A law was introduced into
the Congress for this purpose, but though the Chamber of Deputies
took note of it in April, 1852, nothing was done about it. About the
same time, Manuel Muñoz presented a project for a national bank and
exchange house, which, like Menck's, was tacitly shelved. In the session of the Chamber of July 10, 1854, the deputy Francisco Hordenana
offered a new project for a national bank, which was approved by the
Chamber and the Senate and signed by the president within a week.
The new bank was to have a minimum capital of 2,000,000 "pesos
fortes," its loans were to enjoy the same privileges and rights as the
debts of the treasury, and it could issue notes up to the amount of
money actually in its deposit vaults.

Menck sought to take advantage of the new law, with a proposal
which he made in March, 1855, for the establishment of a National
Bank for Montevideo. The Chamber in its session of April 15, 1855,
approved the charter, which provided for a capital of 3,000,000 pesos,
and the exclusive privilege of issuing notes up to double the amount of
capital actually received in deposits. The bank was to be in operation
within six months of the grant.

Lamas submitted the project to Senhor Irineu for his opinion, who
gave it in a letter dated January 20, 1854 (probably one of the last
he signed as Irineu Evangelista de Sousa, for three months later he
received his title of Baron Mauá).

I shall say now that the Menck project sins in this respect especially,
that an establishment so organized is not required to give guarantees;
neither are the charter and bylaws of the Bank of France acceptable in
any way to govern a bank in Montevideo, since many of their requirements would be inapplicable. The charter and bylaws of the great Bank
of Brazil which is to be founded [the third Bank of Brazil, created by the
forced merging of Mauá's own house with the Banco do Comércio] will
be very much more satisfactory to the requirements of the Republic, suit-
ably modified, and I shall give myself the work of making ready the provisions which must be altered in reference to the requirements of the
Republic, and I shall send the revision to Your Excellency and to your

friends; because this concerns an institution which will exercise a great influence on the destinies of the Republic and which will, if by any chance it should turn out badly, instead of having a beneficent influence, bring about extraordinary evils.

Menck failed, for he did not succeed in raising the necessary capital to make his bank a reality. It is not beyond the realm of possibility that he failed because Mauá did not intend him to succeed. However that might be, within a few years he was an official of Mauá's new bank in Montevideo. For in 1857, after weathering a heated debate in the Chamber of Deputies, the project for a bank presented by Mauá had been approved.

It was founded under the name of Banco Mauá y Compañia, and was a bank of issue, deposit and discount, with a provisional capital of 1,200,000 pesos, which could be raised to 6,000,000. It had the power to issue up to three times the amount of the capital represented by its notes payable in gold on sight. Some estimate of the importance of this establishment can be obtained by comparing its capital with the public income of Uruguay, which at the time was 3,000,000 pesos. By 1861, the Uruguayan government owed the Banco Mauá 2,189,000 pesos. The creation of his bank stimulated the creation of several others: The Banco Comercial, with a capital of 600,000 pesos and the power to grow to 2,000,000, and a number of others founded between 1860 and 1867.

His bank, however, was only the basis for a vast network of industries that Mauá had created in an effort to revive the exhausted country. He built railways, gasworks, and docks for Montevideo, imported pure-bred cattle, and established the first of the great cattle-raising stations in the republic, founded jerked-beef factories and meat-extract plants. He had always been sensitive to the enormous economic potentialities of the River Plate region, always looking for a rapid and energetic expansion that could take place in a region with a vigorous population free at last from the suffocating monopolistic theories of the Iberian peninsula.

Montevideo, it was true, was not representative of the rural provinces, for during the ten years of the siege it had been cut off from the rest of the country. It had become a cosmopolitan colony. In 1842, at the beginning of the siege, said the traveler Zum Felde, 5,218 French immigrants and 2,515 Italians had entered the city. Its population was composed of 11,431 Uruguayans, 15,252 Europeans, and 4,000 Argentines and other nations. In the countryside surrounding the city lived perhaps more than 20,000 Brazilians, the majority of them from Rio Grande do Sul, a number which by 1864 might have grown to around 40,000, a fifth of the population of Uruguay, and they owned one-quarter of the land in the republic.

Sarmiento, the Argentine, who lived as an exile in the besieged city, writing to Fidel López in Chile, was scandalized at the marked influence of the foreign element in the city. In Montevideo Bay, he said, were innumerable foreign vessels. The masters and the crews of the vessels that plied the waters of the River Plate were Genoese; the stevedores were Basques and Galicians; the pharmacies and drugstore were in the hands of the Italians, and the retail trade in those of the French. The English held the wholesale trade; the Basques, the quarries; the Spaniards, the food trade; the Italians cultivated the land under the fire of the batteries, outside the walls of Montevideo; and the colonists from the Canary Islands grew grain, far away from the coast.

"Neither Argentines nor Uruguayans," he said indignantly, "are the inhabitants of Montevideo, but the Europeans, who have taken possession of a part of American soil."

What dismayed Sarmiento exhilarated Mauá. He felt in the diversified activity of the cosmopolitan population of Montevideo the stirring vigor of a new, young people. Undoubtedly it attracted his commercial and financial interest, for it promised possibilities of growth which in speed and scope would quickly eclipse the slower, fumbling course of industrialization in big, awkward, conservative Brazil. This was the thought in his mind, this his expectation when he took over the economic life of the country. Otherwise, as an astute businessman, he would not have sunk his money in a ruin. For he himself described Uruguay thus:

Visiting Montevideo before and just after the constitutional government was organized and traversing the countryside, I was saddened. In the capital the disorganization in all branches of the government was complete. As for the financial resources, the government was dominated by a group of unscrupulous exploiters; as for the collection of the scanty revenues, rapine prevailed. In trade, even in the diminished quantities to which a most limited consumption restricted this element of life, there reigned disorder in all its aspects; there was no agriculture whatever; the rich pasture lands were stripped bare and one could traverse dozens of leagues without encountering a single head of cattle. In sum, the country was a true political, economic, and financial corpse; the ten years of civil war had laid waste everything.

With the defeat of Rosas, Mauá became the creditor of both Argentina and Uruguay, for even the loans made to these governments by Brazil came out of his pocket. Between 1851 and 1867 he himself made loans of hundreds of thousands of pesos to the government which had defended Montevideo and to the succeeding administrations that took over the country. While it lasted, his financial interest in the republic was all-inclusive. In the London Exposition of 1861, the best cattle products of Uruguay came from his ranches, the wool from his sheep surpassed in elasticity that of the woolens shipped from Buenos Aires. His shipbuilding yard in the River Plate produced the first steamboat, the *Dolorcita*, to navigate the great river.

His estate at Mercedes, on the Río Negro, near Montevideo, was a model ranch, where he tried out the newest scientific developments in cattle-raising. In 1861 he thought of selling it, and the letter he wrote to his partner De Castro in Manchester is a good example of his way of thought in such matters:

I have no hope that you will succeed in selling this magnificent property and in fact but for the fall in the price of cattle I was no ways anxious that you succeed. The price I ask is of course extravagant, in reference to the value of other properties, which can be bought in the Estado Oriental [Uruguay], but I consider none as valuable as mine. . . . My idea was, therefore, if a sale for one hundred thousand pounds cannot be made, to create a company—say, one hundred thousand shares of ten pounds each issued, of which I might remain with ninety, or ninety-five thousand shares and the remainder divided by as great a number of people as possible, the Board of Directors to be composed of you and two more gentlemen of character, your friends, whose *sole labor* would be to name a manager and a submanager at Mercedes, the manager to be the present majordomo there, Bento José de Lima, a man from Rio Grande who thoroughly under-

stands his business, the submanager a thoroughly *competent farmer* from
England, who might bring *half a dozen* skilled laborers with him, and all
kinds of superior modern agricultural implements, and as the land is, I
believe, the finest in the world for agriculture, and the transit of the produce which may be raised is by water, I have no doubt that the *yield* of the
estate would vastly increase by such an arrangement. The dividends made
to the shareholders in England regularly *every six months* and the accounts
published would be splendid and naturally attract attention, after a period,
say, at the end of *half a dozen years,* and the shares become sought after
for *investment* eagerly, and during some period of excitement and abun-
dance of money you might be able to dispose of half or three-fourths of
what I held, thus realizing *capital,* the object I have in view without destroying but on the contrary increasing the value of the fine property,
which, even as it stands, is not to be compared to any other in the Estado
Oriental, save in its comparatively small extent (eighty thousand hectares).

By 1861 he was not only the greatest landowner, the greatest
banker, the greatest industrialist, of the River Plate. He was also the
close friend of several of its chief men of state. Andrés Lamas was
always his devoted ally, for besides the fact that Lamas sincerely believed that the support of Brazil was Uruguay's greatest safeguard
(and Mauá was the representative of Brazilian interests within the
country), there was a bond of sympathetic understanding between
them. To Mauá there was something very attractive in Lamas' cou-
rageous, optimistic, dogged, truthful character. And Lamas admired
in Mauá his initiative, his imagination, his forward drive. As Lídia
Besouchet has pointed out:

For more than thirty years they carried on, from London, Rio, Montevideo, Buenos Aires, and elsewhere, a correspondence that gradually lost
the dry, formal tone of the early years of the 1850's to become warm, personal, and full of a mutual trust, surprising in men as busy and as involved
as they in the machinations of their fellows. Mauá had for Lamas an enthusiastic regard and admiration. He was to him what a statesman should
be, cultivated, urbane, trustworthy, openminded, everything that the Brazilian public men with whom he had to deal . . . were not.

In the midst of all the reciprocal animosity that flourished amongst
the public men of Argentina and Uruguay after the defeat of Rosas,
Mauá picked his way with care, and, for a while, with success. He

was on cordial, if formal terms with Mitre, the new president of the province of Buenos Aires; with Urquiza, who, as governor of the province of Entre Rios, was the leader of the Confederation of the other provinces of Argentina; and with the other men concerned in the uneasy transitions in the development of these two countries. But it was only Lamas who heard his real opinions about the others, and Lamas was a discreet man. Mauá's position was awkward, for to the Uruguayans he was *El Peligro Brasileño* (the Brazilian Peril) and to the Brazilians he was the cause of Brazilian trouble in the turbulent Plate, the suspect familiar of Brazilian diplomatic agents. So long as his affairs flourished, these resentments did not trouble him.

His old friend Richard Carruthers wrote to him in February, 1861: "I observe, with pride, how you are estimated in the South . . . and I rejoice at your great successes in that quarter of South America. I must own that I had great fears of your doing well there, owing to the constant motions from diversity of parties. . . . I am most happy to perceive how you keep aloof from all partisanship. This is true wisdom in the Banker and Merchant."

CHAPTER XI

THE
GAMBLER

Under the circumstances, keeping aloof from all partisanship was something much more easily said than done. As a young man, Mauá's political sympathies were probably republican, perhaps separatist, and certainly antislavery. His antislavery convictions survived as he grew older. His republicanism became submerged in his loyalty as a Brazilian to the empire. His inclination toward separatism—in favor, that is, of the independence of the province of Rio Grande do Sul, so different in character and population from the rest of Brazil —was spent in the success of his operations in Uruguay, the projection of his native province. His activities there were bold but they had a solid base in the industrial and agricultural enterprises that expanded so rapidly under his care. That very success, however, led him further and further south and deeper and deeper into the jungle of politics in the River Plate region. In Argentina he became a gambler.

He plunged into the affairs of the Argentine provinces, and his partner in this gamble was none other than the celebrated Büschenthal.

Joseph Büschenthal's career in South America had begun back in the days when Dom Pedro I was Emperor of Brazil. When Dom Pedro abdicated and was on his way back to the Old World, José Bonifacio de Andrada e Silva, his old minister and the patriarch of independence, could not refrain from giving him one last piece of advice. In a letter dated April 11, 1831, José Bonifacio said briefly, with his usual plain-speaking:

Sire, I greatly hope that Your Majesty and all your august family have passed a good night. Sire, Mr. Filipps [Samuel Philipps, an English businessman and banker in Rio, Dom Pedro's man of business, through whose family connections Brazil's foreign-loan negotiations eventually passed into the hands of the London house of Rothschild] showed me the power of attorney which Your Majesty had given him, which I found in perfect order; but he gave me news which afflicts me and which is that the celebrated Büschenthal is also taking part in this business like Pilate in the Credo. Why? and why does Your Majesty want to affiliate yourself with a rascal, such as he is known to be, and the friend of your greatest enemy? Think, Your Majesty, of what you are doing, and don't deliver your financial interests into the hands of such a tool.

Joseph Büschenthal was one of the great adventurers of the early nineteenth century in South America. He began life as a Frenchman in Strasbourg, but the question of nationality did not trouble him. On June 25, 1828, he was naturalized as a Brazilian, when he found himself in Rio, no doubt as one of the many emigrants who had left a troubled Europe for greener pastures across the Atlantic. He went bankrupt, however, and, in April, 1832, departed for London, still owing six hundred contos. It was natural that he should leave Brazil then, for Dom Pedro I, with whom his relations were involved and mysterious, had already left Brazilian shores. In 1834 He set up business in Madrid. When things did not prosper he went once more to the New World, to seek a new fortune in the River Plate, where he was naturalized first an Uruguayan and then an Argentine. In Europe he passed for a German, a Frenchman, a Spaniard as the occasion required.

His wife, Maria da Glória, whom he married in 1831, when she was still in her teens, was said by some to be an illegitimate daughter of Dom Pedro I by Baroness Sorocaba. She was a native of Rio Grande do Sul, where she had been born in 1817. While her husband went to seek a new fortune in the River Plate, she settled in Madrid, where she maintained a political salon that rivaled the famous salon of the mother of the future Empress Eugénie of France. Maria da Glória was noted for her beauty and her social gifts. Her portrait was painted by the fashionable painters of the day, and her box at the Royal Theater was the center of fashion. In the midst of the distractions and intrigue of post-Napoleonic Spain, she watched faithfully over her husband's interests, living in luxury when he had money to send home and in genteel shabbiness when his constantly fluctuating fortunes hit bottom.

Thus when Büschenthal returned once more to Europe, he had a center of operations ready. In 1839 he participated in some of the devious negotiations by which a wife was found for the young emperor, Dom Pedro II. In 1847 he was obtaining a loan for the Spanish crown in London, with the aid of Sir Henry Bulwer, the British minister, and the Marquess of Salamanca, the Spanish financier. In the 1850's he was again busy in the River Plate, negotiating loans for the government of the confederated provinces of Argentina and working to obtain Brazilian support for the Confederation against the powerful province of Buenos Aires. In return for that support the Brazilians were to receive the right to navigate the rivers of the Plate system.

Mauá was his partner in these negotiations. In time Mauá was to regret this association and echo José Bonifacio by calling his partner "that scoundrel Büschenthal." But to begin with he joined Büschenthal in providing money for the Confederation.

When the dictator Rosas had left for Europe in 1851, a political exile, a contest had at once arisen between the city of Buenos Aires and its province, on the one hand, and the other provinces, under the leadership of Justo José Urquiza, the governor of the province of Entre Rios, on the other. Urquiza, ebullient and contradictory, was a good general and an able politician. He was also a shrewd man who realized the importance of economic forces. During his career as the political boss of Entre Rios, he laid the foundation for a public school system and two agricultural colonies, brought an engineer from the United States to plan a railway from Rosario to Córdoba; and made an agreement with the government of Chile for a transandine railway.

Withal, he was subject to violent fits of bloodthirsty passion, when he was capable of massacring his defeated enemies to the strains of music, and he had the typical *gaúcho's* taste for extravagant, unbounded display of wealth and luxury. In him were personified the greatest vices and virtues of the man of the plains. He was touchy, absurdly vain of his prowess as the great chief of a restless, hard-riding, dashing cowboy army. In his own province of Entre Ríos he was a feudal lord, in control of everything political, social, and economic. His *estancia*, or ranch, at San José, where he was finally assassinated in 1870, was a palace, furnished with the richest furniture and ornaments brought from France, and his banquets eclipsed the formal splendors of the government's entertainments in Buenos Aires. He hated and feared Brazil, whose sympathies would normally, he felt, be with his enemies in Buenos Aires.

Very largely because of his disdain of compromise and his jealous pride in himself as overlord of the Confederation, the course of politics in Argentina was during the late 1850's and early 1860's turbulent and unstable. Warfare was intermittent, and when not actually in progress was on the point of breaking out. It was part of his dreams of grandeur that the proud province of Buenos Aires should be taken by his army and forced into the Confederation. There was a party in Buenos Aires that favored this incorporation; to that party Mauá referred when in January of 1859 he wrote to Urquiza and told him of the munitions he could supply:

I assure Your Excellency now that I do not approve of the choice of warlike means to encompass the great purpose that you have in mind. However, if your government should resolve definitely on war, my frank, loyal, and decided aid to your government will not fail, in order that the result may be prompt, thus avoiding the financial ruin that I fear. I have even thought of one means by which I could give Your Excellency efficacious aid. I presume that if Your Excellency's government resolves on war it can surely count on the strong support within Buenos Aires. If that is not the case, I frankly declare to Your Excellency that the war would be an immense danger, whose eventualities no one could control, and that it would therefore not be reasonable to enter into it. Going on the assumption that there is a large party in Buenos Aires to support the reincorporation of the province into the Argentine Nation, things can be arranged so that a movement can take place in the City *on a day and hour* designated. In support of such a movement I would arrange that the two steamboats Manay and Pampeiro (under the pretext of fetching *charque* or other cargo) should leave Montevideo for Concepción del Uruguay, vessels which could carry *two thousand men* without armor and prepared for a *coup de main.* As soon as Your Excellency has these two thousand men ready they can be embarked during the night, the flag of the two vessels being changed on the occasion and at the proper moment by a bill of sale to the Government of the Confederation signed in Concepción del Uruguay. These vessels can enter the port of Buenos Aires on the day and hour previously designated, without anything being suspected there, except by the person who is to head the movement, and can disembark at a stroke the two thousand men, good troops, whose coming no one would suspect, and marching to reinforce the force already in motion within the city, would assure the result of the movement, always presupposing that there existed there a strong party in favor of the incorporation, which appears evident, because otherwise the attempt would be foolish. I believe that if such a plan were adopted without anyone except Your Excellency, your ministers, and the person who was to head the government in Buenos Aires knowing about it, the most complete result would be obtained, thus avoiding the great calamity that I fear, which would be like throwing a great stone from the top of a mountain, causing great damage and no one could foresee where it would stop.

Thus he was playing Ulysses to the Confederation's army. His reasons for such anxious attempts to prevent long-drawn-out and bloody fighting was the fact that he had banking interests in Buenos Aires also, having opened a branch office there. He did not disguise his reasons from Urquiza:

If Your Excellency deigns to accept any aid that may be in my hands to give you, you will understand without a doubt, that since I have interests in Buenos Aires also, money deposited in the Bank, I must be forewarned thirty days *at the very least* of Your Excellency's decision in order to protect my interests there, because given the hypothesis of this beginning, if by some misfortune the stroke should fail through one of the many eventualities to which all human arrangements are subject, the people of Buenos Aires would undoubtedly sweep aside all the laws to injure me, and not being able to reach my person would not hesitate to get into their hands anything that belonged to me in Buenos Aires. I would thus pay dearly for my devotion to Your Excellency and I hope you will coöperate with me in bringing about organization and tranquility in these countries, with whose organization I judge the present state of things in Buenos Aires to be incompatible.

He went on to offer more advice:

Permit me, Your Excellency, to repeat again that in my humble opinion pacific and indirect means, instead of the war which different factions are making in Buenos Aires, would be sufficient to bring about, within a short time, the great end that you have in mind. If, however, Your Excellency considers it proper to work otherwise, it will be necessary to put our hands on all the resources with the greatest urgency, and to arrange sure means so as not to ruin completely the resources of both parties, wasting the vital forces of the Confederation which can be used to so much advantage in the great material improvements which the Argentine Nation lacks. Your Excellency will without doubt excuse my boldness in venturing these reflections, having in consideration that only the hope of doing some good inspires my words.

The anxiety of a man not quite sure that he can manage a wild steed shows through these lines. The war that he could not avert by this persuasion ended in a temporary victory for the Confederation and the decision of Buenos Aires to join with it.

In the lull in hostilities that followed, the branch of Mauá's bank in Buenos Aires began to prosper, and he wrote long letters of fatherly advice to the young Englishman Leslie who was its manager. On June 7, 1861, for instance, he wrote:

I am happy to be informed that the concern under your able charge is gradually but steadily getting onto an improved footing at Buenos Aires, more especially with the Natives, and since the new house is prospering, I am particularly desirous the arrangements should be completed and the changes made, for, with you, I hope a new era will commence when Mauá and Company are installed in the new building. It is strange the opposition we meet with from Armstrong and Lamb, for I do not see in what way my influence will hurt their business, or the operations they carry on. For my part, I am convinced the world is large enough for all, and instead of opposing anybody I am only desirous to work harmoniously with all those who trade in the same community, and I am sure it is again an error and misconception to spend a thought in hurting any one, whilst the doing so cannot in any way serve a good purpose.

His bank in Buenos Aires was doing so well that he was working to obtain a charter for a branch at Rosario, another town in the same province. But in the meantime his deals with Büschenthal were not going well. These joint transactions had a long history and not an entirely happy one. Already by 1861 Büschenthal had aroused Mauá's anger by a clever maneuver that was intended to leave Mauá with a serious loss over a loan to the Confederation. Mauá wrote to him on March 9, 1861:

> If my letter of 8th January is a harsh one, or written in a moment of bad humor, as you say (which I do not deny) you cannot but be convinced that the bad humor was natural, on receiving propositions from you to settle your accounts with us, by which an actual loss of capital was offered as the result of operations entered into by which my position, at one moment, was actually endangered! and above all, accompanying such propositions with assertions trying to convince me that black was white. This was indeed too much! . . . You must allow that the attempt to convince me that I was largely benefited by receiving a large face amount of Confederation stock at 6% which if sold would swallow not only all the pretended profits but all the interest due, and even a portion of the actual amount of capital advanced, was indeed an oversight of yours and certainly offended me, for I considered that I was treated as a contemptible fool!

He had a scheme for the conversion of the Confederation loan which might save both of them loss, and this he outlined to Büschenthal in letters written in March, April, May, June, and July of 1861. The loan, he suggested, could be converted into a foreign loan, payable from custom-house receipts, and he added, "it would be every way desirable to interest Baring Brothers," who already were deeply committed in the River Plate.

But his scheme ran into the difficulty of the rising threat of civil war between the government of the province of Buenos Aires and the Confederation. The Buenos Aires government, in joining with the Confederation, had expected to dictate the terms of the merger and thereby offended the touchy Urquiza. Mauá, uneasy, wrote to Leslie on June 24, 1861:

The news of the probable outbreak between Buenos Aires and the rest of the Confederation is alarming, for I fear that *if hostilities actually commence*, this combat will not be carried on in the spirit of moderation which the last exhibited, and that atrocious acts will be practiced. The absolute want of money on the part of the Confederated Provinces will cause the armies which they raise to live out of a *devastation* of the wealthy Province of Buenos Aires. In fact, I see only calamities and destruction to both parties in this most unfortunate war. Nor can I flatter myself that it will soon be brought to a close. The acts of atrocity likely to be committed and the *devastation* of property will exasperate the minds of the people, so that neither will yield until one of the parties is crushed, which in the end does not bring order but anarchy, for to conquer *is not to convince*, and it is not in the power or resources of whichever party gets the upper hand to keep the other long from revenge, as the idea of a *standing army* sufficiently strong to accomplish such an end is out of the question. The influences at Buenos Aires commit an *atrocious mistake*, even supposing they are *in the right*, for instead of arriving at order and civil government in the end they will only bring destruction and anarchy whatever may be the party who conquered. It is indeed inconceivable! ... The Buenos Aires people would introduce into Congress a number of their most able and influential characters, and by acting with moderation these would soon bring around them a *majority*, I mean in the course of *a few years*, and gradually strengthening their influence in the National Councils, they would be able to serve the principles of order and civilization which they pretend to be their aim; who can doubt that the influence of Buenos Aires would become paramount *if peace was maintained*, and their resources, wealth, superior intelligence in proportion to that of the Provinces would *inevitably* give them every advantage. By going to war they lose *all these advantages!* the influence of the *caudilho* must be the consequence of a state of warfare, and, therefore, the people of Buenos Aires would lose, instead of serving the end they have in view by having recourse to such a way of solving difficulties. I hope I may be wrong, but I dread the combat will not end so soon, and will bring the most serious calamities to the Confederation and Buenos Aires. It would be *infinitely preferable* that a peaceable separation were arrived at.

Peace, in June, 1861, seemed unlikely, though both Büschenthal in

Buenos Aires and Mauá in the Confederation were using their best efforts. Mauá wrote to Büschenthal on June 24:

It is indeed a calamity both to you as well as to me [that the River Plate has been getting ready for another civil war] but it is not in your nature, nor in mine, to lose courage. We have unfortunately both risked too much on a single card and we pay or suffer the consequences of our independence; to lament over the past, however, does not mend or help anything as regards the future. Unless we make some new arrangement with the government of the Confederation, we need not look forward to receive interest or amortization on the Bonds we hold for years to come; let us by all means try to obtain an order against *all the customs houses and public stations* throughout the Confederation or in all the Provinces so as to make up the interest and amortization of the three millions of bonds in yours and my possession (I suppose no more were issued?) for this is the only way to get the matter on the tapis, for if we allow them to stop one or two quarters, we are done for.

Büschenthal apparently still hoped to deal with the governments on the brink of war, but Mauá's remarks were uncompromising when he replied to Büschenthal on June 24:

"The idea of trusting another *real* to the belligerent parties does not, I hope, enter your head, be the conditions *what they may!*" And on July 8, he added:

It is to be hoped that an amicable arrangement between Buenos Aires and the Provinces will be arrived at. I have, however, lost all faith in such lawless governments, and do not consider that any peace can be arrived at that can be relied upon. Faith amongst a parcel of bandidos is really a word without sense. How any man *in his senses* can trust his fortune and much less capital, not his own, into the hands of such people, is now a matter of astonishment to me. The lesson was a terrible one, but I hope will be useful.

Mauá undertook, nevertheless, to write persuasive letters to Urquiza, trying to mollify that touchy general's ire over what he considered the insolence of the people of the port city. Mauá had told Büschenthal on May 24, 8161:

I hope you may be successful in your endeavor to conciliate these people of Buenos Aires with the Provincials. I also wrote a long letter by the last

Packet to Urquiza, touching on all the chords of the better part of his nature, urging him to extend his hand to the Buenos Aires people. I fear that a new separation will be immediate, followed by the stoppage of payment of interest and amortization on our Bonds, and that we shall find ourselves with *papal sujo* [dirty paper] on our hands for a while, at all events, which is a most serious business to reflect upon.

Mauá, with his usual urbanity, had cultivated the General's goodwill. His wife and the General's family were on a friendly footing. About this time Dona Maria Joaquina, Baroness Mauá, sent Doña Dolores, the General's wife, a little present for the children, "a modern stereoscope which contains a great number of curious views which are presented to one's view when the handle on the side is turned and two little boards on top are lifted so that the light catches the mirrors, throwing a reflection on the pictures which produces the visual impression, whether by daylight or by candle light." Or so Mauá himself described the toy in a letter to Urquiza dated December 14, 1861.

These blandishments succeeded in maintaining the friendship between them but not in preventing war. Mauá, seeing his own efforts with Urquiza failing and Büschenthal equally unsuccessful in efforts at conciliating his friends in Buenos Aires, wrote to MacGregor in July, 1861, that he saw nothing for it but war, and "this combat will not be like the last. It will be bloody and protracted."

He was partly right. The forces of the Confederated Provinces under Urquiza and those of the province of Buenos Aires under Mitre, its president, met in September, 1861, on the battlefield of Pavón in the province of Santa Fé. The result was Mitre's victory and the final union of all Argentine provinces.

Mauá and Büschenthal remained the new government's chief creditors.

Mauá's financial dealings in the River Plate were well-known to the Emperor's government. In February, 1861, Francisco Otaviano, then the Brazilian agent in Buenos Aires, wrote to José Antonio Saraiva, the Brazilian special envoy in Montevideo, saying flatly: "Mauá and

Büschenthal are the *owners* of the internal consolidated Argentine debt."

For the moment affairs were quiet in Montevideo under the control of a president of the Blanco party, Bernardo Berro, whose alliances were with Urquiza and to whom the Brazilian government gave circumspect support. But it was the calm before the storm, for contentment by no means dwelled among the Uruguayans. Some of them had taken part on either side of the struggles in Argentina, those of the Colorado party with Mitre and those of the Blanco with Urquiza. Among the men who had distinguished themselves at the battle of Pavón was Venancio Flores. He was an Uruguayan, an intrepid cavalry raider and uncontrollable firebrand, who now sought refuge with his friend Mitre in Argentina. With Mitre's moral support, he began to prepare an invasion of Uruguayan territory, with a party of disgruntled Colorados and Blancos, to seize the government in Montevideo. Bernardo Berro, the Blanco president, more intelligent and an abler man than many of his political supporters, had kept Uruguay neutral during the war between Urquiza and Mitre. But matters were rapidly getting out of hand. Public opinion in Buenos Aires was on Flores' side, the newspapers were in favor of gun-running to help his forces arm, and recruiting campaigns were opened to promote his cause.

Andrés Lamas, as the representative of the Uruguayan government, pointed out to the Argentine Minister of Foreign Affairs, Elizalde, that Flores was gathering an expeditionary force in Argentine territory to attack Montevideo. The Argentine government merely replied that it "had taken measures intended to fulfill its duties imposed by neutrality with a friendly government." Then the Portuguese chargé d'affaires, the Italian minister, the British chargé d'affaires, and the French minister called on Elizalde in a body, to protest against the aid given to Flores, but this effort also had little effect.

Things went from bad to worse until Lamas persuaded Elizalde to sign a protocol in Buenos Aires, on October 20, 1863. It named the Emperor of Brazil as arbiter if these difficulties were not resolved. Lamas' hand had been strengthened by a visit to Buenos Aires of the

Brazilian minister to Montevideo, João Alves Loureiro. This visit had been inspired, said the British chargé d'affaires at Buenos Aires, by the influence of Baron Mauá, "who is one of the most influential men in his own country and is daily increasing his pecuniary connection with governments of both these republics, to both of which he has already made considerable loans."

In fact, in November, 1864, Mauá made a new loan to Berro's government in Montevideo, a loan of 6,000,000 pesos at 6 percent interest, with a guarantee of an additional 3 percent on import duties and 2 percent on export duties.

But Lamas' protocol failed, for it was not accepted in Montevideo. It had offended Berro, who was well aware that Dom Pedro II's personal sympathies were with Flores.

"Since when," asked Berro, "has Señor Lamas the right to elevate the Emperor of Brazil into a supreme tribunal for the international affairs of the Uruguayan people?" In vain did Lamas point out that Brazil had used her influence to bring about a peaceable settlement; that geography and common sense made Brazil the natural mediator. The protocol lapsed, and Uruguay and Argentina were no nearer an understanding than they had been before.

In the meantime, Flores (whose success Mauá, in a letter to Lamas, had erroneously declared to be materially impossible), during the night of April 19, 1863, landed at Rincón de las Galliñas, a small village at the mouth of the Rio Negro, and began his invasion and civil war in Uruguay. He had started on the road that led to the Paraguayan war, his own assassination, that of his enemy Berro, and that of Urquiza.

It was no wonder that Mauá wrote in a letter of November 8, 1864, to his managing partner in Montevideo, Ricardo José Ribeiro: "Above all, the affairs in the River Plate cause me the greatest concern, because the policy of the Imperial government is always equivocal, incomprehensible, maddening, which keeps me much preoccupied with the great interests I have in the River Plate."

Its policy was equivocal, incomprehensible, maddening, because the Emperor's government would not make up its mind, in the maze of conflicting interests in the River Plate, which course to take. Buenos

Aires was inimical to the empire, Urquiza hated the Emperor, Berro's government in Montevideo was fearful and touchy. Paradoxically, Brazil's two friends were on opposite sides of the Uruguayan political fence: for Flores was sympathetic to the Emperor, and Lamas favored Brazilian intervention to protect Montevideo from entrapment by Buenos Aires.

The policy of the Emperor's government, in fact, was the result of the Emperor's effect on his public men. He could neither be ignored nor disobeyed. He could seldom be persuaded, without great difficulty, from the path he chose to follow. Yet he seldom gave his ministers unequivocal advice. Now, confronted with the developments in the River Plate, remembering the history of Portuguese and Brazilian intervention there, acutely aware that the people of his southernmost province were inextricably involved with events across the border, he waited, watchful and suspicious. To him no man was more suspect than Mauá himself, the partner of the notorious Büschenthal, the man who by hearsay had been the partisan, in his younger days, of the secessionists of Rio Grande do Sul, the man of money behind the jealousies and counterplots brewing south of the Brazilian border.

CHAPTER XII

SOWING
THE WIND

DOM PEDRO II was not a man who cared much for change. He had been brought up to have great respect for constituted authority, and no doubt his unchildlike childhood had given him a feeling of inner insecurity, so that he preferred familiar scenes to remain familiar. He carried this feeling to the point of disapproving of any city improvements for the capital of his empire. André Rebouças has recorded the difficulties he and his brother encountered when, as engineers, they went in 1870 to see the Emperor and to suggest that studies be made to improve the water supply of Rio:

"We also combated the false idea, which the Emperor had, of giving water to the poor people gratis in fountains and demonstrated to him that it was much more liberal and hygienic to give the poor people water in their houses at a nominal price."

Like Queen Victoria, also, Dom Pedro disliked new faces around him in responsible positions. The old ministers of the Regency lingered long into his reign as the most powerful statesmen. Three former regents were the men upon whom he chiefly relied in moments of stress in his government, until they failed him by dying: Pedro de

Araújo Lima, the Marquess of Olinda, the taciturn, antisocial old former deputy to the Côrtes at Lisbon, who was a sort of vice-emperor of the realm; José da Costa Carvalho, Viscount Mont'Alegre, the man of the world, whose special gift was common sense and an ability to keep his friends; and Honório Hermeto Carneiro Leão, the redoubtable Marquess Paraná.

In the 1860's Dom Pedro had become self-confident enough as Emperor to dominate even these former regents among his ministers. Yet his personal preferences led him to listen attentively to the more conservative, the more familiar, the less innovating. Thus, Viscount Itaboraí was his favorite financial adviser, not Sousa Franco; Caxias was his favorite general, not Manoel Luiz Osorio (Marquess Herval) or Manoel Marques de Sousa (Count Pôrto Alegre), equally good generals but leaders of some rather ebullient elements in Rio Grande do Sul; José Antonio Pimenta Bueno (Viscount São Vicente) was his favorite reformer and abolitionist, since his views were not as sweeping nor called for such immediate measures as those of the men of the Liberal party. Dom Pedro's personal power probably reached its peak during the Coalition Government, in the late 1850's and early 1860's. In this idea of the Coalition (the *Conciliação* of Brazilian parliamentary history) he had largely succeeded in embodying his dislike of party politics and the consequent rise of public men to power without his immediate backing and control. The supreme moment had passed with the death of the Marquess of Paraná, the Prime Minister of the Coalition Government, in 1856, but still his personal prestige had not greatly diminished.

For ten years his realm had been quiet, fixed in its habits, with a basic prosperity that seemed unchanging so long as its foundation, the sugar- and coffee-growing slavocracy, remained undisturbed. Now there were disquieting signs which "this grandson of Marcus Aurelius," wrapped up in his scholarly pursuits, nevertheless observed. For though he hated change, change was overtaking him and his empire, and it was emanating from the troubles in the south.

Though all might be enlightenment and civilization in the Emperor's court, far to the south bloodshed was still the order of the day. Down

on the border of Rio Grande do Sul and Uruguay the old vendettas
that had commenced in colonial times between the Spaniards and the
Portuguese continued to flourish, with sometimes whole families
being wiped out in raids from one side to another. When it was not
murder and mutilation, it was cattle-raiding and arson. The border
was never quiet, and for years the Brazilian Minister of Foreign
Affairs had kept the records of outrages committed by Brazilians on
the Uruguayans and the Uruguayans on Brazilians, impartially. The
situation created a continuing dilemma for the government in Rio. If
the Emperor's government failed to satisfy the demands of Montevideo for reparations, the Uruguayan government would be a right-
eous enemy. If, however, the empire censured the men of Rio Grande
do Sul, the unruly province, where separatism ever flourished, would
be set afire in a new war of independence.

In the winter of 1863-64, old General Felipe Neto went to Rio de
Janeiro as the spokesman for his fellow cattle barons in Rio Grande
do Sul. He was powerful, and rebellious against the imperial government's tendency to favor the enemies of his *gaúchos*. His interests
were *gaúcho*. His sympathies would naturally be—in any conflict in
the River Plate region between the forces of Montevideo and Buenos
Aires on the one hand and the *gaúchos* on the other—with the *gaúchos*
across the border. He was also very wealthy, having been a war
profiteer during the siege of Montevideo, in the 1840's, when he had
supplied meat to Oribe's besieging army. Now in Rio he gave banquets of great luxury to the imperial senators and deputies, who could
not resist the temptation to attend. He was eloquent; he could talk
burningly of the outrages to which his countrymen were subjected
by the wicked Uruguayans. His eloquence and the magnificence of
his entertainments made an impression on the Brazilian parliament,
which dry, official reports, listing murder, rape, cattle-rustling, arson,
had never stirred.

Besides, when the year 1864 dawned, the Emperor found himself
confronted with a Liberal party majority in the Chamber of Deputies. By the rules of the parliamentary game which he so carefully
played, this meant that he must call a Liberal party cabinet into office.
This he did, though with considerable mistrust, since the province of

Rio Grande do Sul was a Liberal party stronghold. He named Zacarias de Góes e Vasconcelos, the cold, austere, self-appointed Cato of the Second Reign, his new prime minister.

Zacarias had begun his political career in the bosom of the Conservative party, but had switched over to the Liberal. In 1862, because of his very peculiarities, he had become a leading figure. He was a characteristic product of Dom Pedro II's government. For Dom Pedro had certain fetishes and taboos in governing and one of these concerned the freedom of attack upon himself by discontented politicians. He had no objection to outspoken criticism, provided that the attacker was a man of honest, if misguided, purpose and that the attack was not fortified and directed in such a way that it posed any real threat to the imperial regime. Both these elements were present with Zacarias. He was proud, disinterested, narrow, strengthening his own self-importance by becoming the searcher-out of knaves in public office, the smeller-out of interested motive in the most exalted.

It was Zacarias, however, the implacable enemy of impulsive action, who was betrayed by the situation in the River Plate. His ministry yielded to the pressure from the south, to the emotional excitement stirred up for the vindication of Brazilian rights, to the desire for revenge for the horrors committed on the border which just now had finally touched the imagination of the deputies in the Chamber. Zacarias yielded to the pressure and undertook to send the Uruguayan government an ultimatum, demanding reparations and guarantees for future conduct.

The man selected to deliver this ultimatum was José Antônio Saraiva, who received his instructions on April 20, 1864. Saraiva had been raised an orphan, without family and almost without friends. This fact gave him a taste for impartiality, and he made a virtue of necessity. He liked to make his contemporaries aware of the fact that he was immune to family influence and party influence, and that the good of his country alone and not the demands of his friends weighed with him. Now he had a task on his hands that would have tested the capacity of the most practiced diplomat. His instructions left him no leeway for bargaining; if the Uruguayan government did not punish those who had caused damage and injury to Brazilians, compensate

Brazilians who had suffered losses, release Brazilians who had been impressed into the Uruguayan army, then the imperial government would use its troops to protect the life, honor, and property of the subjects of the empire. It could make good this threat, for Brazilian troops had been concentrated on the border of Rio Grande do Sul, to prevent Brazilians from going to join Flores' revolutionary army in its invasion of Uruguay.

Gabriel Aguirre, another Blanco, had succeeded Bernardo Berro as President of Uruguay, and his party was the ally of Francisco Solano Lopes, the dictator of Paraguay, the third republic of the River Plate region. Uruguay was a mass of intrigues, and Flores was invading its borders. Saraiva saw all this at a glance and realized that Brazil was not at the moment popular in the River Plate. He began his mission by presenting the terms of his instructions in much more polite language. But Juan José Herrera, the Uruguayan Minister of Foreign Affairs, gave him little help, denying a good many of the charges brought against his country.

Saraiva, in May, 1864 wrote home, asking for an extension of powers, so that he could temporize and compromise. He suggested bringing Argentina into the settlement, because Argentina, also, had claims against Uruguay. The British minister to Argentina, Sir Edward Thornton, was asked to coöperate with Saraiva and with Elizalde, the Argentine Minister of Foreign Affairs, but all their efforts were in vain. Aguirre's Blancos were frightened of Flores and no temporizing succeeded. Saraiva then suggested that Argentina and Brazil should intervene together to keep the peace in Uruguay, but Mitre of Argentina, although agreeing that Brazil might take independent action, refused to join. On August 4, 1864, Zacarias' cabinet held a council of war, and in September the Brazilian army invaded Uruguay. The empire had now accepted Flores as an ally and sent its army to join his in the taking of Montevideo.

Mauá, like Saraiva, from the beginning saw the war between Brazil and Uruguay only as a calamity which would inevitably bring in its wake disaster for Brazil. He was neither patient nor reserved in his opinions of the actions of the imperial government. He had gone to

Europe in 1864 an angry man. So shaken was his financial structure in the River Plate that he went to London to see what he could do about reinforcing his credit and his financial alliances. His scheme of the moment was the merger of Mauá and Company with the London and Brazilian Bank, a coup which, as has been told, he brought off in London with brilliance, to the surprise of international money circles, but which fell to the ground for want of approval by the imperial government. He had left the New World in a rebellious frame of mind, as his letters to his old friend Lamas indicate. He spoke of going to England, "because among the *English* I am still worth something," and of the efforts of friends "to save my house from the ruin in which certain malevolent persons wish to involve it," a ruin that would also involve the whole of Uruguay and the River Plate.

Confronted with the embroilment of affairs in the River Plate from 1860 on, Mauá was concerned first and foremost with defending his financial interests. The question of party interest was unimportant to him, as he made plain to Lamas. He had a sentimental attachment to his native province and a lively friendship with several of the *gaúcho* figures—General Osorio, whom he considered slighted when the Emperor made Caxias a duke; Count Pôrto Alegre, another stalwart of the plains. But this predilection was tempered by a fear and a dislike of *caudilhismo*, the thinly disguised banditry of the great cattle barons, even of Urquiza, whom he personally liked. *Caudilhismo* was unfortunately both the connecting link between Rio Grande do Sul and its neighbor and the source of international antagonisms, for it was characteristic of both sides of the border. It made *gaúchos* in Rio Grande blood brothers of *gaúchos* in Uruguay, but it also provoked between them long and undying feuds that resulted in the general lawlessness that disturbed the relations between Montevideo and Rio.

Neither did Mauá look on war or civil disturbance with any favor. He remembered what the country was like when he first moved into Uruguay on the heels of the victory at Monte Caseros in 1851. Then the country had fallen into his hands, not as a ripe plum, but as a withered fruit:

On the termination of the war, I found myself compromised for a pretty big sum as creditor of the Uruguayan government, and the economic con-

dition of the Republic was such—something I had to take into account at
the time—that the country was veritably a dead body, and I seriously feared
that I should lose my money, I had therefore to plunge into the weakened
economic system of that nation, a fact that created for me difficulties which
in 1868 produced the first violent shock to the House of Mauá. I was as-
suredly led by noble motives to commit the original sin of putting foot in
that country; there is no limit to the sacrifices demanded by the aspirations
of patriotism, when they are enthusiastically pursued. Only he can understand the force of that feeling who possesses it deep in his soul; those are
few who feel it sincerely. In the period to which I refer the superfluity of
my assets gave me the power to cover any eventuality.

He could, with reason, point out that it had been his readiness to
take over the finances of the exhausted country that had given it new
life, had created out of nothing an economic basis for the new nation.
Now these very interests—for he was a landed proprietor, the master
of cattle ranches, the owner of meat-processing factories and wool-
export houses, the banker of both the government and of many private citizens—made him fear the renewal, or rather the continuance, of
warring political conflict.

His ties had at first been with the Colorado party, the party traditionally more open to coöperation with Brazil, traditionally linked
with the Liberal party in Rio Grande do Sul. But party lines meant
little to him. When the Emperor preferred the Blancos—and at first
he did, for there was a bond of affinity, in conservatism and respect
for constituted authority—Mauá found no difficulty in dealing with
them. Before 1863, Mauá and Company in Montevideo had subscribed 2,500,000 pesos of a public loan floated by the Blanco Government of 6,000,000 pesos (the Uruguayan peso at this period was
valued at about 50 English pence on the London exchange) at 6 percent guaranteed interest, to be secured by customs house receipts,
with a 3 percent duty on imports and a 2 percent duty on exports,
and with a further provision that if the House of Mauá was named
intermediary in the conversion of the debt into a public loan with
shares to be issued in London, it would receive one half of the profits.
A few months later, Berro received yet another loan from the Mauá
bank.

Affairs were far from static in Montevideo. Berro was replaced as President of Uruguay by Gabriel Aguirre, a more timid, less able man. And Montevideo was under threat of military assault by Flores' forces. Mauá, in his letters to Lamas, did not hesitate to call Flores "a bandit." In fact, he went so far as to call him "that thousand times wicked Flores who comes to disturb the peace of the Republic under the pretext of obtaining guarantees for the Colorado party!" But indignation could not stop the march of events, and "that stupid and miserable *gaúcho* Flores" had the whip hand. Montevideo was cowering before his threatened attack.

It was a black moment for Andrés Lamas. Lamas, who had spent a lifetime jockeying with the great powers surrounding his beloved little country in an effort to keep it alive, saw what looked like the final catastrophe staring him in the face. He wrote to Mitre of Argentina on January 28, 1865:

From the ruins of Montevideo (if they finally make out Montevideo a ruin) it will be necessary to raise the Uruguayan nation, revivified and strengthened by a fraternal policy, for only fraternity can cure the wounds of this horrible fratricide. That is the clear interest, the *legitimate* interest of Brazil, as well as of the Argentine Republic.

Poor Montevideo, my dear friend! . . . Montevideo was the ark of salvation in that flood of blood and barbarism, which was called the dictatorship of Rosas. And they are sacrificing our Montevideo on the altars of Paraguay!

Mauá, watching things from London in constantly increasing anxiety, when he wrote to Lamas on March 20, 1865, referred to Flores' invasion of his own country and the armed intervention on his behalf by the imperial government, as a mistake. It was a mistake, he said, that would put Brazil in a bad light and create mistrust and fears of annexation, something which he sincerely believed neither the imperial government nor the Brazilian people, with the exception of a handful of *gaúchos* from Rio Grande do Sul, really wanted.

"In fact, my friend, I am uneasy and even confounded," he said, "at seeing what is reserved for me in the presence of such fearful complications. As for Brazil, its finances will be ruined for *twenty years!* even supposing that the imperial arms should triumph completely."

He was in a gloomy enough frame of mind to add in a discouraged tone unlike his usual cheerful self: "I have the pleasure to communicate to Your Excellency that my good wife has one more little daughter, without any ill news, which she has asked me to let you know so that you may tell Dona Telesphora. Such an increase in my family I could well dispense with at such a moment, when my future is presented to me so full of uncertainties."

At this strategic moment, however, there arrived in Montevideo the only man whose energy and skill could avert the disaster. He was another of Mauá's friends, in spite of the fact that he was one of the men most trusted by the Emperor. He was José Maria da Silva Paranhos, and so closely linked was he in friendship with Mauá that whenever he was in the River Plate, Mauá's house was his headquarters. It was another case of the affinity that always seemed to exist between Mauá and any of these public men who were gifted with imagination and endowed with self-confidence and energy. Like Lamas, like Sousa Franco, Paranhos was on a footing of affectionate and long-lasting regard with the banker of the River Plate. Mauá once described him (in a letter to De Castro) as "a regular *Frenchman*." "Baron Mauá's guest in the River Plate," the newspapers in Rio called him, suspicious of this close link between two such prominent men.

José Maria da Silva Paranhos was the Emperor's favorite diplomat. He was born a poor boy on March 16, 1819, in Baía, for his Portuguese forbears, originally well-to-do settlers in the province, had lost most of their possessions as a consequence of their unwavering loyalty to the Portuguese crown at the time of independence. With the help of an uncle he went to Rio and gained an education by entering first the Naval Academy and then the Military School. By the time he was twenty-five he was a teacher in the Military School, a major in the army, a journalist.

He was a big man, for a Brazilian, well over six feet tall, blond, fair, with blue eyes, and his only personal vice was cigar-smoking. He smoked thirty Havana cigars a day, imported especially for him. He was neither an impulsive man, nor an effusive friend, but he could charm friends and enemies, while following his own line of action, tenaciously and tactfully. In politics his was the iron hand in the velvet glove, and he was in politics early. He was elected to the Legislative Assembly in the province of Rio de Janeiro—that strategic proving ground for Dom Pedro's future ministers of state—by the time he was twenty-eight, and vice-president of the province in 1846. In 1847 he was elected deputy to the imperial Assembly. His debut was completely successful. In fact, he went up so fast that Quintino Bocayuva later ironically remarked: "His Excellency did not rise; he skipped lightly to the top."

He rose not only politically but in the esteem of Dom Pedro, who never preferred anyone to him except his old friend Viscount Bom Retiro. Paranhos had started out in his political career as a Liberal, but when, during the 1840's, the Liberals had become obviously the party of the separatists and the republicans, he changed over to the Conservatives. In his personal attitude, however, he was always a moderate. His was the gift of compromise. He was also durable under political attack, for his conservative, temperate spirit saved him from feeling too keenly the barbs thrown at him by political enemies. In a country dedicated to extremes in feeling in politics as in everything else, he deliberately chose the middle of the way. Perhaps nothing else quite so much accounts for his impregnable position in the Emperor's esteem than this unshakeable impassivity.

His political career was a steady accumulation of importance and prestige. His family background, though modest, also made him particularly acceptable to the Emperor. In 1855 he became Minister of Foreign Affairs, the role he was to make famous, forever associated with his name in Brazilian history, and as such signed treaties with Paraguay and Argentina concerning boundaries and commercial relations. In 1858 he went to Paraguay as the Brazilian envoy to sign another treaty. In 1861 he was again Minister of Foreign Affairs. In 1862 he was named senator for the province of Mato Grosso, the vast, empty land in the wilderness heart of Brazil, important to him because it had boundaries with Paraguay. He pleased the Emperor, for he had the Portuguese virtues of temperance, tenacity, and industry and above that a breadth of view concerning international affairs that was remarkable among his contemporaries. Some years later, in

1871, the Emperor was to recognize his talents and make him Viscount Rio Branco. For his title he chose the name of a small river that had figured in one of the boundary disputes he had settled (between the province of Mato Grosso and the Republic of Paraguay). He has remained in history as the elder of the two Rio Brancos, being to the empire what his son, Baron Rio Branco, was to the future republic, the major diplomat and the builder of a traditional foreign policy. One element of that foreign policy was a preference for the peaceful arbitration of boundary disputes instead of boundary warfare. Thus he, like Saraiva and Mauá, opposed the Paraguayan war.

The Emperor's thoughts turned naturally to Paranhos as, with his government, he watched the affairs in the River Plate steadily deteriorate. Saraiva's task had been too great, for on the one hand he was handicapped by the drastic and warlike character of the instructions given him by the Brazilian cabinet and on the other by the intrigues and political folly of the reactionary Blanco party in whose hands the Uruguayan government was placed.

Saraiva departed from Montevideo in September, 1864, and things grew rapidly worse. The Brazilian admiral Tamandaré, hearty and brave but wanting in forethought, who had originally been sent to the River Plate to back up Saraiva with a show of force, precipitated warfare by joining the revolutionary general Flores in attacking the town of Paysandú on the Uruguay River. His actions immediately aroused fear and indignation in Argentina, where mistrust of Brazilian motives was always alive, if in temporary abeyance. Brazil was confronted with a very dangerous situation, for Paraguay had declared war on her, hostility in Argentina was increasing, and intervention from abroad, a reflection of Brazil's difficulties with England in the acrimonious quarrel about the suppression of the slave trade, was always threatening.

The Brazilian cabinet, under Zacarias de Góes e Vasconcelos, was Liberal, but nevertheless Zacarias, frightened by the real danger, asked Paranhos to use his already enormous prestige in a mission to the River Plate. Paranhos hesitated, for he was a member of the Conservative party in good standing and he had a political future to think of, but he went, with instructions "to obtain an alliance with the Argentine government or a joint intervention of Mitre and the empire in Uruguay, using the revolutionary element as the foundation, and, if neither of these measures were possible, to obtain the formal alliance of Flores." It was the latter alternative that Paranhos succeeded in bringing about. For Mitre of Argentina did not want to enter into the war against Montevideo, whereas Paranhos could hold over Flores the threat of a withdrawal of Brazilian aid, without which Flores could never take Montevideo. Paranhos' great task was to prevent a bloody attack on the city that would arouse the anger of the whole River Plate against Brazil and prevent aid for Brazil in the war with Paraguay. In these efforts he had the support of Andrés Lamas, who saw the danger even more clearly. Through Lamas' persuasions and the efforts of the British ministers in Buenos Aires and Montevideo, Thornton and Lettsom, the Italian minister at Montevideo, Barbolani, called on Aguirre, the Blanco president of Uruguay and suggested that he accept Mitre of Argentina as a mediator in the troubles with Brazil. But Aguirre was a personal enemy of Mitre's and refused. By then, however, Paranhos had concluded a formal agreement with Flores and was no longer interested in Mitre's intervention.

It was Paranhos who saved the day for Montevideo. He was successful in holding back the bold and dashing admiral Tamandaré and in soothing the alarm of the Brazilian cabinet, now under the leadership of Francisco José Furtado. He succeeded in bringing about the resignation of Aguirre and an agreement between Flores and the new president of Uruguay, Villalba. It was one of his most brilliant successes, for he had cleared up the danger of bloody war in Uruguay—had, in fact, conquered Uruguay for Brazil by peaceful means, and had thereby prevented the creation of bitter enmity against Brazil in the strategic region that must serve the empire as a route of supply and a base of operations against Paraguay. Not only had he done this, but he had succeeded in sugaring the pill so that in general his settlement was received in Montevideo and Buenos Aires with good grace.

His efforts, however, were not so well appreciated at home. Admiral Tamandaré had been denied a chance for a beautiful naval

battle and some military glory. Also the public in Rio, afire with wartime fervor, was disappointed at so tame an ending to so exciting a
spectacle. The Liberal cabinet therefore was not slow in recalling
Paranhos and sending in his place Francisco Otaviano de Almeida
Rosa, on March 11, 1865, on a special mission to Buenos Aires.
The change in envoys—the replacement of Paranhos by Otaviano—
was not a great blow to Mauá, for Otaviano was also his personal
friend and at one time his lawyer. Mauá did not permit his dislike of
Flores to prevent him from doing business with the new provisional
government in Montevideo, since Flores now held office with Brazilian support. Through Otaviano's intermediation, the Mauá bank made
a loan to the Flores government, and Flores continued to deal with it
between February, 1865 and the beginning of 1868. But Mauá remained gloomy. There was no prospect of real tranquility in the
affairs on the River Plate.

In October, 1865, Mauá wrote to Lamas from London:

From now on the Uruguayan Republic is a country from which all
should fly who can, saving as best they can their interests. *Unhappily I cannot do that;* I have not been content to put only my arm under the execu-
tioner's axe, but my breast, too, and now I can only await events with
resignation. If things had run another way, trimphantly and without suc-
cumbing to the principle of authority (neither *parties nor proper names*
have any importance with me), at the time when the same generous flag of
conciliation protected all the Uruguayans, without a single exception, I
should see nothing on the horizon of the Republic that would inspire me
with great fear.

His success in London in bringing about the merger of his house
with the London and Brazilian Bank restored some of his old self-confidence. But his exhilaration was short-lived, cut short by the refusal
of the imperial government to give its approval. Invincibly conservative in its attitude toward financial problems, it wanted no such aid in
the constantly increasing troubles in the south.

For the God of War once aroused was impossible to appease. There
was another party to these intrigues in the River Plate—the Republic
of Paraguay.

At the time when the Spanish dominions in southern South America revolted against the crown of Spain, they had not only achieved independence but fragmentation also. The old administrative region in the Spanish empire known as the viceroyalty of Buenos Aires had been split up, at first into many small political divisions, each seeking autonomy—the genesis of the modern states of Argentina, Uruguay, and Paraguay. Thus modern Argentina was in the beginning a group of independent provinces, later united into a single nation only after much bloodshed and civil war. The city of Montevideo had remained loyal to the king of Spain; it was only after her devious course in and out of Portuguese hands that she became the capital of an independent nation. There was still a third fragment of the viceroyalty. Up the river from Buenos Aires, almost lost in the wilderness, the small republic of Paraguay brooded in its self-imposed isolation.

Paraguay had been made into an independent Guaraní Indian state in the early part of the nineteenth century by her first dictator, José Gaspar Rodrigues de Francia, who, with the resentment of the colonial patriot, hated the Spaniards who had once ruled his country and who remained after the independence as the principal landowners. Especially did he hate the Spaniards who lived in cities near the seacoast and who now as Argentines still dominated the life of the region around the estuary of the River Plate. His hatred was logical, for he knew that the Spaniards and their attendant creoles in Paraguay were far closer in sympathy to these foreigners of their own class than they could ever be to the Indian peasantry within Paraguay. With this implacable hatred as the cornerstone of his policy, he had made himself dictator of Paraguay—a successful dictator, as Horton Pelham Box in discussing the origins of the Paraguayan war has pointed out, because he earned the gratitude and loyalty of the Guaraní peasant.

His successor, Carlos Antonio López, had maintained this enmity towards the inhabitants of the Argentine provinces and, as a counterpart of this feeling, Paraguay might be said to have favored Brazil in intra-Plate affairs. But boundary disputes with Brazil had made her as much an enemy as the Argentine provinces. Brazilian interest centered on the fact that the river system of the Plate and its tributaries, including the Paraguay River, was the only practicable roadway into the great interior regions of the southern Brazilian provinces, Rio Grande do Sul, Paraná, Mato Grosso. In 1865 the Brazilian government discovered that Lópes was intending to seize as contraband the cargoes on Brazilian vessels going up the Paraguay River. Paranhos was dispatched to Asunción, the capital of Paraguay, to straighten the matter out. He succeeded, and Lópes, albeit unwillingly, withdrew the regulations he had made closing the river to navigation.

But trouble was brewing. Lópes had inherited from Francia an Indian nation trained to the blindest obedience and devotion to their leader. He himself was suspicious and capricious, disliked foreigners, and was determined not to permit any influence in his country that might corrupt the absolute loyalty of his Indians, kept in the blackest ignorance so that new ideas might not arise to trouble their pristine savagery. Now he was growing old and falling under the persuasion of his son, Francisco Solano Lópes.

Solano Lópes, who succeeded his father in 1862, numbered among his personal qualities a love of violence and a phenomenal taste for cruelty and brutality that finally ended in madness. His two predecessors had created elaborate spy systems in the country; Solano Lópes added a savage and unremitting scrutiny of all the actions of his subjects. When Paraguay's old boundary disputes with Brazil again flared up, he did not follow the advice his father is said to have given him when he died, to try the pen and spare the sword. War, savage, man-consuming war to the death, alone could satisfy Solano Lópes.

Now, with Montevideo at war with Brazil, he stepped into the affairs of the lower Plate. For he had declared that "any occupation of Uruguayan territory by foreign forces was an attempt against the equilibrium of the states of the River Plate, which would interest the Republic of Paraguay as a guarantee of its peace and prosperity." He suited actions to words by seizing the *Marqués de Olinda*, a Brazilian vessel which was in his territorial waters, and invaded the Brazilian province of Mato Grosso. He then declared war on Argentina. On May 1, 1865, Argentina, Brazil, and Uruguay signed a secret treaty of triple alliance to make war on Paraguay.

Like all such wars, it was, in the enthusiastic imagination of the

Brazilians, to be brief and glorious. Two powerful countries, Brazil and Argentina, against weak and backward Paraguay could not produce any other result. But the allies had not counted on the facts that Francia had so carefully consolidated his Indian state, that Lópes senior had preserved it in its isolation from any corrupting influence, and that Lópes junior had made every able-bodied man in Paraguay a warrior.

But it was not a moment for sober views. The war spirit in Rio was high, and the talk was all of glory, sweeping and prompt victory, in defense of Brazilian honor. The Emperor, much against the counsel of his government, went south as the first "volunteer of the fatherland," with his new son-in-law the French Count d'Eu, the husband of his elder daughter and heir, Princess Isabel.

By the middle of 1866 the first rosy picture of a quick and easy victory for Brazil had faded. Brazil found herself alone in fighting Paraguay, for Montevideo was a conquered city and Argentina had withdrawn from the war. Nor were the Paraguayans easy to defeat. The war was costing heavily in money and men, and still it did not come to an end. Complaints and murmurs against its continuance were beginning to be heard in Brazil itself. A good many Brazilians were ready to arrange a peace but not so the Emperor.

"We did not provoke the war," he said, "and we will not propose the peace! If the sacrifice is enormous, the humiliation would be greater." He was a little tired, no doubt, of always being compelled ignominiously to bow to the pressure of more powerful countries. In the years past, Brazil had not come out well in such disputes with foreign powers. The Paraguayan war seemed a chance to assuage the smarts in the national pride and in the imperial pride. The Emperor was going to see this international complication to a triumphant end.

For a brief period, the war brought a certain prosperity to Uruguay. The year 1866 did not start off very well, however. The air was filled with rumors about the financial panic in England, especially concerning the bankruptcy of Overend, Gurney and Company, rumors which precipitated a run on the banks in Montevideo. Within a few days the public withdrew more than 1,500,000 pesos from the Mauá bank, so crippling its funds that the firm was obliged to notify the government that if it did not pay over the one million pesos pledged to the bank, the bank would have to close its doors. This the government could not do, for its own resources were exhausted.

So to save the Mauá Bank from bankruptcy, a decree was passed prohibiting the conversion of paper money into gold for a period of six months. By December, 1866, however, such conversion was again allowed, for the country was again in an excellent economic condition. The wartime trade through the port of Montevideo was enormous and the customs house warehouses were bulging with goods for which sufficient ships could not be found. Profiteers made fortunes, for immigrants were pouring into the country, land values were rising, Montevideo was building itself a new and modern city, and the government had begun construction of the excellent system of highways for which thereafter the country was to be famous. Therefore, there had been little depreciation in the notes of the Mauá Bank, although it had issued the equivalent of 4,000,000 pesos worth against a fund of only half that sum.

This exhilarating moment did not last long. The Paraguayan war was dragging on too long. The land began to feel the effects of the devastation of war, the price of cattle products fell, herds and flocks were slaughtered for want of hands to care for them, the Argentines were jealously putting obstacles in the way of the trade through its rival port, the cholera epidemic spread from Buenos Aires and the province of Corrientes into Montevideo. The result was the flight of gold specie to European markets, £2,500,000 passing through the money market of Buenos Aires alone in six months. The exchange rate of the Uruguayan peso on the London market dropped from fifty English pence to forty-eight between July and December, 1867.

A new cholera epidemic, said to have been brought into the country by the Brazilian army, spread first to Mercedes and then to Montevideo, and as a result the country's finances went from bad to worse. The Uruguayan government decreed another six-month period in which paper money could not be converted into gold. At the time the Mauá Bank had a fund of more than 1,000,000 pesos and notes in circulation representing more than 2,000,000. In June, 1868, when the conversion of notes into specie was once more permitted, the

Mauá Bank had 600,000 pesos in its fund and had issued notes representing 7,000,000. The day that conversion was once more permitted, the Mauá Bank closed its doors. It was promptly imitated by all other banks in the country except the Bank of London and the River Plate and the Commercial Bank. Among them all, paper money representing 13,000,000 pesos was issued against a total fund of 7,000,000 pesos.

Mauá could hardly watch all these years pass by, with their constantly increasing difficulties, without complaints, bitter and heartfelt. He wrote to Lamas from London in April, 1866, that if the war lasted even to the end of the month it would cost Brazil sacrifices which would upset its finances for a quarter of a century.

When he was in Buenos Aires in November, 1866, Mauá entertained Caxias, the Emperor's Chief of Staff, who was on his way to join his army up the river. Reporting the occasion, Mauá told Ribeiro, the manager of his bank in Montevideo, that he hoped the marquess' (for Caxias was not yet a duke) operations would hurry things along, "for I fear that if the war lasts much more time we shall lose the shirts off our backs." It was weary work to see the slow attrition of his great industrial empire in the Plate, without the power to stop it. To Lamas, as usual, he opened his heart:

"On the 6th of March [1867], I shall complete forty-one years of a *commercial career* in which I have not had the least rest—I have made a great deal, but today I can say with all my soul that I should have preferred to have *made less, a hundred times less!* I should be happier! In my present condition I must seek some rest, and I cannot get it!"

The House of Mauá, like the empire of Brazil and the Republic of Paraguay, was a major victim of the disastrous war.

CHAPTER XIII

REAPING THE WHIRLWIND

DOM PEDRO II had inherited from the days of the Regency, besides men of state, a first-class professional soldier, Luiz Alves de Lima e Silva, made Baron Caxias for his success in the pacification of the rebellious provinces on the eve of Dom Pedro's coming of age, and marquess for his subsequent achievements. In tradition he is the Bayard, the Iron Duke of Brazilian military history, the ideal soldier, loyal, brave, a martinet for discipline. But he had, too, the shortcomings of the professional soldier: he was extremely conservative, without a wide acquaintance of the world, with an ingrained sense of hierarchy. In his faults as in his virtues he merited the Emperor's confidence; he was a "safe" man, in his background, in his political opinions, and in his personal history of devotion to the security of the throne, and he was eventually rewarded by being made the only duke in the Brazilian empire, the Duke of Caxias.

Even Caxias, however, did not seem able to win the war. In 1868, the Emperor, uneasy with a Liberal party cabinet, with Zacarias de Góes e Vasconcelos as Prime Minister and Sousa Franco as Minister of the Treasury, men who represented neither his ideal of maintaining the status quo nor the *fazendeiro* wealth of the country, dismissed his ministers. Never at home with people who wanted to experiment, he felt this was no moment to rely on men unsympathetic towards him. His chance to make the change was given him by Zacarias himself. For in the beginning of 1868, Zacarias made the following statement to the Emperor in the presence of the Council of State, against which there was considerable popular feeling, for it was looked upon as the stronghold of the Emperor's dyed-in-the-wool conservative favorites:

Sire! By the transport which arrived yesterday from the South, the Minister of War received from the Marquess of Caxias a notification in which the General asks leave to resign, alleging illness, but he received at the same time a private letter in which the Marquess frankly explains the real reasons that have caused him to take such a step. These reasons may be briefly stated thus, that the Marquess believes, in view of the newspapers and his private correspondence, that the government, far from having in him the same confidence which at first it showed, seeks by various means to withdraw its moral support from him.

When in October, 1866, the government invited the Marquess of Caxias to go and take command of the Brazilian forces in Paraguay and he accepted the invitation, with no condition except that of the full and complete trust of the government in him, I declared to him, in conversation, that his presence in Paraguay seemed so necessary that if he had refused the commission and if to us this refusal had seemed to come from an unwillingness to serve with us, we should be disposed to resign, because for us the war was not a party question and what was essential was to finish it honorably, whoever should be in power.

The government now thinks, as in 1866, that the presence of the Marquess of Caxias in Paraguay is of the greatest importance, and because the General shows himself persuaded, although without reason, that the government has withdrawn its moral support, the ministry wishes to resign rather than use its right to demand an explanation from the General, thus wiping out his unfounded apprehensions.

The Emperor seeing Brazil in the midst of a financial and economic crisis and hearing revolutionary talk in the air, called a new cabinet, made up of members of the Conservative party under the reliable Rodrigues Torres, Viscount Itaboraí. He had made his choice between a Conservative general whom he trusted and a Liberal party cabinet which gave him considerable anxiety. But Caxias was really tired and old. He made a final effort, and, with the loss of a good many men, took Asunción, the capital of Paraguay, in January, 1869. The city was half-deserted, and López, the dictator, had taken to the jungle to raise another army. To the old duke, the war at last seemed over. He resigned his command to give place to the Emperor's French son-in-law, Count d'Eu.

The Frenchman, never popular in his adopted country, where he was always a foreigner, nevertheless was a good enough soldier to see that the hunt through the jungle, after a constantly vanishing enemy, would cost more, in men, horses, ammunition, and food than the army could afford. But the Emperor was adamant. López must be killed. He was, hunted down in the jungle like the wild beast he so ably imitated, on March 1, 1870, by a Brazilian corporal. Paraguay had lost her entire male population except for small boys and old men. Solano López left Paraguay a broken country, at the mercy of its neighbors and with a legacy of bitterness that was to endure to modern times.

He had cost Brazil the lives of fifty thousand men, uncounted invalids, an enormous debt, and an economic crisis. The throne itself had been so severely shaken that it never regained its former stability.

The unpopularity of the empire, in fact, was not restricted to Brazil. In Uruguay the old mistrust and dislike flourished, and Brazil was blamed for the economic consequences of an unnecessary prolongation of the war.

The House of Mauá was the chief manifestation of Brazil within Uruguay, and Baron Mauá himself was the focus for the general discontent. His economic and industrial empire was too big, too widespread, not to arouse jealousy and envy. Since the reëstablishment of Uruguay as an independent nation in 1852, after the battle of Monte Caseros, he had been the country's chief creditor, the owner of most of her profitable resources, the builder of most of her industries. Such octopus-like power does not engender affection and gratitude in those not sharers in its profits, and Mauá was no exception.

When on June 1, 1868, the government of Uruguay had permitted the conversion of paper money into specie, this had been a bad blow to Mauá and Company, but it was not the worst. For in 1868 Uruguay had acquired a new president, Lorenzo Batlle, to whom the Mauá Bank was indeed *el peligro brasileño*. He was a thoroughgoing nationalist, fearful of Brazilian interest, and his first aim was to drive the Mauá Bank, with its vast ramifications in the country's industries, out of the life of Uruguay. Mauá, with his characteristic want of insight into political men and their motives, had written to Lamas on March 16, 1868, that the "election of Batlle was a good step, since he is an honest and moderate man, but whether he will have the strength to dominate the bad elements which surround him to influence the progress of the country remains to be seen and only events can show."

Batlle, it turned out, was no friend of his. On July 13, 1868, the Uruguayan government gave Batlle extraordinary powers to deal with the banking crisis. On July 16, he passed a law requiring the banks to issue only up to double their paid-in capital; whereas, in the past, the Mauá Bank had been granted the privilege of issuing up to three times the total of its capital. To meet the situation Mauá sent abroad for 2,000,000 pesos in gold. This did not suit his political enemies, who obtained the passage of a decree on January 21, 1869, suspending the authorization for an increase in the capital of banks of issue.

There was no doubt that the Batlle government intended to ruin the Mauá Bank.

Mauá did not, of course, accept the situation docilely. He began his protest by publishing his opinion of these governmental actions in the Montevidean newspaper *El Siglo*, but something more effective than newspaper articles was called for. His bank in Montevideo closed its doors for the second time on February 11, 1869, and its liquidation was already begun under the supervision of the Public Credit Board *(Junta de Crédito Público)*. Mauá protested to the Brazilian officials in the Plate.

The Brazilian diplomatic agent in Montevideo, Araújo Gondim, wrote a private letter to his chief, José Maria da Silva Paranhos, the Brazilian minister of Foreign Affairs in the cabinet headed by Viscount Itaboraí. Gondim described the run on the Mauá Bank and a visit he had paid, accompanied by Mauá, to President Batlle of Uruguay.

"The Baron," said Gondim, on February 11, 1869, "made a very clear exposition of the state of his affairs. As for me, I strongly urged that His Excellency should take immediate steps to save [the Mauá Bank], but I only obtained fair promises that he would do what he considered to be within his powers." About the same time, Paranhos received another letter, dated February 12, 1869, from Andrés Lamas, who told him: "I must ask Your Excellency to give attention to the situation of our excellent and worthy friend. There exists here in Montevideo an old scheme to kill his house. . . . Do not fail to do what you can for Mauá."

But it was an awkward moment for Paranhos to act. Between February 10 and April 30, 1869, he was temporarily substituted as minister of Foreign Affairs by Baron Cotegipe, for the Emperor sent him to Paraguay to conclude the negotiations that would bring the Paraguayan war to a formal close. On February 28, 1869, therefore, Mauá sent his protest to Viscount São Vicente (Pimenta Bueno), the Emperor's favorite legal adviser, who showed it to the Emperor. The Emperor acknowledged it thus, in a note to Baron Cotegipe: "São Vicente delivered to me the enclosed representation in Mauá's name, which I judge to be worthy of consideration."

Cotegipe himself wrote to Paranhos on March 8, telling him of the fact that São Vicente had personally delivered the demand for aid which São Vicente himself had signed. The government, Cotegipe said, had agreed not to make an official claim in the question of the Mauá Bank against the Uruguayan government, but it did not forbid the Legation in Montevideo to take some step. Paranhos, replying on March 24, from Asunción, the capital of Paraguay, where he was on his special mission, defended São Vicente's action, which Cotegipe had not liked, saying that it showed the great displeasure the viscount felt at the situation.

"Mauá is the victim of an unjust war," said Paranhos, "being waged not only against the banker but also against a Brazilian citizen." If the English, he added, "were willing to risk the life of a naval officer to go and rescue British subjects in Paraguay, it certainly behooved the Brazilian government to protect the good name and interests of its own subjects."

But Cotegipe did not agree with him. He replied in a letter of April 7, 1869:

> I feel I must disagree with Your Excellency concerning the aid that we should give Mauá, against whom I have no prejudice. I authorized Gondim to do everything in an unofficial guise, and this for two reasons: (1) because I don't know how far the question will go and what influence it would have on our political relations with the Republic of Uruguay, whose good will we need; (2) because I am not convinced of Mauá's *right* to require that the government should grant him what it has properly restricted, that is, the privilege of issuing *paper money*.

It was a very delicate matter, he pointed out, and if the imperial government should intervene, it could not then withdraw. It was better to let things take their course. "Your Excellency may, if you like, intervene to make some arrangement; but we certainly will not authorize any official action."

Mauá, in the meantime, was in the midst of the embroilment, and he could not look upon the matter with such cautious detachment. In March, at the time Paranhos and Cotegipe were exchanging their views, he wrote and thanked Paranhos for his support: "I thank you from the bottom of my heart for the friendly expressions and sentiments of your letter of the 28th past, which I have just received. They are balm to my soul and a consolation which encourages me in the struggle in which I am now involved."

He was still hopeful, when he wrote that letter, on March 4, 1869, that with the support of the Brazilian government he would survive the worst. But by April 14, 1869, he had decided that it was time for strong measures. He wrote a long and explicit letter to Viscount São Vicente:

> I am grateful for Your Excellency's repeated proofs of friendship, of which I have been informed by my friend Alfredo. The conduct of the

men in the government here disgusts me naturally, because not only do they fail to protect me as they should, but they have made a parade of this fact *here*, so that no less than four firms here will have news of my abandonment by the same medium by which my friend Alfredo gave me the news in *extreme confidence*.

Happily, they are in an ambiguous situation here in attacking my position, now as in May of last year (when Zacarias did not fail *ostentatiously* to demand that I should be protected). Simply because I am being abandoned by Viscount Itaboraí does not mean that I am being abandoned by the vast majority of the *Uruguayan people*, nor by the many Brazilians who inhabit this Republic; and if it were necessary, some thousands of people from the province of Rio Grande would come to my aid, independently or even against the will of any Ministry that might be hostile to me in *Rio de Janeiro*. Your Excellency can see that my position is not so precarious as Snr. Itaboraí believes, and what he calls my imprudences do not diminish my prestige here. The truth is that I am struggling against the *declared and formal* war prosecuted by the Government of the Republic and I am cruelly treated as an enemy of the so-called conservative circle, which here means the men of the *United States of the Plate*, those who would prefer to seek an alliance with Argentina, rejecting one with Brazil. Happily, this faction in the Colorado party is small. The Colorado party properly so-called and the Blanco party (which rejects all *foreign* influence) give me help because they recognize the services that chance has permitted me to give this country. I am, therefore, Your Excellency will please believe, strong, and as for my struggle during the past month, this has been to prevent any divergence from the legal path adopted by those who, because of the public distress, are determined to have the Mauá Bank close its doors. The triumph by legal means is secure although delayed. The government was in despair at the ascendency of the interests linked to my house, and finally the Minister of the Treasury, who is a madman fit to be chained up, hurled at me and the other banks (also persecuted, on paper, in order to keep up appearances) the greatest outrages, and this in a report to the legislative body! *I sprang forward* to contest every point, *as usual*, and in the same daily paper are published corrections of the errors made in the translation of my letter addressed to the Minister in reply to his attacks. Some say this is too strong; I say that I do not know how to reply to such insolence in any other way. The government gave itself out as offended and ordered the *Fiscal* [a police official] to accuse me of abusing the freedom of the press! Both the civil and the criminal *Fiscães* [police officials] will find themselves suspect. Five lawyers have been named by the Supreme Court of Justice, and they have all rejected the case. It looks as if the government will not find anyone willing to bring suit against me! a consequence of its own rash actions. If it should succeed, my plan of action is drawn up; the bandits who govern this Republic will not bring me to the criminal's dock. The government's right to attack me for any act not provided for in the four cases expressly set forth in the Law of the Press will be denied before the Judge of the Criminal Court. If the Judge of the Criminal Court says the government is right, I shall appeal to the Supreme Court of Justice; if the latter (since it is composed of Conservatives) says the government is right, in such a case of the *denial of justice* (in the opinion of all the lawyers of importance here) I shall appeal to the Legation. If the latter denies me the protection to which I have so much right and which it grants *every day* to any *fugitive negro* who has obtained a Brazilian certificate from a vice consul (which is very easy here), then another alternative arises. A declared enemy of all kinds of armed resistance, I am nevertheless not one of those who fail to recognize the *right of revolution* in extreme cases. The extreme case for me will have arrived in such a circumstance, because I cannot nor must I abandon to pillage the Brazilian interests which I represent. Fortunately, in the present state of public sentiment in this country, I should not have to do much; I should merely cease from making continuous efforts to prevent discontent from spreading. Tomorrow the Chamber will either reject the bills presented by the government or return them to the Minister without discussion, declaring them to be unconstitutional and absurd. In the next few days a law will appear which grants to the Mauá Bank much more than I suggested, on the grounds that the country *needs* it. Thus the State fails at one blow. This nonsense cannot go on indefinitely. However, if it does, it will reach the *extreme case*, so far as the *elements of disorder* are concerned, seeing as the government in such a circumstance would be a revolutionary one, and the result would not be in doubt.

It seems to me that there is someone here who doubts the legal position of the Mauá Bank. For this reason, I send Your Excellency all the papers. To resolve this question of the increase of capital it is not sufficient merely to read article 2 of the decree of July 16. For I too was in doubt before the Ministers explained it, and, later, facts confirmed this, the increase being granted to four banks. This was told to me by the Minister of the Treasury in reply to the letter which I published. In view of this, I am no longer in any *doubt*. Here there no longer exists, even among the friends of the government, any defense on legal grounds, but only on that of the convenience of the country!

This undisguised threat of extreme action had its effect, apparently. The Council of State, asked for an opinion on the case, was favorable to Mauá claims. Nabuco de Araújo, once his adversary, went so far as to declare that the imperial government should intervene amicably to cause the Uruguayan government to indemnify the Mauá Bank for the damage it had suffered.

On May 4, 1870, Lorenzo Batlle's government in Montevideo passed a law providing for the liquidation of the notes issued by banks of account, notes for which the nation was liable according to the decree of July 16, 1886. Mauá, always fertile in inventing a way out of financial difficulties, circularized his creditors with a proposition. He invited them to accept, instead of their shares in his bank, income securities based on his own individual liability. Such was the confidence in him that not a single creditor protested the idea. The bank shortly thereafter once more took up its transactions, for, legally speaking, it had no more creditors; they were now all personal creditors of Baron Mauá himself.

But the government in Montevideo had the last word. The law of May 4, 1870, had provided that banks would have to deliver to the Public Credit Board securities corresponding to the value of the notes issued and in circulation. This delivery was to be made, preferably, in public securities according to the price set in the last amortization payment on the public debt or at the rate of exchange at which the loans had been floated, the banks having the choice of basis of payment. If such public debt securities were not available, the banks would have to deliver other securities, to be chosen by the board. The Mauá Bank had in its local and foreign funds a greater sum on hand than the total of its notes in circulation, but this availed it nothing. The government forced the liquidation of the notes in circulation. Mauá protested to the Brazilian legation.

In the meantime, there had been a change in the Brazilian government. A new cabinet under Viscount São Vicente had taken office on September 29, 1870. It resolved to approve the energetic notes

which, during the administration of Viscount Itaboraí (otherwise so
cool to Mauá's proposals), the Brazilian minister to Montevideo,
João Alves Loureiro, had handed the Uruguayan government. On
January 30, 1871, the new Brazilian minister to Montevideo, Araújo
Gondim, was given a new and sharper note to deliver to the Uruguayan Minister of Foreign Affairs, Julio Herrera y Obes. Herrera y Obes
solved the awkward situation in which he found himself on receiving
the new note by keeping silent for twenty-two months. On October
19, 1872, he made an ironical reply, saying that there was no truth in
the accusation that a personal animosity against Baron Mauá was the
basis of his government's actions.

The matter hung fire, with sharp diplomatic notes back and forth,
but though the Brazilian minister dutifully kept up his barrage of
official protests, the Brazilian government took no active steps to
pursue the dispute.

All these negotiations did not pass without comment. There was
one man in Rio who made it his business to make them as widely
known as possible.

The Emperor at the end of the Paraguayan war had done more
than dismiss his Liberal cabinet; he had made a mortal enemy. For
Zacarias de Góes e Vasconcelos was a man to whom a grievance was
dear. He was not mollified when the Emperor, in another of his
attempts to suppress sharp party feeling, invited him to be a member
of his Council of State, that august body which many members of
the Liberal party considered to be a fortress of the Emperor's conservative favorites.

"In normal times," said Joaquim Nabuco, in the biography of his
father, the imperial senator, "an ex-president of the Council would
have refused a nomination to the Council of State, which he knew to
come from the Emperor, with every deference." Not so Zacarias.
Smarting under what he considered injustice and a lack of appreciation of his efforts, he published in the journal *A Reforma* on January
15, 1871, an explanation of his reasons. It was his manifesto to the
Emperor and the Conservative party.

Zacarias was a man from the province of Baía who began his career as a professor in the Law Faculty at Recife, but who switched to politics as giving more scope for his idiosyncracies. He started out as a member of the Conservative party in Baía, a deputy in the provincial assembly. He arrived in Rio in 1850, became a member of the Liberal party, and by 1862 had risen, by his very peculiarities, to the top of the political tree. He was a man who made a religion of regular habits; his contemporaries called him a Jesuit in a frock coat. Baron Cotegipe, who found in this figure of preternatural solemnity a welcome object for his nimble wit, claimed he owned thirty frock coats, which he changed every day. Cotegipe, in fact, once had to defend himself against a sarcastic attack by Zacarias on his luxurious habits. He did it with his usual barbed good humor:

I am sorry, Mr. President, not to have heard the minute report the noble senator made on my daily life, because I could have corrected various inaccuracies. Up to a certain point, however, it was correct. In the meantime, I have had the opportunity to make a conscientious investigation, and I am now able, on my side, to tell the Senate the mode in which His Excellency spends his day. He gets up early, at six in the morning, takes his cold bath, drinks coffee with milk, and eats a little plate of toast. Afterwards he breakfasts and goes to dress, in doing which he wastes some time, while he tries on various coats to see which suits him best. He comes to the Senate and takes until four o'clock in the afternoon to burn everybody up. He returns home in his carriage, dines at five, and picks his teeth. At half past six he goes out to the Misericordia Hospital. At eight he shuts himself up with the Sisters of Charity there and converses with them until half past nine. He goes home at ten and goes to bed, sleeping the sleep of the just, since he has carried out well all his duties.

Zacarias was a tall, thin, angular man, with hard eyes and a sardonic mouth. There was always a biting, wounding mordacity in his attacks on his fellow legislators. When he rose to speak in the parliament, said Machado de Assis, he always drew blood from somebody. The seeking out of other people's mistakes and sins was balm to his narrow soul. He was the Grand Inquisitor of the words, the actions, the lives of his associates and political brethren. He had an inexhaustible memory for details, which at the most unexpected moments he could bring forward to confound his victims.

The situation in the River Plate was particularly his meat. The war had been the cause of his loss of power and in the person of José Maria da Silva Paranhos he had a target for all his rancor against the Conservatives, whom the Emperor had favored at his expense. Nor had he forgotten that he had an old personal score to pay off with Mauá. What was this wily banker doing? he demanded, living in the pocket of the Emperor's most powerful diplomatic representative, drawing on the resources of the Brazilian government to bolster his banks, using the prestige of the Emperor's government to threaten the men of Montevideo.

To Mauá he was that "unworthy, wicked Zacarias," and "my rancorous enemy." Mauá had first earned Zacarias' animosity during the presence in Montevideo of the Saraiva mission on the eve of the Paraguayan war, when Mauá, on April 22, 1864, published in the *Jornal de Comércio* in Rio, just as Saraiva was about to depart, an article in which he took to task the Brazilian cabinet, Zacarias' cabinet. "What I lament," said Mauá, "is that the policy of my country concerning our neighbors continues to be the same haphazard policy without a fixed plan, without clear and definite ideas." These were not words calculated to win the friendship of a man like Zacarias. Mauá became one more in the list of public men of whose actions Zacarias constituted himself the judge and critic.

He had at his fingertips the most minute details of the transactions in the River Plate involving the House of Mauá. The loan asked of the imperial government by the Flores provincial government in 1866 through the intermediation of the Brazilian diplomatic agent, Francisco Otaviano Almeida da Rosa, gave him an excellent opportunity for attack. When Otaviano presented to the Zacarias cabinet the treaty which included the terms of the loan, ratification was refused on two grounds: that the imperial government had already refused such aid to Argentina and that the imperial treasury itself was in difficulties. The real reason, said rumor and newspaper speculation, was that the cabinet had its doubts about the eventual goal of the money, for the Mauá Bank had in the last few years been the inexhaustible money chest for Flores' government. Three times during the 1860's, just before and during the Paraguayan war, while Mauá's fortunes in Uruguay were crumbling, Zacarias had headed the Brazilian government: from May 24, 1862, to May 30, 1862; from January 15 to May 12, 1865; and from August 3, 1866 to July 30, 1868. He had combatted, during the incumbency of the cabinets under his leadership, any favors for the Mauá Bank, ignoring the fact that Flores' government had come into power with the support of the empire, and that Mauá's loans to it were thus made to an ally of Brazil.

The bitterness that Zacarias felt over the dismissal of his last cabinet was increased by the triumphant emergence of his archenemy, Paranhos. Paranhos was now Viscount Rio Branco, for the Emperor, pleased with his successes in foreign negotiations, had given him the title on June 22, 1871.

Viscount Rio Branco, then, the sagacious and imperturbable, had one vulnerable link in his political armor. The newspapers were fond of calling him "the Baron's lingering guest in the River Plate." It was true that he had been a frequent visitor south of the border and that Baron Mauá's house was always at his disposal. There can be no doubt of the close alliance that existed between him and Mauá, for in his letters to the banker, that discreet statesman wrote candid opinions on the political events in the Plate and on the other men concerned in the negotiations, a latitude in expression that Rio Branco rarely permitted himself. He even spoke familiarly of the Emperor, in commenting on his hesitation in dismissing the Zacarias cabinet, calling him "our friend" and "*bonanchão*" or "good-hearted fellow."

In 1868 Paranhos had been Minister of Foreign Affairs for the second time and had been sent on another special mission to Montevideo. In 1870-1871 he had gone to the Plate again, this time as minister plenipotentiary to sign the final peace treaty with Paraguay. In March, 1871, the Emperor called upon him to form a new cabinet. The Emperor felt a great relief in having Rio Branco thus at hand. He wanted to go to Europe, and he knew that Rio Branco was dependable, that he could be counted upon not to go too far in any direction, that he knew how to temporize and to manage the idiosyncracies of his colleagues. Even perhaps if the Emperor was not fully aware of the fact, he probably felt he could depend on Rio Branco to recognize inevitable change and yield just so much and no more.

Beyond this, the Emperor was somewhat bored by politics. His favorite recreation was fraternizing with men of learning, playing the humble patron to the great minds of his day. Undoubtedly he had a sincere admiration for scientific investigation, the pursuit of the history of past ages, learning in general. He invited great Frenchmen—Pasteur, Lamartine, Ernest Renan—to come to Brazil. He was fond of reading American poets—Longfellow, Lowell, Whittier. He gave every encouragement he could to scientists of all countries—so much so, that Charles Darwin (who had once visited Brazil) remarked that "the Emperor has done so much for science that every scientific man is bound to show him the utmost respect." Digging up the past, as done in the great archeological expeditions of Schliemann and others, fascinated him. He liked to discover talents among Brazilian boys and to provide an education for those who could not otherwise afford it. But to him learning and scientific advances were theoretical matters. He did not envisage their use and adaptation to the practical concerns of his country. The great discoveries in medicine, for example, were marvels to be much appreciated and admired, but the idea of a public welfare service, which would bring the benefits of such discoveries to the multitude never crossed his mind or, if it did, was not entertained with serious effect.

When he left for Europe, on a jaunt to indulge his favorite recreation, he left Viscount Rio Branco with a number of serious problems on his hands, including the new agitation for the abolition of slavery and the active revivification of a political party that sought the overthrow of the monarchy and the creation of a republic. Party feeling was rising with a strength that no amount of maneuvering could suppress. And Zacarias did not cease to make himself heard. He searched out every weakness in the government's actions, questioned every bit of evidence of friendship between Rio Branco and Mauá. He wanted to know about contracts for army supplies that the imperial government had made with the House of Mauá during the Paraguayan war. He scrutinized the appearance of the Baron's name in every offer of new contracts with the government.

Rio Branco maintained his usual good humor, but privately he wrote many letters to Mauá—letters of friendly admonition, counseling a more cautious policy than Mauá, exasperated by his constantly accumulating troubles, displayed. On June 16, 1872, Rio Branco wrote to him about two major projects then on foot, the submarine cable to Europe and the contract for the improvement of the water supply of Rio de Janeiro. Neither of these schemes was going well, for Mauá was encountering more opposition among men in official positions who were unfavorable to him or who saw in his loss of power a chance for their own enrichment. The bid he had put in for the water contract had met serious competition. An English engineer named Gotto had presented a bid, as had a Brazilian named Castro. Then unexpectedly a third bid had appeared, put forward by three Brazilians powerfully placed: Borja Castro, Baron Carapebus, and Viscount Lage. The decision was made in a long report by a committee presided over by Francisco de Sales Torres Homem, Viscount Inhomerim (who, with Viscount Itaboraí had in the middle 1850's opposed the creation of Mauá's first banks), a decision later discovered to be unfavorable to Mauá. Rio Branco at the time of writing his letter had not seen the report, but his words were full of caution:

> It was to the latter [a Senhor Braga] that I once said that I do not wish you to present yourself at one and the same time in many enterprises depending on the government, not because of a lack of desire on my part to help you, nor because I have more confidence in someone else, but because I am your sincere friend and saw the rivalries which your name arouses. There is here now a great demand for enterprises and I cannot struggle in the Ministry against these interests, protecting various candidates. Mine was the counsel of prudence and friendship.

Rio Branco continued as head of the Emperor's government until June 25, 1875. During that time, well aware of the fact that he who holds the purse strings holds the power, he was Minister of the Treasury also. While he was in office the claims of Mauá and Company against the Uruguayan government were kept alive.

Uruguay, in the meantime, had acquired a new president, Ellauri, and a new minister of foreign affairs, Pérez Gomar, and, in September, 1873, Mauá had talks with them concerning his bank's affairs. The discussion went so far that the Uruguayan government now admitted the claim but argued about the method by which it should be assessed and paid. Pérez Gomar wanted the matter settled by an Uruguayan court. Mauá wanted a disinterested party. He suggested the Bank of France, the Bank of England, or one of the large banks of the United States, but the Uruguayans refused.

Two years later, in May, 1875, Mauá and Company of Montevideo closed its doors for the last time. Later in the same year, Andrés Lamas, now Minister of Treasury in the revolutionary government of Pedro Varela, proposed to allow the reopening of the Mauá Bank and to grant it certain privileges. These were: permission to issue notes up to three times its capital; the acceptance of the notes of the Mauá Bank as the only paper money to be received in the government offices; and the appointment of the Mauá Bank as manager of the public debt. The notes exchanged for those of the Mauá Bank would constitute a national debt in favor of the bank, without interest. On its side, the government could draw up to two million pesos at sight and be freed from the diplomatic demands of the Brazilian government in behalf of the bank.

But in the beginning of the following year—1876—five months after the Varela administrations adopted regulations for the law that granted the Mauá Bank these privileges, a new military *coup* (on March 10, 1876), headed by Colonel Latorre, put Varela out of office. Latorre, who governed Uruguay as a dictator until February, 1879, and thereafter as constitutional president until March, 1880 (when he resigned the office, because, as he said, the Uruguayans were ungovernable), rescinded the agreement with the Mauá Bank. He made, instead, a new contract, according to which the Mauá Bank received as indemnity 1,070,000 pesos. The government of Uruguay assumed liability for the 12,000,000 pesos circulating in paper money issued by the bank.

Thus died the last hope for a revival of Mauá's financial empire in the River Plate.

PART FOUR

"FATE DID NOT WILL IT SO"

CHAPTER XIV

FRIENDS
AND
ENEMIES

Bγ 1875 Mauá had lost most of his powerful political friends and his seat in the Chamber of Deputies.

Twenty years (from 1853 to 1872) is a long period for any man to hold a seat in his national legislature, especially for a man without political ambitions. From the beginning, Mauá had another purpose in mind when he had heeded the advice of his old patron, Richard Carruthers: "How gratifying it is to me, you may imagine, that in our old local, the Candelaria [a ward in the city of Rio de Janeiro], your honored name was so justly estimated. I trust, however, that you will be elected from your native province, and that you will accept thereof if you purpose to stand as Deputy from any place." (Letter of February 8, 1861.)

Mauá himself had written, early in 1861, to his partner De Castro in Manchester. In that letter he said, among other things, in his easy English:

The government and Conservative party has been completely defeated in the elections of the 30th ultimo in this city, the *chapa* [ticket] of the Liberal party having triumphed in all the *freguesias* [parishes] except two.

This will have a great moral effect in the Empire and probably brings about the calling of the Liberal party into power. At this moment I stand well with both, the Conservative party being alive to the folly of their hostility to me in consequence of my liberal economical ideas. The Liberals, of course, surround me with all the attentions possible. The Conservatives have lost their ground completely in consequence of their restrictive views and the meddling in every man's right to act and work according to his own idea instead of having all his actions and doings regulated by Government and the law, in which nonsensical ideas the Ferraz cabinet has gone further than any of its predecessors.

When he wrote that letter he had already been a deputy in the national parliament representing his native province of Rio Grande do Sul. In 1853 he had been elected to substitute for another deputy, and again in 1856. In 1857 he was elected in his own right. He was to keep his seat until 1872, although between 1869 and 1872 the Liberal party in Rio Grande do Sul, because of conditions arising from the Paraguayan war, abstained from taking part in the national elections.

He was in parliament for one openly avowed purpose: to promote legislation that would improve the position of private enterprise in the country, including his own interests. He spoke infrequently in the Chamber and then only on subjects concerning financial affairs— the reform of commercial legislation or the passage of bills providing loans for companies in which he was interested. In committee he was far more effective, and he was active in preparing reports and opinions on financial affairs.

His early training had prepared him for a commercial, industrial, and banking career, but it left him somewhat at sea in the political world of the empire. He was the poor boy from the wrong part of the country, who had not grown up within a family important for its political ramifications, the best, the only school for political men in the Brazil of the mid-nineteenth century. Lídia Besouchet has hit upon two symptoms of the weakness of his position, when, in discussing the letters that passed between him and Andrés Lamas, she refers to his constant misjudgments concerning the maneuvers of professional politicians, and to what she calls "his picturesque spelling, revealing splendidly his self-taught education and the confused culture he imbibed among Englishmen and Spanish Americans." His letters in English, especially those to his partners, De Castro and MacGregor, are equally revealing.

There was nothing in this training that he had received among strangers that would fit him for a place in the world of Dom Pedro II—that could make him sympathetic to "this society made aristocratic by the social system of a slavocracy and by the influence of European court circles," which disdainfully displayed a complete "want of interest in effective, practical work." Politically, he was in total disagreement with the fundamental concepts of government as understood in Brazil and with the current practices of its public men. The duty of government, he sincerely believed (in agreement with the majority of businessmen in both England and the United States in the nineteenth century) was to provide stable social and political conditions in which the commerce and industry of a country could pay the greatest possible profits on the money invested in them. Brazil, however, was the inheritor of a philosophy of government that called for a far greater participation of the public authorities in any private enterprise. It was based on the theory that the government, as representing the crown, was the principal owner and landlord of the wealth of the country; that individual initiative must in the smallest details be supervised and regulated by constituted authority. Profits for the individual were always subject to the interest of the government. This fundamental theory never changed, no matter how many might be the innovations in the form that government assumed.

A sharp realization of this divergence between his ideas and the weight of Brazilian tradition caused Mauá to seek and retain his seat as deputy. It gave him a vantage point from which to confront a situation otherwise altogether outside his reach. He was, he said, the true liberal, for he never tried to stand in the way of liberal ideas which the government (whether the Liberal or the Conservative party was in power) had attempted to put into effect. Certainly he was a liberal in the sense that he espoused the principle of economic liberalism. He was against slavery, for free white immigration, and in favor of the incorporation of large companies to open up the vast interior of the country.

His statement is a key to two things: to his own failure to understand the world of politics; and to the anomaly of the party system in Brazil during the empire.

Though Mauá grasped the significance of slavery as an economic problem, he failed to grasp the true role of the existence of the servile regime in the political structure of Brazil. In this, Dom Pedro was shrewder than he, for Dom Pedro intuitively understood its importance in the political and economic life of the country. All problems of the empire were linked to this fundamental question. The economic forces which underlay it were far more powerful than the formal division of political parties. It was economic interest that made the slaveholders conservatives. They were a remnant—a powerful and numerous remnant—of the regime that had created the wealth of Brazil in colonial times and in whose hands it still largely remained at the time of the independence: the sugar planters of Baía and Pernambuco. As the century wore on, the center of gravity of this regime tended to shift south to the province of Rio de Janeiro, across the bay from the imperial capital and equally prosperous, first in sugar and then in coffee and in the possession of slaves. When Dom Pedro was still a gay young spark—or the closest equivalent to such as he ever was—in the late 1840's and 1850's, he had made a celebrated progress through the province of Rio de Janeiro, stopping at one great *fazenda* after another, the guest of the local Croesuses and Midases, who built new palaces, sent for new clothes from Europe, provided the most sumptuous entertainments in his honor. It was a splendor that could not have existed without slave labor. Undoubtedly Dom Pedro early learned the importance of this point. As a moral man he regretted slavery; as Emperor of Brazil he understood the place of slavery in the foundations of this throne.

In the course of time, the center of wealth in the country traveled on further south, for coffee was displacing sugar, and the province of São Paulo was the best place to grow this new great export crop. With coffee something else came into São Paulo which had not figured in the sugar-growing north: industrialization, for the railways came to São Paulo to carry the coffee from the interior to the seacoast. Coffee was a hybrid; it, too, depended upon the labor of slaves,

but it was half-linked to the age of the machine. The south of the
country, particularly from the provinces of Baía and Pernambuco,
from Europe as existed, so that coffee-growing, when it lost its slave
labor, had free labor to depend upon. It thus constituted a new regime,
with a rising order of bankers, brokers, importers, and exporters,
whose interests were largely associated with an England violently opposed to slaveholding and at odds with the old regime in the sugar-
growing north.

The result of this ill-defined evolution was confusion in the Brazilian world of party politics. Typically it might be said that the
member of the Conservative party was a man from the north of the
country, particularly from the provinces of Baía and Pernambuco,
the scion of a family vastly ramified throughout the sugar-growing,
slaveholding country and powerful through inherited wealth (albeit
steadily diminishing with the encroachments of modern industrial developments) and family alliance. The Liberal party man, on the other
hand, was probably from the south, an advocate of the abolition of
slavery, even in favor of a republican form of government. Yet on the
principal questions of the day—abolition, republicanism, free trade—
there was no such uniformity of opinion within the ranks of either
party. Nabuco de Araújo, typically a man from the north in other re-
spects, was a leader of the Liberal party and an advocate of abolition.
So was Zacarias de Góes e Vasconcelos. This confusion spoke of one
thing: the political structure of the country was not geared to the
economic, and in the gap between the two was lost the successful operation of a true party system. Political events—the rise and fall of
cabinets, the passage or failure of proposed legislation—were the
results, not of deep feeling, but of collisions between the personalities
of the men involved or between them and the Emperor.

On the surface, parliamentary rule, under a constitutional monarch,
was the form of government in Brazil under Dom Pedro II. It was an
exotic plant, transplanted from England long experienced in the sub-
tleties of such a system and France accustomed to the problems of
adapting parliamentary procedure to a government fluctuating between republicanism and constitutional monarchy. Both England and

France were old countries, densely populated, with a large and quickly growing literate middle class. The days of an economic system based upon the ownership of land by a privileged few and the working of that land by an enormous servile class, had passed in both. To transfer the governmental system adapted to them to a huge, almost unexplored, empty land in the New World, furnished with a sprinkling of Europeans along the seacoast and with an economic system based on latifundia and slave labor, was bound to produce an unreal political world, which had no basis in the economic realities of the country or the necessities of the majority of its people.

That world of political fantasy was a success—or at least maintained itself in existence—for so long a period because of the Emperor. He was probably better educated than the majority of his ministers and certainly than the majority of his countrymen. Like Queen Victoria, or Emperor Franz Joself of Austria, he had the advantage of always being in office, no matter how often his ministers, his deputies, and his administrative officials might change. He reigned for forty-nine years, from 1840 to 1889. As his reign lengthened, he acquired an immense fund of well-learned information that only long experience could provide. This gave him an advantage none of his ministers of state could circumvent, though they might accuse him of absorbing all real power in the government.

No better example of this absorption of power, of this suffocation of the initiative of other individuals exists than the fate of the political administrations that alternated in office during his reign. Whoever the minister and whatever his party, while a member of the Emperor's cabinet he bowed to the Emperor's will. Joaquim Nabuco, himself in later years one of Brazil's most able public men, writing the biography of his father, who at one time was Dom Pedro's Minister of Justice, expressed the matter as follows:

Primarily, the realm was the Emperor. Certainly he governed directly and on his own behalf, binding himself by the Constitution and by the forms of the parliamentary system. But he alone was the arbiter of the term in office of each party and each statesman, and as it lay in his hands to make or unmake ministries, the power was his as it lay in his hands to make or unmake ministries, the power was his as a practical matter. The period in office of cabinets was short, their title precarious so long as it should please the monarch; in such circumstances there was only one way to govern—in conformity with him. To be opposed to him, to his plans, to his policy, was to renounce office. Any minister could leave the government suddenly, although holding a portfolio; the cabinet, however, would remain, and the party would impute to it compliance with the imperial will through a love of political plums, of patronage. In spite of themselves, the ministers acquiesced thus in the role the Emperor assigned to each in his realm. To break with him for long was impossible in politics. The Senate, the Council of State lived by his favor, by his grace. No chief wanted to be *incompatible*. The tradition, the continuity of government was with him alone. As the cabinets lasted but a short time and he was permanent, only he was capable of undertaking a policy that required time; only he could wait, temporize, continue, postpone, sow seeds for a future harvest.

On one point, Dom Pedro was very touchy: he must never be suspected of playing favorites. He reduced all his ministers to subordinates, ignorant of the whole history of any government maneuver, some part of which might have preceded their taking office or survive their dismissal. Unlike Queen Victoria, he was not obliged to submit to the power of a Gladstone or a Disraeli, fortified by the support of well-organized, powerful political parties, able to overthrow the government and force a new election. No one knew from one day to the next what might take place, except the Emperor himself. Thus only he could lay a course for the ship of state and only he could name its port of destination.

This subtle form of absolute power, as Joaquim Nabuco pointed out, was the natural result of the political and social condition of the country. It was impossible, in a country like Brazil, to create a real electorate, and if there had been a real electorate, it would have been, through sheer inexperience, even more dependent on the Emperor. Only one thing could have broken his almost indestructible power: the rise of legislative chambers independent enough to have challenged him, to have placed themselves in opposition to his will. Under the circumstances, such a thing was impossible. It was nevertheless the great chimera that deceived those who fought for direct elections, and the Emperor, with a mixture of shrewdness and good intentions, was always careful to exercise his power strictly within the constitutional forms and to bow to public opinion and sentiment strongly expressed.

"What distinguished his government," said Nabuco, "was the sacrament of form: from the day on which he declared himself of age until the day on which his deposition was made known to him, he did not go outside his role of constitutional monarch. Furthermore, the course of politics in the realm was not his doing; he was only the clock; he marked the hour or gave the rhythm."

In fact, the Emperor did not want to act. To act meant to bring about change, and though he yielded to change where it was not to be withstood, he did not favor it. He kept himself aloof from the politicians and from political parties. Party politics were anathema to him, especially when they tended to create a powerful man in his government. He and his ministers, so long as they were his ministers, seemed thus to operate in a vacuum outside of the growing pains of a country learning the first steps in self-government. By 1853 his manner of governing was fixed. The old statesmen of the days of the Regency no longer completely dominated him; he instead was beginning to dominate them. Powerful though they might remain and long though they might linger into his reign, they were not powerful enough to escape the impress of his will. He preferred to have them about him, for he knew them thoroughly and understood the economic and social elements they represented. New men he instinctively disliked, but new men or old men alike, the characteristic feature of his manner of handling them was the regularity with which he destroyed the growth of power in a man and a group by removal from office and the calling of the opposition.

In 1853 the Marquess Paraná formed a mixed cabinet of Liberals and Conservatives, which went by the name of the Coalition Cabinet (A Conciliação). It had a double distinction: it lasted longer than any other cabinet (until 1857); and some of the most sweeping legislative reforms were made under its aegis. Nabuco de Araújo was the Minister of Justice in it and as such the prime mover in the adoption of a new commercial code, of the creation of the commercial courts, of the reform of legislation dealing with crimes committed by Brazilians abroad, marriages between Catholics and non-Catholics, and the reform of the Brazilian national church. The old Marquess of Olinda once declared that the Coalition cabinet was the "august idea," the Emperor's own brain child. It had all the earmarks of such a thing, since in its very character it leveled party distinctions and destroyed some of the power of the individual ministers. It was a highly controversial experiment, the focus of many debates, many bitter attacks, and much fulsome praise.

This coalition government, however, suffered a serious setback in 1856, for on September 3 of that year its chief, Marquess Paraná, died suddenly, some months before the election scheduled to take place before the end of the year. His death threw the political world into confusion, for the coming election was to have been the test of the success of his government. Whatever would have been the course of politics if the Marquess had lived no one can say. As it was, the Coalition Cabinet went out of office six months later, to be replaced on May 4, 1857, by a cabinet formed by the old Marquess of Olinda, always ready to accommodate the Emperor when he needed a reliable chief of government. The Liberals, however, had gained considerable ground in the Chamber of Deputies. Baron Mauá was among the new deputies from Rio Grande do Sul, his election assured by Marquess Paraná and by the influence of Count Pôrto Alegre, a powerful man in the province and a hero of the battle of Monte Caseros.

Throughout the 1860's Mauá held his seat. He was not a very assiduous deputy, for frequently he was away, in Europe building up his financial standing in the money markets of London and Paris, or in the River Plate, trying to stem the tide flowing relentlessly against his interests in Uruguay and Argentina. Thus by temperament and necessity he was unable to enter fully into the evolution through which the Emperor's government was passing. Five times during the 1860's the Liberal party came to power, and Liberal cabinets controlled the course of events in the international troubles in the south. But though this was nominally his party, its leaders were not men especially friendly to him, and in Zacarias de Góes e Vasconcelos, three times prime minister, he had an avowed enemy. The Emperor did not like this surging up of men and forces not entirely devoted to the maintenance of his throne. He always seized the first opportunity to reinstate his more reliable conservatives.

Toward the end of the 1860's, the Liberal party had lost its prestige and the Conservatives had gained an overwhelmingly powerful position at the expense of their rivals. But new changes were coming. In 1869, the *Manifesto* of the *Centro Liberal* had been published in Rio and Baía. It was the Liberal party's program, and it pledged the party, among other things, to the reform of the electoral system and the abolition of slavery. In these terms it may be read as a direct attack upon the Emperor himself, an attempt to break the absolute power he had so skillfully built up. The *Manifesto* represented the resurgence of the Liberal party from the limbo into which it had fallen with the dismissal of the last Zacarias cabinet during the final stages of the Paraguayan war, when the Emperor, uneasy at the marked lack of popular enthusiasm for the pursuit of the war, had sought the support of sympathetic opinions, appointing Viscount Itaboraí to head a new cabinet. Now, with the *Manifesto*, he felt again the breath of inimical forces. It marked the growing strength of real party feeling, of the antimonarchical element in the Liberal party, of the rise in importance of the south of the country at the expense of the north.

It was again the province of Rio Grande do Sul, the traditional stronghold of the Liberal party, of republicanism, separatism, rebellion against the centralized power of the imperial government, that brought about the change. The province was the part of the country where the cattle owners ruled like petty chieftains within their own domains, expecting their relatives, cowhands, friends to rally round as henchmen whenever there was an old score to be paid off with shooting. The climate, the countryside contributed to this frame of mind, since the one was cool and invigorating and the other open rolling plains, a horseman's country, a country that encouraged violent outdoor exercise and put a premium on the frontiersman's virtues of hospitality, a touchy sense of honor, and self-reliance. It was natural that this frame of mind should be carried over into the party politics of the province. Political leaders were warrior chieftains. The political candidates were a body of henchmen closely bound together and to their leader by this carry-over of a feudal, personal attachment. Furthermore, the province had been in a ferment throughout the 1860's, for the Paraguayan war was fought on and across its borders. Now in the elections of 1871, the war over, the province was returning to the political world of the empire. It did so as the only province to send a solidly Liberal delegation to the imperial Chamber of Deputies: Gaspar Silveira Martins, Count Pôrto Alegre, Florencio Abreu, Luis Flores, Araújo Brusque, and Baron Mauá. With the exception of Baron Mauá, they were all men whose associations were thoroughly with their province, whose lives had been lived within the politics of the Liberal Party in Rio Grande do Sul. Mauá was a stranger to such intimate provincial loyalties. All his life he had maintained connections with his native land, but it had been at a distance and impersonally.

The only other Liberal deputies in the Chamber were two from the province of Minas Gerais. The Liberal party was fighting against odds.

On December, 27, 1872, the lobbies, the corridors, even the enclosures reserved for members of the Chamber of Deputies, were overflowing with people, excited, expectant, chattering with curiosity. They were waiting to hear a new member make his maiden speech, a new member whose reputation as an orator, as a stirrer-up of the multitude, as a dynamo of energy, had preceded him from the south. When he rose to speak, they were not disappointed. He gave his audience the first taste of the fiery eloquence for which he was to remain famous for many years. It was an aggressive, showy manner of speaking that could stir up enthusiasm or animosity. Said Viscount Taunay, in his reminiscences of the occasion:

"That larynx and those lungs of iron! One could feel in his voice the rude, violent countryman's nature, capable of dangerous impulses, always full of life, of vigor, and of power; the hot note, ardent, vibrant, sharp, unreasonable, too much exaggerated, but irresistibly compelling and attractive."

This was Gaspar Silveira Martins. At that period he was thirty-

eight years of age. He was a man made for political life. His personality made an impact on his contemporaries that survived in their ad-
miring remembrance of him. To Nabuco de Araújo he was colossal—
"nothing gracious, modest, humble, little. Everything about him was
vast, ample, super, dominating." In the offices of newspaper editors
and in the coffee shops in the Rua do Ouvidor, he was to be seen and
heard, talking, gesticulating, unruly, exuberant, surrounded by a fascinated audience of young men and old men alike. His first foray in
the Chamber had the "effect of an earthquake." His method of address in the Chamber was to attack, with energy and a facile use of
innuendo, driving his opponents into responding by the audacity of
his remarks, entertaining the visitors in the galleries until the House
was in an uproar.

He was another son of the border, born in the midst of the turbulence of the War of the Farrapos, of a family whose name figured in
the heroic annals of the province. Though there is some dispute about
the exact date of his birth, he was probably born August 5, 1834, on his
father's ranch, which had been the scene of the signing of the peace
treaty between the generals Rivera and Lavelleja, the Fazenda de
Asseguá. When he was thirteen, he traveled to Rio de Janeiro to present himself as a candidate in the then famous preparatory school
maintained by Vitório da Costa. He knew what he wanted, and, without waiting for the director of the school to question him, he said that
he was from Rio Grande do Sul, that his parents had allowed him
to choose the school most suitable for his training, had put at his disposal the money needed for his fees, books, and other expenses. The
director, with the canny sense of character that had made him at that
time the best-known of native teachers, raised no obstacles. Instead he
asked the boy what he wanted to be when he was a man.

"I want to be Minister of State," Gaspar replied, "and I shall make
you Councilor of his Majesty the Emperor." Thirty years later he
had achieved both ambitions.

He was a brilliant student in the Law Faculties of Recife and São
Paulo. He was a great reader, who could seize upon what he read to
use in public addresses. Fresh from law school, he returned to Rio de

Janeiro and toyed with the idea of settling down to practice law or
to be a judge. But his childhood ambition stayed with him. In 1862
he was elected by the Liberal party as a member of the provincial
assembly of Rio Grande do Sul. In the years that followed he learned
to make political capital out of the resentment in the province against
the imperial government. Nine years later he was the leader of the
provincial delegation to the imperial parliament.

As a man whose meat and drink was party politics, who understood the strength of party organization, he was acutely aware that
within the group he was leading to Rio de Janeiro in 1872 there was,
from the point of view of strict party discipline, a dangerously weak
spot. Baron Mauá had been absent from Brazil during the elections
of 1872, and he was a stranger to the internal politics of the province.
As had been the case previously, his seat in parliament had been
obtained by the influence of a powerful friend, this time Viscount
Rio Branco, who had passed the word along to General Osorio
(Marquess Herval), a hero of the Paraguayan war and now political
boss of Rio Grande do Sul.

When Mauá's name had been included in the ticket, Silveira
Martins had objected. When Osorio informed him that the deed was
already done and could not be undone, he did not mince words in
his reply: "In that case, Your Excellency has done a lot of harm. The
place belongs to Dr. Camargo and not to Baron Mauá. He is in
Europe, he will take no part and has taken no part in the first session.
His banks, his businesses, his various affairs make him a less independent man before the government. The Liberal party must send fighting
men and not spiked guns to the Chamber of Deputies."

Silveira Martins did not let the matter rest at that when he arrived
in the capital. His maiden speech was an attack upon the actions of
the imperial government in Rio Grande do Sul. Especially it was an
attack upon the Conservative cabinet led by Viscount Rio Branco.
The Emperor was just back from abroad, from his first trip to
Europe, as a royal tourist sampling the pleasures and relaxations of a
grand tour after the fatigues of the wartime years. Party politics,
sharpened by the bloody troubles in the River Plate, had reached a

stage of bitterness they had up until then never shown in the Second Reign. There was real significance, therefore, in this attack upon the government by a new leader of the Liberal party.

This opening address, said Viscount Taunay, one of those who heard it, was "a real explosion, a sort of pampas gale, coming in through all the windows and doors of the big house of the Chamber of Deputies, a hurricane that made the old building . . . shake." His fellow deputies from Rio Grande do Sul applauded him vigorously— all except Mauá. The omission was not overlooked. It meant only one thing: Mauá was not prepared to attack Viscount Rio Branco. Since at the same time rumors and open accusations were circulating that Rio Branco's negotiations in the River Plate were too much influenced by the interests of his friend Mauá, that the Viscount was too often the guest of the Baron in Montevideo, the implication was obvious to all.

It was a situation which presented Mauá with an adversary with whom he could not compete. He had no gift of words to stir the multitude, no gift for drama sufficient to compare with Silveira Martins'. In fact, few of Silveira Martins' contemporaries could have competed with him successfully. With him public speaking was an art carefully cultivated in a very special manner. Alberto Faria describes him as

. . . a great figure in the meetings in the house of Senator Tomas Coelho, which gathered around the dinner table. He lived nearby, in Praia da Botafogo, and he was in the custom of going to drink coffee in the house of his political adversary who was nevertheless his old friend and admirer. He came to converse, he used to say. His table companions were transformed into an audience; he orated. Once he began, no one could leave, for he held them spellbound with admiration for his rhetorical gifts. For hours and hours he could talk. He allowed his audience to applaud, but he rarely tolerated an interruption. If anyone was bold enough to try to interrupt and disagree, he paused only long enough for a polite monosyllable. These were not conversations, in reality, nor even lectures, in which the student was allowed to comment for himself on what he heard. They were instead like sermons from the pulpit, in which no truth outside the dogma affirmed was admitted. His eloquence was especially fervid if he was speak-

ing of the fanatical devotion which his compatriots had for him or the
depths of the admiration in which he was held in Rio Grande.

This command of words, this ability to construct subtle, magnificent illusions in the air out of mere words, was a gift typically and
passionately admired by his contemporaries. It was part of the phe-
nomena of the romantic, literary social tradition of the Second Reign.
It held a fatal weakness for a people already too much given to self-
delusion where economic problems were concerned; it caused them
to lose, in the emotional exuberance it created, any grasp they might
have had on the unpleasant actualities of the financial and economic
crises through which, as a new, half-developed country, Brazil must
inevitably pass. Mauá, who by nature and by training lacked both
the gift and an appreciation for it, was irritated by the weakness it
promoted. He confessed later that he seldom spoke in the Chamber,
"for I well knew that it would have been a sheer waste of time to
combat the ideas that dominated then." For, indeed, he added, all
was lost in long-winded oratory, full of banalities and absurdities.

Mauá was seriously handicapped when goaded into open warfare
on such terms. Yet he could not ignore the attack, since the implications behind it touched on the very sore point of his dealings with
Viscount Rio Branco. One trait of his character, a reflection of the
energetic enthusiasm with which he undertook new enterprises, was
a sudden firing up of temper, especially where he felt his opponent
foolish or vindictive. Viscount Taunay, the indefatigable observer
of the political scene of the time, has left a description of the unequal
match with Silveira Martins, coming as it did when Mauá was sixty
years of age and under the strain of the accumulating financial difficulties that would culminate in his final bankruptcy several years
later.

In spite of the sincere sympathy that he awakened and the air of benefactor that surrounded him, Mauá, then already old and tired, every time
he took the floor [in the Chamber], obviously lost the duel and prejudiced
his own position, through uncertainty of phrasing, through the accent and
mistakes in language acquired by residence in foreign countries, especially
in the Plate, so that he would say *bussóla* instead of *bússola*, *rato* instead of

momento, de cerca instead of *de perto,* the result being that his formidable
rival, in the prime of life and with his public speaker's prestige every time
greater, gave him tremendous blows and succeeded in carrying with him
not only the galleries, but even his political adversaries in the enclosure of
the Chamber, fascinated more by the showy, burning words than by the
value of the arguments put forward.

In contrast, Councilor Sousa Ferreira has left a description of Mauá
in the speaker's box: he was "discreet, restrained, proficient, spoke
with conviction and sought to impress his ideas on the minds of his
hearers, speaking with the authority of some one who knew and had
studied his subject." His voice was low, and he spoke calmly, except
when some idea fired him with enthusiasm.

A month after Silveira Martins' original attack on the government,
Mauá spoke in parliament in defense of Viscount Rio Branco and the
Conservatives. He accused the Liberal party of having deliberately
fomented trouble within the province of Rio Grande do Sul, of being
disaffected to the national interests. He declared himself to be the
true liberal since he had never tried to stand in the way of the liberal
ideas which the government had attempted to put into practice.

Silveira Martins interrupted him: "Your Excellency should have
made your feelings known to the voters before they sent you to
parliament," and added: "The question is between me and Your
Excellency. Let us appeal to the voters. If they judge that I have not
fulfilled my mandate, I resign my place. Your Excellency must do
the same."

Mauá replied: "I accept the challenge Your Excellency has thrown
at me. If the majority of the voters believe that I do not serve the
interests of the country, that I have gone outside the mandate in
following the dictates of my conscience (which is the only judge of
my actions in this Chamber), I resign my seat, however high may be
the honor of representing my province."

It was a safe thing for Silveira Martins to undertake. He controlled
the Liberal party in Rio Grande do Sul. Even General Osorio could
scarcely refuse to support him. Unfortunately, the true character of
the dispute was then obscured by a violent and bitter undercover

war in the newspapers. This was inevitable, for this falling out with the leader of the Rio Grande delegation in the Chamber of Deputies was merely the reflection of a far-reaching attack both on Mauá and on the government for their dealings in the River Plate during and immediately after the Paraguayan war. Mauá's activities as an intermediary between the imperial government and several of the public men of Uruguay, the pressure he had brought to bear to safeguard his financial interests within the neighboring republic—these were used as a basis for an attack upon him in the newspaper *A Republica*, an attack generally attributed to Silveira Martins.

Mauá, irritated, demanded an inquiry in the Chamber. The quarrel was reduced to name-calling. Mauá, said Silveira Martins, was disloyal to his party, had received favors from Rio Branco that were prejudicial to Brazil, had used his financial power for personal advantage. Mauá, in a letter to Osorio, the political boss of Rio Grande do Sul, replied with bitterness: "Your Excellency will be able to form your own judgment of the ideas of justice that are pent up in that rancorous soul. I am proud that I am not in agreement with such a person and the blame will not be mine if he is able tomorrow to erect, in the name of liberty, the guillotine in the public squares as a means of government."

Silveira Martins had the undeniable advantage of an appeal to the local prejudice, in Rio Grande do Sul, against the imperial government.

"We were, I and Baron Mauá," he said to the voters, "elected by you in the name of the same ideals, in the name of the opposition party which has been so atrociously manhandled by the government. I attack the policy of the ministry, he applauds it."

The Liberal party machine settled the matter. It confirmed Silveira Martins' mandate and rejected Mauá's. General Osorio, aware of the local temper in political affairs, made no effort to intervene. It was obvious that he could not openly support, within Rio Grande, the avowed friend of Viscount Rio Branco, the head of the Conservative cabinet. Mauá himself did not hesitate in recognizing his own defeat. He sent in his resignation to the Chamber as soon as he heard the result of the election. Requests of friends, the opinion of the reporter of the legislative committee on the legality of the run-off election, the persuasions of various political men—none of this was sufficient to make him retract. His prestige was at stake, and he had a very sound view of which choice would leave him with the greater share.

He may also have been relieved at the chance to leave politics. The old simplicity was going out with the passing of the century. There were new forces, new ideas, a different temper creeping into the empire of Dom Pedro II. In the echoes of Silveira Martins' voice the note of a new concept of political power could be heard.

CHAPTER XV

THE CRASH

A BUSINESSMAN and banker in the South America of the middle nineteenth century, forever sensitive to the slightest variations in the international money markets in London and Paris and aware of the rising financial power of the United States, must have felt himself isolated indeed. Certainly Mauá felt himself cut off, for his letters to his partners, De Castro in Manchester and MacGregor in London, reflect the carefully cultivated patience with which he awaited news about financial events abroad. There was an English packet steamer and a French packet that connected Rio with London and Paris in 1861. By their means he was able to send information abroad and receive news every two weeks, and he gave keen attention to the days of their arrival and departure. The era of steam navigation was a great improvement over the sailing ship days in which he had begun his commercial career. Yet it was hard to wait days for some vital news item, and tantalizing to know that elsewhere in the world the telegraph and cable were practical realities. The knowledge must have put a sharper edge on the impatience of the banker, waiting for news in a continent still dependent on slow steamers to bring it into contact with the world outside.

In August, 1858, Queen Victoria, sitting in Sandringham House, had been able to send a message to President Polk in the Capitol Building in Washington, D. C., and to receive his reply through the submarine cable which Cyrus Field, after the expenditure of great sums of money, had succeeded in laying. This first attempt to set up permanent cable communication between the old and the new worlds did not entirely succeed, for the cable broke. Six years later, however, a permanent connection was achieved. Wall Street in New York could know what went on in Lombard Street in London and the Bourse in Paris almost as soon as the brokers in the other capitals of the Old World.

In Brazil, in the meantime, experiments had been going on with the telegraph as a means of communication within the country. In 1852 there was wire communication between Rio and Petrópolis, its two promoters being Eusébio de Queiroz, the Minister of Justice who had made the contract with Mauá for the illumination of the city of Rio by gas, and Baron Capanema, a renowned mathematician of the day. The first proposal for a submarine cable in Brazil was made in 1853, for a link between Rio de Janeiro, Recife, Belém do Pará and the European continent. In 1850 the North Atlantic Submarine Telegraph Company was organized in the United States. It proposed to connect America and Europe with two submarine cables, one to cross the Atlantic by way of Greenland and the other by way of the São Roque Cape on the Brazilian coast. None of these schemes succeeded.

In 1863, an Italian, Pier Alberto Ballestrini, made a proposal to link several points on the Brazilian coast with North America and Europe. Brazil signed a convention with France, Italy, Portugal, and Haiti, in 1864, to make such a plan possible. But Ballestrini failed to organize his company, and his franchise lapsed. In 1870 Charles Bright, an Englishman, obtained a renewal of the franchise for a cable to connect the north and south of the empire, with a preferential right to lay a transatlantic cable. But though his franchise was extended for two years beyond the original date of expiration, the coastwise cable failed to materialize. Ballestrini and Bright both failed because they did not themselves have the financial resources necessary to float such an enterprise, nor were they successful in finding other backers, although the wealthy French chocolate manufacturer Meunier is said to have been interested in Ballestrini's scheme. The idea attracted Mauá. He had thought about submarine cables before, being all too well aware of their value in the financial world.

"It made me sad," he said, "to see Brazil cut off from the civilized world and outside the enjoyment of the finest invention that the nineteenth century could show, all because franchises had been given to speculators who wanted to make a fortune at one stroke."

He went to Europe, "carrying with me the firm intention of not returning home without being assured of the carrying out of an idea that appeared to me to be of transcendent importance in the political, economic, and financial life of Brazil, and this is what I told His Excellency, Viscount Rio Branco."

In London he found a group of investors who had entered into negotiations to buy Ballestrini's franchise. However, the speculations in which Ballestrini and his associates had become involved so discouraged them that the scheme failed. Mauá had a happy inspiration. His friend Viscount Rio Branco was then head of the Emperor's cabinet, and without much delay he was able to obtain an official declaration that the Ballestrini franchise had lapsed. A new franchise was granted directly to Mauá in August, 1872. These maneuvers were not carried out without considerable uproar in the parliament and in the newspapers. For there were numerous people who looked with suspicion on the close association that the Prime Minister maintained with this banker, whose affairs, so it was said, were in bad condition.

Mauá, ignoring the attacks made on him by men whom he considered to be enemies with interested motives—he had just been defeated in his parliamentary battle with Gaspar Silveira Martins and he was the object of violent accusations made by less honest men than Zacarias de Góes e Vasconcelos—went on with his plans. Together with Sir John Pender he founded a company and laid the submarine cable, from Caravelas in Portugal to Recife in the north of Brazil and thence to Rio de Janeiro. On June 23, 1874, the Emperor, seated in the National Library in Rio, sent his first messages over it to the

heads of several European countries. It was a gala occasion. During
the first three months thereafter, traffic over the cable amounted to
about twenty-three messages a day. Mauá made no profit from the
promotion of the company, although his name figured in the board
or directors. On June 18, 1873, he transferred his rights to the Brazilian Submarine Telegraph Company, the ancestor of the modern
Western Telegraph Company.

His payment was in the formal thanks of the Emperor, made more
honorific by a decree of June 23, 1874, the day of the inauguration
of the new cable, granting him the title of Viscount. In the increasing
cloud of difficulties that were gathering around him, the new honor
gave little satisfaction, except as one more proof of the friendship
of Rio Branco. For he knew that it was not a spontaneous display of
the Emperor's goodwill and appreciation. Just as, in 1854, it had
been Viscount Bom Retiro who had obtained for him the title of
Baron, so now it was Rio Branco who had proposed the new honor
to the Emperor. Mauá, aware of the growing animosity toward him
of many men in the government, was particularly touched by the
fact that Rio Branco himself brought the imperial decree to him at his
house. Always a man to feel acutely the sympathy of a friend or the
hostility of an enemy, his heart overflowed at this simple but sincere
gesture on the part of the Emperor's chief minister. But toward the
Emperor himself he grew more adamant than ever.

There were some people, in fact, who thought the Emperor should
not have given him the new title at all—certainly not to a man whose
bankruptcy was openly talked about.

One of the last great enterprises that Mauá undertook was the
creation of a company for the organization of agriculture and cattle-
raising as big business. In the provinces of Rio Grande do Sul, Paraná,
Santa Catarina, and Mato Grosso there were vast plains, extensive
forests, empty land, uncontaminated by the regime of slave labor. But
so long as those lands remained empty, cut off from the rest of the
country and the rest of the world for want of means of communication and hands to work them, their value must remain merely potential. To Mauá there was only one reasonable method by which this

wealth could be exploited: by the creation of companies with sufficient capital to build roads and houses for the immigrants, to transport the immigrants and give them the tools, seeds, and machinery without which they could not hope to start in farming and cattle raising.

This he had already done in Uruguay, where he owned many acres of land valued at ninety thousand contos. In 1873 he launched in the money market in Rio the prospectus of the Companhia Pastoril, Agrícola e Industrial, for the development of commercial farming, cattle-raising, and fishing. The shareholders, who were chiefly himself, his relatives, and friends, were guaranteed an interest of not less than 5 percent. His company in 1877 owned in Uruguay forty-eight lots of land and in Argentina seventy, with a total of one hundred thousand head of cattle. He continued to manage this company throughout the 1870's. In 1882 it had receipts amounting to 864 contos, with expenses of 297 contos, showing a net profit of 566 contos. But he never succeeded in extending this lucrative enterprise to the vacant lands of the southern provinces of Brazil.

The reason he did not was that in May of 1875 the Mauá Bank in Rio, finally overwhelmed by the troubles in Montevideo, had had to ask for a three-year moratorium and to suspend payment. Its assets were 88,000 contos in unliquidated capital, and its liabilities were 78,000, of which 6,859 were owed to the Brazilian treasury.

The immediate cause of the moratorium was a request made by the Mauá Bank to the Bank of Brazil for a credit of three thousand contos to cover the bills drawn on London by Mauá and Company of Argentina. As security, shares in the prosperous Companhia Pastoril, Agrícola e Industrial were offered. Viscount Rio Branco, still Minister of the Treasury, made representations to the bank in favor of the loan but it was refused. Mauá himself, in his statement to his creditors, merely remarked with emphasis: *"The rigidity of the charter of the Bank of Brazil* did not allow the aid requested." In point of fact, it was refused because he no longer had friends (with the exception of Rio Branco) who could help his cause, and the enemies of the Rio Branco cabinet saw in his difficulties excellent political capital with which to attack the government. Zacarias allowed no one to forget

that this man on the brink of bankruptcy had been so embroiled in
the troubles in the River Plate that his good faith was impugned. He
had, Zacarias charged, mysterious dealings with the Treasury over
supplies for the army in Paraguay, and he had coerced and suborned
public officials into giving diplomatic protection to his demands on
the Uruguayan government.

The element of personal revenge also was not lacking, for one of
the directors of the Bank of Brazil was J. M. Pereira da Silva. Pereira
da Silva was now a councilor of state. Years before, in the 1850's, as
a deputy he had opposed the bill proposed by Mauá to provide a government guarantee of interest for the loan for the Petrópolis railway.
Pereira da Silva was not a man who hesitated to use the perquisites of
his position. In 1868 he had been one of the shareholders in the company formed to build the new customs house docks, a favorite scheme
of the Brazilian engineer, André Rebouças, who, in his diary remarks:
"A discussion followed, in which Comendador Mariano Procópio distinguished himself by his talents as a promoter and the ex-deputy
Pereira da Silva by the complete ignorance of the subject and the
craftiness he displayed." In 1873, Pereira da Silva had hoped to make
a profit out of the submarine cable, a hope that Mauá had firmly
dashed by refusing to have any business dealings with him. Now he
took his revenge, for a unanimous vote was required to grant the
loan asked by Mauá and Company.

So closely were Mauá's fortunes tied to the Rio Branco cabinet
that people said they contributed to its final fall. Viscount Rio Branco
was not easy to disturb with political polemic, which was fortunate,
for he was the target for a good many attacks. His term of office was
filled with incident. His was a modernizing government, sponsoring
legislation to revise the system of weights and measures and the
emancipation law. He had to withstand also the rancors arising from
the vexed question of the Masonic lodges. Freemasonry had been traditional in Brazil; throughout the early nineteenth century most of
the public men of the country had belonged to Masonic lodges, including many priests. But now Pope Pius IX declared them pro-
scribed. The resulting schism within the Brazilian church and among

the men of political importance produced a dispute which weakened the structure of the throne itself.

By 1875 Rio Branco was worn out by the incessant political quarrels. He finally withdrew from the government in disgust at the increasingly personal character of the invective directed against his cabinet. His dealings with Baron, now Viscount Mauá, were not forgotten. In the Chamber, a deputy, Cesário Alvim, accused him of "having confided, without guarantees, seven or eight thousand contos of the Treasury's money to an almost bankrupt banker. A little while later, that banker suspended his payments, an operation displaying an excessive and censurable trustfulness on the part of Viscount Rio Branco."

Zacarias did not allow the opportunity to pass without improvement. He said in the Senate, in the session of May 14, 1875:

When a bank extends itself everywhere in the old and new world—and would have extended further had there been more world—when it has a house here, another in Belém do Pará, another in London, another in Montevideo, three in São Paulo, and three in Rio Grande do Sul . . . the Minister who has any self-respect cannot constitute himself a broker in bills of exchange on European markets for the benefit of that bank.

Rio Branco defended himself on the ground that he was convinced that the Treasury would suffer no loss and that the Mauá Bank could be depended upon to pay up. But Zacarias was not satisfied: "And notwithstanding the fact that his protégé, his intimate friend, caused the Treasury a loss of seven thousand contos, the noble President of the Council and Minister of the Treasury, *cool as a cucumber*, seeks to defend himself by making that declaration to the Chamber and afterwards throws his cloak around the criminal, saying 'He is a benefactor of the Fatherland.' "

Rio Branco could only repeat: "He is a benefactor; his bankruptcy is a national misfortune."

Whatever Mauá's enemies might find to accuse him of in the events immediately preceding the moratorium, they were hard put to it to find the least shadow in his dealings once his house had closed its doors. His whole purpose, with unquestionable sincerity, was to safeguard his creditors. This had been a cardinal principle of his throughout his financial life, expressed over and over again in his public writings and in his confidential letters to his partners in England and the River Plate. Present losses, he always argued, could be made up in the future if confidence was maintained and the dissatisfaction of creditors avoided. He clung to the belief that people who had been induced to invest money on the strength of his name should not lose it through his failure to make an enterprise successful.

In 1877, he wrote to his managing partner in Montevideo, Ricardo Ribeiro:

> I shall not have a *vintem* [farthing] to send to market, whatever may be the conduct of the creditors towards me. My friend will believe that the only idea that afflicts me is that there should be any deficit whatever in paying in full the capital and interest which has been obligated in my name wherever the firm of Mauá and Company exists. The family has in any case the support of my son Henrique, which is a good one; for myself, nine *palmos* [six feet] of earth will be enough whenever God appoints.

A year later, he wrote to Baron Cotegipe, at that time Minister of the Treasury:

> A little more steadiness would have been enough to have allowed me to hand my children an honored name. Fate did not will it so. Fifty years of back-breaking work, during which I always sought to do some good, were entirely lost to me, while Your Excellency will believe that the efforts that I still make will not fail for want of energy and are made exclusively with this end: to fulfil my obligations towards the creditors of my house. If I succeed, I shall die resigned; if I do not succeed, I shall die impenitent.

He did not stint anything of value to bring about complete satisfaction of his creditors. In the report of the Bank of Brazil, which was in charge of the liquidation of his bank, Councilor José Machado Coelho made the following statement: "Before finishing with the information of Mauá and Company, I have the pleasure to state that the head of the house is currently credited with a favorable balance of 100 contos, whereas in the balance sheet of 1875 he was charged with a debit of 180 contos; that is to say, Viscount Mauá has brought forward as assets of Mauá and Company securities which he owned in his own name and which can now be liquidated." By 1878 this credit had reached the sum of 1009 contos. During the three years of the moratorium, Mauá paid 66 percent of his liabilities. These affairs, however, took time, and the period of the moratorium was drawing to an end. Mauá asked for an extension of time. According to the letter of the law—as found in the Commercial Code—such an extension was impossible without the consent of an absolute majority of the creditors, who must personally appear in the jurisdiction of the headquarters of the firm in order to give their consent. The Code was obviously out of date; at the time of its adoption the idea of a bankruptcy that would take in creditors, thousands of them scattered far and wide over the great sprawling empire, had not been thought of. Modern financial developments had overtaken the Code's draftsmen. Mauá and Company had more than three thousand creditors, most of them spread throughout the provinces, with less than seven hundred and fifty resident in Rio de Janeiro. To gather so many people together for such a purpose was a physical impossibility.

Two alternatives were tried. One was the presentation to the administrators of the company's affairs of a petition signed by twelve hundred creditors who resided in Pôrto Alegre, the chief city of Rio Grande do Sul, in São Paulo, Santos, Campinas, Baía, Recife, Belém, and abroad. The other was to change the law. Both failed, for the first was considered to be ineffective, and the second, again, required too much time. Nabuco de Araújo himself introduced a bill into parliament which sought to make the suitable change. It was supported by Silveira Martins, now ready to forget the bitter dispute of several years before. But the Chamber of Deputies, for reasons connected with the contemporary political crisis, was dissolved. When finally the law was passed (it received an almost unanimous vote in favor), it was too late. Mauá and Company was already in bankruptcy.

The bankruptcy once declared, Mauá held nothing back. He delivered up all his possessions, including much which a more cynical, less proud man would have found some legal ground to exclude. He handed over the shares of the Companhia Pastoril, Agrícola e Industrial, tracts of land and buildings in Santos, São Paulo, and Rio, including valuable commercial and waterfront property; the furnishings of his house, the jewels he had bought his wife at Farani's in Rome for thirty contos, the house in which he was living (formerly the home of Dom Pedro I's mistress, the Marchioness of Santos), sets of china with his coat of arms, gold and silver-handled umbrellas and walking sticks, leather trunks, table linen, mementos of silver plate given him by his old patron, Richard Carruthers, even the gold insignia of the Order of the Rose and the Order of Christ, with which the Emperor had decorated him—everything was offered in the forced sale of his effects.

Much of it was offered against the will of his friends and employees, in whom he was always able to inspire the most devoted loyalty. One of the latter, Francisco da Costa by name, could not restrain his indignation at seeing one familiar object after another fall under the judge's power. Viscountess Mauá—May—had a hobby, the collection of little earthenware water bottles, samples of native craft from various places. It was put up with the rest of the things at auction. Da Costa could stand the strain no longer and jumped up, declaring: "No, this is not possible. This is too much. This can't be the law of a civilized country." But the judge, though sympathetic, was adamant. If the objects were offered, he was bound to accept them, however clear might be the bankrupt's right to retain them. Whereupon Da Costa cried, "No, this is not for sale," and dashed the cabinet on the ground, smashing the objects into a thousand pieces. He was censured for disrespect for the court, but for the moment he was happy. The judge himself drew the line at accepting Mauá's gold-rimmed spectacles.

By the end of the proceedings, Mauá had paid off 80 percent of his debts. He offered to pay off the remainder at 51 percent; this is, 7 percent in money and 44 percent in shares of the Companhia Pastoril, Agrícola e Industrial, with a face value of a hundred milreis each and paying a dividend of 6 percent (they were quoted on the market at forty milreis). By the time he received his discharge in

bankruptcy on January 30, 1884, he had paid off more than 90 percent of his debts and until his death he did not cease striving to pay
off the remainder.

Though most of his friends among the great of the land were dead
or dying, he was not friendless. The judge who signed his discharge,
another Miguel Calmon du Pin e Almeida, gave him a friendly embrace in the courtroom. Baron Cotegipe, at the time Minister of the
Treasury, sent his daughters to help Viscountess Mauá and her family
move. In fact, he and his family were homeless now. He had never
succumbed to the passion that overtook so many of the *fazendeiros*
of Dom Pedro's empire for building palaces in Rio to display their
wealth. Early in his career he had taken over from a bankrupt creditor
the old dwelling of the Marchioness of Santos, situated almost at the
gates of the São Christovão palace in the northern suburbs of the
city. When Petrópolis was founded and he was building the railway
that linked it so conveniently with Rio, he had been one of the first
to build himself a summer residence there, a prosperous banker's
house surrounded by elaborately landscaped gardens and wide lawns.
Now the house in Rio was sold for the price of the furnishings and
that in Petrópolis went on the block for forty contos, although it had
a market price of two hundred.

He moved his family into a rented house in a new street at the
foot of Mount Tijuca (Rua Haddock Lobo), an unpretentious new
suburb of the growing city. His creditors, most of whom remained
his friends, bought up his wife's jewels in the auction and returned
them to him as wedding presents for his daughters. There must have
been an echo in all this for him, of those far-off days when, as a
sharp boy he had observed the breaking-up of his old master Almeida.
But now he was a man past middle-age, tired from a decade of constant struggle against financial disaster. He was thinner than he had
been in all his active life, and his eyes, instead of sparkling with the
half dreaming, half brilliant light that had been characteristic of them
earlier, were baffled and disillusioned, as though he could not believe
that his business life was over.

He went back to earning his living. With his eldest son, Henrique,
and three friends, Inácio de Tavares, J. Frias, and Simeão de Porci-

uncula, he gathered together two hundred contos, money lent by friends, and set up a stockbroker's office in Rio. There were still many people who had faith in the extraordinary financial skill and personal integrity that he had shown throughout more than thirty years of business adventure.

In his explanation to his creditors he named five reasons for his bankruptcy: first and foremost, the decree of 1854 which forced him to abandon the corporate form of organization for his bank and create in its place a simple partnership, with all the attendant risks; second, the too rigorous governmental supervision to which all private enterprise was subjected; third, various "unjust decisions of the courts of my country," which milked his firm of needed resources; fourth, the loss suffered through the wasteful methods used in the construction of the São Paulo Railway; and fifth, and most immediate, the troubles in the River Plate.

In 1878 there was still one more source from which he hoped to obtain some financial relief. The São Paulo Railway, he contended, still owed him money which he had advanced in the difficult years of its construction. This was to prove a will o' the wisp, a cause of extra bitterness in his last days, but at the time it seemed to offer a ray of hope.

The São Paulo Railway had been built in the late 1850's and 1860's, in the golden dawn of the coffee boom in the province of São Paulo, and it was to connect the coffee-growing center of the province with the port of Santos, then and now the world's great coffee port. It had been built with extravagant waste. Not only were there the problems of conquering the mountain barrier of the Cubatão, but the men who built it, English engineers and skilled workmen, were bemused with the visions of vast wealth that coffee was producing. Mauá had remonstrated with the manager of the line, Robert Sharpe, concerning the lavishness of appointments, remonstrances that had apparently no effect. Twice during its construction he had advanced money to the company, on one occasion £76,000 and on another more than £338,200.

Now, in the 1870's, Mauá sued in the Brazilian courts to recover the old debt, for the money he had advanced had never been repaid. The company's chief defense was an allegation that the Brazilian courts lacked jurisdiction over the suit, since the company's legal domicile was in London. In May of 1876, the São Paulo court upheld this contention, a decision that was naturally applauded by the friends of the shareholders in England, to whom the São Paulo Railway had been a speculative investment that had paid remarkably well. On July 27, 1877, the Supreme Court of Brazil upheld this decision, reversing a former decision it had made, earlier in the litigation, in support of Mauá, the judges composing the court having in the meanwhile been changed, as the result of the death or retirement of members of the original bench. To the company the importance of the decision lay in the fact that, according to English law, the debt was outlawed by the passage of time. If the Brazilian courts refused to assume jurisdiction over the case and in the English courts the right of recovery was barred by the lapse of time, Mauá was left without any recourse.

In 1883 he made one more trip to England, in the hope of convincing the managers of the company that they had a moral duty to repay the sums he had forwarded to the company nearly twenty years earlier, when it had been threatened with complete stoppage of work for want of money. He suggested arbitration, with as referees three lawyers or three directors chosen from the governing boards of the three largest banks in England, but the company refused. Had the suits in the Brazilian courts not consumed ten years, he would have had a legal ground for further court action in England. As it was, he was out of court and out of pocket.

He returned to Brazil in 1884, anxious for one more try in the Brazilian courts, but his lawyer, Francisco Otaviano de Almeida Rosa (the same Francisco Otaviano who in 1869 had been the Brazilian diplomatic agent in Montevideo) convinced him that nothing more could be done there, either. He gave some relief to his feelings by publishing an article in the *Jornal do Comércio* on December 6, 1884, restating his case. It was the final word of a defeated man—defeated, he felt sure, by a combination of enemies.

The article aroused the ire of the Brazilian minister in London, Carvalho Moreira (Baron Penedo). On January 23, 1885, Penedo

wrote him from London, taking him to task for remarks made in the
article and reminding him of an occasion back around 1858 when he
had saved the Mauá firm (so he said) from serious embarrassment by
using his influence with the Rothschilds to delay a demand for payment of bills drawn in Rio on the London branch, a contention he
documented with an undated letter signed by Mauá. Mauá replied
that he had no recollection of ever having written such a letter, and
went on to answer Penedo's further recriminations. In this letter,
dated from Montevideo on April 2, 1885, he speaks, perhaps for the
last time, with his old fire, with his old gift for characterization. But
whereas twenty years before he could chastise Büschenthal for
"taking me for a fool," with an ebullient spirit, his tone now held the
resentment of an old man without the sense of an expanding future
to give him energy and assurance:

> Your excellency is surprised that I should know what took place in the
> private meeting of the Board of Directors of the Company [the São Paulo
> Railway, of which Penedo was a director] when I was last in London. You
> forget, however, that in the notice which was sent to me by the Secretary
> of the Board concerning the matter, he wrote me that the meeting had the
> honor of Your Excellency's *presence*, as I would have asked, and the *ad-
> vantage of your vote*, which could not fail to show me what attitude Your
> Excellency had assumed, something which is now *clarified* by your asser-
> tion in the letter to which I reply, that my *attempt was absurd!* Absurd,
> Baron, a demand which at all times and even in the last event I was always
> ready to turn over to arbitration by independent men of the London
> market? If the demand was *absurd*, why not give it the *coup de grâce* by
> accepting the impartial judgment of third parties! Since when must the
> judgment of only one of the parties in a question be accepted as the only
> one which must prevail? No, Baron, a Directing Board of *thieves* in London
> handed over a letter of marque to the entrepreneurs, who were without
> conscience, money, or position, to come and carry out a great work in
> Brazil. And the Directors, using one of their members who was known to
> have great influence over me, prevailed upon me to supply in loans the
> money they lacked, and in this manner, not one but many Brazilians were
> robbed.... To decree civil death for me was a stupendous robbery. God
> gave me courage to face the misfortune and thus to be able to demonstrate
> who are the thieves. This at least I will do—and carry conviction to the
> minds of *all honest men*.

But there was nothing but words left. The money had gone, political influence was gone. Once this final dispute was out of the courts and out of the newspapers, even the drama of his spectacular crash was quickly forgotten. For the empire was dying by attrition, and with it the simple world in which Mauá and Company had first been launched and in which its triumphs had been gained.

Not even Rio Branco was there any longer to give him sympathy. In 1878 Rio Branco went to Europe, to seek treatment for cancer of the mouth, which the doctors said had been induced by his habit of chewing on a cigar. The treatment was temporarily successful. The day he arrived back in Rio, June 30, 1879, was a real return of the hero, for he had achieved a popularity with the multitude that the Emperor himself might envy. Newspapers printed special editions in his honor, speeches were made in the streets in his praise, masses were said for the restoration of his health, the Freemasons held a great feast. There were fire works and public demonstrations, and the criticisms of four years ago were forgotten. His popularity hardly diminished after that. He died on November 1, 1880.

He was the last of Mauá's chief friends, except Andrés Lamas. Lamas, whose office as Minister of the Treasury in the Varela administration in Uruguay had been his last political post, had retired. The victim of heart disease, he sat now in his study engaged in nothing more strenuous than scholarly writing. He outlasted his old friend by two years, dying in Buenos Aires on September 23, 1891. Sousa Franco had died on May 28, 1875. Even Urquiza was dead, assassinated in 1870 in his stronghold, the Estancia of San José in the province of Entre Rios.

CHAPTER XVI

MAUÁ EXPLAINS
TO HIS
CREDITORS

W HILE THE bankruptcy proceedings were going on in Rio, Mauá removed himself and his family from the scene and withdrew to his *fazenda* at Sopapemba in the nearby countryside. There, during a fortnight he set himself to writing his *Explanation to his Creditors* [*Exposição aos credores*]. He worked alone, as he always had done when engaged in his commercial correspondence, without a secretary, covering the pages rapidly with his neat, small, even handwriting, the words flowing onto the paper with the naturalness of a sincere man speaking his mind. It was a job which absorbed all his attention, night and day, and only under his wife's persuasions would he stop for a moment to take food or rest. Occasionally he would stop to bathe his head with cold water, in an effort to clear his ideas in the crowd of memories that the task called up. His private papers and professional correspondence were not at hand. He wrote with the retrospective clarity of a man with a good memory.

The result was a remarkable document, these hundred and fifty-nine pages addressed to his creditors, probably a unique document in the annals of bankrupt financiers. In it he told his story of his own enterprises, of the companies he had founded, of the companies for whose early beginnings he had found money, of the services he had given Brazil as an industrialist and financier and in support of its public men. This "species of financial and industrial autobiography," as Baron Penedo called the document, was his own brief, a synthesis of his professional career as he saw it now at its close. In that statement is preserved, also, and probably without his being aware of the fact, some of his personal history, the traces of the accidents of his early youth that made him the man he was. For, as his letters to his old friend Carruthers and to his partners De Castro and MacGregor were written in an English as native to him as his own thought, so this explanation is clothed in a Portuguese as peculiar to himself, a direct, headlong style, in its grammatical structure frequently and curiously close to an English mode of expression. He plunged into his narrative thus, after a brief preamble:

It is not in this solemn hour, when the victim of a great and unmerited misfortune comes forward to give explanations to those who have a right to require them, that it would occur to me to make an unfaithful account of the facts with which I judge it my duty to occupy your attention, for the truth has always been the shield with which I have protected myself throughout the vicissitudes of a long life. In that new sphere of work into which I was thrust by the force of destiny [his abandonment of trade for industry and finance in the 1840's], it fell to my lot to take part in the carrying out of many important ventures. It is certainly not mere fatuity, which would be really ridiculous in the circumstances in which I now find myself, that leads me to record the services that I have given to my country and obliges me to enter into a consideration of some operations of which I was the instrument, passing by in silence many others which could advantageously be presented, since they were indirectly concerned in the financial and economic life of Brazil. Thus I limit myself to those operations that have enough public notoriety to provoke open dispute, in order to reply categorically to my attackers while there is yet time before the cold grave stone is placed over the worn-out remains of one who, during his whole life, has had one major aspiration—to do some good—and who is now thrust into the criminal's dock. The explanation of the causes which may have brought about the disaster, which I consider a great one, since I am not the only one to suffer, and the interests of third parties stir me to the bottom of my soul.

Under such circumstances, this explanation is at one and the same time
a right and a duty. Since I know that not all of these undertakings have had
a favorable result, I have the further right and duty of making better
known the reasons under which I acted, for I am anxious to be judged according to the real truth [*verdade verdadeira*] and not according to interpretations inspired by malice.

At the advanced age at which I am now [sixty-five] and in the presence
of the event which is the motive for this explanation, I cannot have any
other object in view than the saving from shipwreck of that which is to me
more valuable than all the gold that has ever been extracted from the mines
of California—my good name; for I insist on believing that misfortune is
not criminal.

He proceeded then to list twenty-four major enterprises which he
had either founded or helped to found, pointing out, quite accurately,
that the list was not complete. The list was: the iron foundry at
Ponta da Areia; the Steam Towage Company of the city of Rio
Grande do Sul; the Gas Illumination Company of Rio de Janeiro;
services given in aid of the imperial government's policy in the River
Plate, at the request of the Emperor's ministers; the Fluminense Trans-
port Company; the so-called Mauá Bank of Brazil; the Petrópolis
Railway Company, commonly called the Mauá Railway; the Amazon
Steam Navigation Company; services given to the organization of the
Pernambuco Railway Company in London; services given to the Baia
Railway Company; the Floating Dock Company; the leather tannery
company; the Luz Estearica Company (which manufactured stearine
candles); the Montes Aureos Brazilian Gold Mining Company; the
Santos a Jundiaí (or São Paulo Railway) Company; services given to
the Dom Pedro II (now Central) Railroad Company; services given
to the Tijuca railway; the Botanical Gardens Railroad Company;
prospecting done for the railway from Paraná to Mato Grosso; the
submarine cable; supplying water to Rio de Janeiro; the Rio Verde
Railroad; the Mauá Bank and its ramifications inside and outside the
country; services given in the development of agriculture.

He had, he said, been dissuaded originally from making this explanation by friends who declared that it would be received as the act
of an angry man. He denied that this was the case, yet certainly

anger flashes out now and again in his pages. As Castro Rebelo has pointed out, one does not go to such a statement for a dispassionate consideration of a banker's financial career. The explainer, under such circumstances, is innocent; he presents to his creditors only those aspects of his story that favor his own case. But, because Mauá was Mauá, because everything he wrote, even his letters to his partners, is a crystal-clear window displaying the temper of his mind, because his statement was struck off in a last burst of the generous enthusiasm that carried him so successfully through thirty-five years of an adventurous life, his remarks are worthy of the most respectful attention. In them may be found, without equivocation, the principal elements of his business philosophy. In them may also be heard the man as he saw himself and the man as others saw him.

Mauá was attacked, both at the time of his bankruptcy and after, by critics who believed that he had been able to build his financial empire only because he had the favor of the government. In his statement to his creditors, though he frequently speaks of his friendship with this or that public man—with the Marquess of Paraná, with Paulino Soares de Sousa (Viscount Uruguai), with Sousa Francisco— he denied that he had had the consistent support of the Emperor's government.

To illustrate this fact he told the story of one of the contracts he failed to receive. It was one for the further development of the water supply system of the city of Rio, fourteen years after his first success in canalizing the Maracaná River. There was again a noticeable lack of water in the city's fountains, especially when the customary amount of rain failed to fall. His chief engineer in the gasworks at this time, an Englishman by the name of Ginty, was interested in the scientific problems involved and, under Mauá's encouragement, undertook a detailed study of the situation. Unfortunately, before his scheme could go forward he died of an apopletic fit. Mauá was then approached by another Englishman, Gotto, the engineer for the City Improvements Company, who had published two works: one, in 1871, a *Plan for the City of Rio de Janeiro Surveyed in 1866;* and the other, in 1878, a proposal for the furnishing of water to the city. Mauá said:

Mr. Gotto indicated that he wanted to join with me in carrying out such a desideratum, saying to me that he had already made some valuable studies of the matter; and his ideas being fortified by an old friend of mine from England, these plans were continued at my expense, I supplying everything required of me by Mr. Gotto. Two partners later joined with me, so that I did not have to carry the whole expense alone, but these latter had the good sense to withdraw shortly afterward, since they did not wish to continue to spend money with no security.

When these new plans were completed and the proposal made to the proper government bureau, we were required to trust the whole voluminous mass of graphs and blueprints to the Bureau of Public Works. When I was consulted by Mr. Gotto about this, I, without hesitation, authorized the turning over of everything that had been done, because not to have done so would have been to distrust the honesty of the imperial government. The only condition I made, and I believe even that was verbal, was that we were to be indemnified if the Bureau should carry out the works itself.

Time ran on and each day the question of a water supply became more urgent, while deliberations were held on the proposals.

At this point in the negotiations Antonio Gabrielli stepped into the picture. He was an engineer who had proved his abilities in developing the waterworks for the city of Vienna, and now he had come to Rio with recommendations from the Rothschilds, the Emperor's financial agents in London.

It was then, while absent in Montevideo, that I received a letter from Mr. Gotto in which he presented me Mr. Gabrielli, to whom I could within fifteen days declare whether I considered him bound by the proposal we had made, or whether he could get out of his promise. Surprised by this intimation, I did not hesitate to send to say that I accepted his withdrawal. Neither Gotto nor anyone else could have forseen the magic power with which this happy warrior [Gabrielli] came armed. The fact is that he had Caesar's happiness—he came, he saw, he conquered! For in fifteen days he had obtained the contract for which I and competent persons for me had employed long years in vain solicitation, I not receiving one farthing of indemnification for the expenditures laid out. That is one of the evidences of protection from high places which, according to many, was dispensed to me during the fifty-five years of my industrial career.

The government's defense for its actions was simply that at the time Mauá was involved in financial difficulties, and the work had to be done at once to avoid the risk of leaving the city without water. As a crowning touch, since Gabrielli had made no plans or blueprints and prepared no budgets, he was furnished with those submitted by Mauá. Arriving back in Rio from Montevideo, Mauá sought out the minister who had made the contract with Gabrielli, Councilor Tomas Coelho, and asked for explanations. These were given to him: Rothschilds had promised the financial backing necessary for the job, in letters addressed to the Emperor and to the Minister of the Treasury, Baron Cotegipe. Coelho admitted that Mauá had a grievance and indicated that the government would favor his claim if he cared to make one. It was the merest sop to offer to a man whose lifetime in industry had included some of the greatest enterprises Brazil had ever seen. Mauá declined it and declared the matter closed.

If Mauá's early commercial and industrial training had been English, his financial methods were French in origin. The period between 1848 and 1870 in France was that of the most active experimentation in paper credit manipulation. It was the age of fortunes suddenly made and lost with equally dramatic speed, the age when speculation on the stock exchange took precedence over gambling in any other form. In a little more than fifty years France had passed through its Revolution and the Terror, the First Empire, the Restoration. Money, ready money, had come to be the controlling factor in determining her ruling class. Frenchmen were experimenting, often wildly but always imaginatively, in investment banking, and none of them more successfully (until their great crash) than the Pereire brothers, Emile and Isaac, who covered France with railroads and otherwise did for France, through their Crédit Mobilier, much that Mauá did for Brazil. For France at the time the road to heaven was paved with the new wealth derived from these new methods of banking transactions.

Even the new emperor, Napoleon III himself, was not immune to the fever. He was indeed one of the chief gamblers. So much a part of French life was this mania for speculation that it entered into the romantic history of the period; in the novels of Dumas and Balzac and many lesser writers the banker who made a fabulous fortune one day and blew out his brains a bankrupt the next is a common figure. It was the great day of the *nouveau riche*, of the suddenly well-to-do who could buy titles, build great houses in Paris, take over the provincial estates of the decaying gentry of the old regime. But the golden dream could not last forever. After 1870 the frequent vicissitudes of its career—the violent financial crises of the late 1850's and middle 1860's—proved too much for it.

Unquestionably Mauá was one of the aptest of pupils. With his genius for financial problems, he quickly picked up the new ideas and put them to work, with suitable modifications, in his own enterprises in Uruguay and Brazil. Thus, in 1851, speaking in the first shareholders' meeting of the Banco do Comércio, which was later to merge with his own first banking house to form the third Bank of Brazil, he said: "The spirit of association, gentlemen, is one of the strongest elements of prosperity in any country; it is, in fact, the soul of progress." When he spoke, therefore, of capital for investment as "the most powerful instrument of modern civilization"; when he described to his partner Ribeiro his ideal of a banking system that would provide a means for the little man to invest his modest sums where they could have the greatest effect; he was echoing the Pereire brothers. For the creation of the Crédit Mobilier, early in the 1850's, according to Isaac Pereire, came from just such a philosophy: the need for a powerful financial organization to gather capital from all sources to be used in the carrying out of great enterprises.

Mauá expressed his theories on credit and its place in the development of industry and national weath frequently, in public and in private. In his explanation to his creditors he said:

In Brazil the action of credit and of capital itself is besieged by oppressive financial legislation. From this fact arises the clamor for the intervention of the government when necessary demands come knocking at the door, and as in the present case [the development of agricultural resources] with such force as to work the ruin of the best and most legitimate interests of the Brazilian nation. . . ."We do not have capital," some say. I believe that we do, otherwise the country would have foundered before this. . . . The country has internal credit within the country and an advantageous position abroad. I know perfectly well that *credit* is not capital . . . but who is going to maintain that *it does not create* capital?

He was frequently attacked as the prime mover in schemes to produce an endless supply of paper money to aid financial dealings of his bank. Again his words are an echo of the Frenchman's. Isaac Pereire said: "[It is necessary] in fact, to introduce into circulation a new agent, a fiduciary coin, with interest, to make profitable the savings of the humble and the money of large capitalists." The new agent of circulation, the new fiduciary coin, must be the creation of bank notes, and to forward this end, the establishment of a banking company.

These theories are obviously those that Mauá adopted in the creation of his own banking house. The most complete and mature statement of his views on the subject is contained in the pamphlet, *The Circulating Medium* [*O meio circulante*] which he wrote in support of emergency financial legislation sought by Silveira Martins as Minister of the Treasury in 1878. In it he said:

If specie and banknotes convertible at the will of the bearer constitute the best possible motive force for the money transactions of any country . . . it does not follow that they are the only such force. These are the most excellent conditions for the best circulating medium of countries which possess ample resources to back them up. It does not follow that they cannot be substituted with advantage, sometimes with great advantage, by temporarily nonconvertible paper money issued by banks enjoying internal credit and possessing large capital, banks which, because of the special circumstances prevailing in the country, find themselves compelled to hold in their vaults, in place of gold, private securities of sound value and government securities, to cover their notes in circulation.

After all, in the last analysis, he said, what was specie except merchandise, subject to the economic law of supply and demand?

The manifest deficiency in precious metals in the amount necessary to accompany exchange transactions, or the exchange of drafts, on the vast scale that civilization has produced, has brought about the creation of new agents or expedients intended to serve as supplementary instruments to achieve the same useful end.

One of these instruments was paper money, beyond a doubt the best arrangement that could have occurred to the human mind, to provide a powerful agent endowed with immense advantages (the principal one being flexibility, a desideratum not yet wholly achieved) for the transfer of assets.

The crux of the matter lay in the quantity of such paper money that he considered necessary. As a businessman, subject to the inexorable demands of business dealings and the aberrations of international money markets, he frequently felt the need for a good deal more circulating medium than did the gentlemen in charge of the Emperor's Treasury, whom he once wished would show less wisdom and more common sense. He had in fact more than once complained bitterly of the lack of a sufficient supply of circulating medium within the country; there was a middle road, he insisted, between too much paper money and too little.

"It is not my thought [that paper money is a panacea]," he said. "I wish to see in circulation only that quantity necessary to serve as motive power for money transactions throughout Brazil; my reasoning has always been based on the state of the empire as a whole and not merely on that of its capital [Rio de Janeiro], which is not the case with the men who govern Brazil."

Real wealth, he added, could only be created by an increase in production, and for that capital was necessary. He had an answer for those who feared him as an embodiment of foreign capital in Brazil:

I want [foreign capital], and the more the better, provided that all such capital in Europe [is brought forward by men who] weigh the conditions of our nation, and that it comes here to compete with the country's capital in spheres of activity most conducive to Brazilian interests, because all capital aids directly or indirectly the creation of wealth. What I do not wish is the importation of transient European capital which does not remain in the country, or if it remains, will create major financial embarrassments for us.

In his letters to De Castro and MacGregor he gives interesting details concerning the practical methods used in his banking house. To MacGregor he wrote, on May 8, 1861:

A banking house on this side [of the ocean] is justified in making every combination of credit to raise money at a low rate of interest to invest on this side at a higher rate. This is quite a different thing from raising the wind for speculative purposes. You clearly see that our operations with the London firm have this object in view, viz., raising as much money as we can at five percent in England to have it employed at nine percent here. The operations from the Plate are more profitable, for the money is employed there in equally good bills at twelve percent or given on account to persons of unquestionable credit. This is the plain truth which might be told out and out to anyone who may enquire, if the truth was wanted. In some points, however, men prefer being deceived, and *other parties* will make combinations to *save appearances*. We might also do the same, but I conceived that operations based *on the truth* and *real means* to fall back upon are presented. The end of business is profit and every *honorable way* of securing such an end is legitimate. If we were men of straw, and endeavored to get hold of other people's money by such combinations, there might be something unjustifiable in it, but in our position, with the *moral conviction* and *material proof*, that, should disaster or losses occur, *we pay the losses* and not the holders of our bills, under, almost, *any circumstances,* what scruple can I have in endeavoring to carry out my views?

And to De Castro he said, on the same date:

We must submit to the dictates of the great men Rothschilds who have their own way in London. After taking the drafts on Paris with your endorsement, to refuse them was indeed an insult, and I am half-disposed to write them a letter stating that if the bills did not represent the wealth of Rothschilds, they (the names on the bills) certainly represented as much honor and honesty as they can boast of. . . . The credit we enjoy *in Europe,* with exception of what is granted us by the Union Bank of Manchester and one or two friends, is based on the *good bills* we send as remittances, and as long as we send such bills they will be easily discounted. As to *Rothschilds,* from the time of Paraná [the incumbency of the cabinet headed by Viscount Paraná in the middle 1850's] they have complained against receiving our paper, and Paraná answered them that our paper was the only paper in the market with which the government could take so large sums with perfect ease. They complained to *Sousa Franco* (about receiving so much of our paper) and he sent them 200,000 pounds by the same packet which had brought the complaints. Ferraz sent them 340,000 pounds by our drafts the moment he came into power (1859), and to their complaints he answered that the Brazilian government endorsed the bills, which, besides, were second to none. Since they first remarked against out bills to Paraná they have received close upon one million and a half sterling of our bills, which have all been duly paid. What more do they want?

Another accusation made by his critics was that Mauá's great financial power arose from the fact that, because of his close friendship with many Brazilian statesmen, he was the banker to whom the government by preference had recourse to carry out its obligations abroad. One of Mauá's most serious complaints, however, was that with the Brazilian government he had no official standing as a banker. His help was accepted at moments of stress and certainly during the various incumbencies of Viscount Rio Branco as Minister of the Treasury, he was a confidential agent in government finances. But he could have been, and should have been, he believed, much more. His company, if it had been given the confidence of the government and relieved of the anomalous legal position into which it was forced by the mistrust of the Emperor's favorite financial advisers, could have, he said,

constituted the center of all monetary and financial movements in South America in close touch with the principal money centers of Europe. Had the idea been carried out, Brazilian enterprises, protected by the credit of the imperial government, would certainly not have had to grovel before the unmerciful usury of evil financial elements in the London market; a five percent guarantee and not seven percent would have been the basis sufficient for me and my agents to have succeeded in obtaining European capital for our transport companies and other enterprises, of a well-demonstrated usefulness for the employment of capital, which would have encountered easy and efficacious aid, since the Mauá firm represented in Europe a first class Brazilian interest. How many hundreds of thousands of contos would have been saved to the public wealth of Brazil merely by the difference represented by the interest guaranteed to the enterprises actually created within the period of the prospective contracts, I invite anyone who understands figures to calculate.

To those who may greet with a smile of incredulity this declaration of the services which I was ambitious to give my country and which would have been a reality had not the confiscation of acquired rights come about to upset all my calculations, I extend an invitation to accompany me through this brief account of the transactions of the establishment on which, however false its basis, I was embarking [the Mauá Bank, Banco Mauá & Cia.] I believe that no one in good faith would dare to deny that if, with such scanty resources I succeeded in lifting the House of Mauá to the position of a real national monument, I would have succeeded in doing much more had not the public authorities, who have the duty of protecting and aiding legitimate interests, interfered to confound me, from the beginning, with the governmental action to which I have referred. [He was referring to the nullification of the charter originally granted to the *sociedade anonima por açes* which he attempted to found after the absorption of his first banking house by the Bank of Brazil.]

But the Emperor was fundamentally opposed to the idea that Mauá should have any official connection with his government in financial matters, and especially was he determined that Mauá should have no part in the public loans which from time to time Brazil was forced to raise abroad. These borrowings had always been handled by foreign bankers, since the first Brazilian loan was raised in 1824, during the reign of Pedro I, by the three London firms of Bazeth, Tarquard, Crawford and Company, Fletcher, Alexander and Company, and Thomas Wilson and Company, the money they advanced being secured by the customs house receipts. In January, 1825, Nathan Meyer Rothschild, merchant in the city of London, as the Brazilian documents described him, took over the debt and became the agent and depositary for the service of the loan. In 1829 a new debt of £400,000 was contracted for with Rothschild and Thomas Wilson, to provide funds for the payment of interest on the original loan.

In 1825, the Marquess of Barbacena, on his trip to Europe in search of a second wife for Pedro I, discussed a new loan with Rothschilds, Thomas Wilson, Samuel Phillips (who had a banking business in Rio), and Baring Brothers. In his report he commented on the cold and unfriendly attitude of Rothschilds and spoke admiringly of Baring Brothers. Samuel Philipps raised another £312,200 for the Brazilian government in 1839, and Sir Isaac Lyon Goldschmid another

£622,702. The London agents for the Brazilian debt in 1847 were Goldschmid, Thompson, and King. In 1852 Nathan Rothschild and Sons once more entered the negotiations with a new loan of £1,040,600 to be used in the amortization of the loan made to the Portuguese crown in 1823, a legacy of debt which Brazil had inherited from Dom João VI. In 1855 all the service of the loan was turned over to Nathan Meyer Rothschild, who thus became the official banker of the Brazilian government. In 1858 Rothschilds lent the Brazilian government £1,526,500; in 1859, 508,000; in 1863, 3,389,906. It was Rothschilds who supplied most of the funds to prosecute the Paraguayan war, raising £6,363,613, with the help of Becker and Fuld of Amsterdam, in 1865; and they supplied other sums in 1871, 1883, 1886, and 1888.

All loans up to that of 1858 were for the purpose of covering the existing national debt, to finance the indemnity that Brazil had had to pay to Portugal as part of the price for the recognition of the empire as an independent nation, and to meet the payments due on prior loans. The loan of 1858 was the first for the purpose of developing the natural resources of the country. It was intended for the building of the Dom Pedro II Railway and in the negotiations surrounding it, Mauá first came into direct conflict with the interests of the government's official bankers.

The Brazilian minister to London during many years was Francisco Inácio de Carvalho Moreira, Baron Penedo, well-liked by the Emperor and popular at the Court of St. James, where the Brazilian Legation during his incumbency enjoyed success as a center of society. He had the Emperor's confidence in financial transactions and he preferred to deal strictly with the Emperor's bankers. In this he no doubt was correct. But in the end this preference got him into trouble, for he was accused in the Chamber of Deputies in Rio of having received an agent's fee from Rothschilds, and as a result of this accusation, was dismissed from his post by the implacable Zacarias, against the Emperor's wishes. He has been defended, particularly by the historian Oliveira Lima, who pointed out in his own memoirs that Penedo did not enrich himself, that his commission was not charged to the Brazilian government, and that he spent the money to help support the expenses of the Legation in London in a becoming style, himself dying poor.

The fact remains that he was opposed to any increase in Mauá's influence with the government at home. He apparently did his best to minimize as much as possible any part that Mauá's banking house could have in the matter of the loans for the Dom Pedro Railway; so much so that Mauá, in 1885, remarked in a letter to him, "in my repeated voyages to England to treat of various and many important affairs, I never remember that I could ever obtain any service from the Minister of Brazil." In 1860 a situation arose concerning payment of the installments on the loan which was the genesis of their disagreement.

From August 10, 1859, to March 2, 1861, the Prime Minister and Minister of the Treasury in the Brazilian government was Angelo Muniz da Silva Ferraz, later Baron Uruguaiana. He was a man from Baía, with a notably successful political career and some reputation as an originator of financial theories. Mauá was not impressed by these ideas, which in his private correspondence he characterized as "nonsensical." "At no time," said Mauá, "was I one of the intimate friends of Councilor Ferraz. Our relations were those of simple courtesy."

Their common friend, however, Count Pôrto Alegre, smoothed the way for more cordial relations, and

one day when the packet from Europe came in, I received a message from His Excellency to go and talk with him—which I did at once, and I found the honorable Minister of the Treasury angry and irritated. His Excellency said to me: I have just received letters from our financial agents in London, which place me in an embarrassing position, and make me indignant; because they require from me by return of post the balance of their account, which at this moment is considerable. It is impossible to carry out this request without producing a violent disturbance in the Exchange (which at the moment was extremely soft). Otherwise, the government would be under the necessity of delivering up the balance of the securities on the

last loan, which could not be issued in *toto* except at an enormous difference in price of the securities so issued, five or six percent below the quo-
tation in London, in order to pay off the balance.

As a Brazilian, I also was indignant at the procedure of the financial
agents of Brazil, and I declared to Councilor Ferraz that within an hour
His Excellency would have in the Treasury a proposition which, in re-
moving the threat, would enable him to satisfy the demand without any
sacrifice on the part of the Treasury; it would also prevent the powerful
bankers from making the least reflection on the imperial government or
spreading complaints against it. And I fulfilled my promise. The proposition was sent—in obedience to the impulse that dominated me and placing
my feelings as a Brazilian above my position as a banker.

Baron Penedo, reading this passage from Mauá's *Explanation to his
Creditors* in London, was highly incensed. He wrote off a long letter
to his old friend João Cansanção de Sinimbú (Viscount Sinimbú)
who in 1878 was Minister of the Treasury and Prime Minister:

I, however, was the negotiator of that loan to whose fate he alludes. I
have at my disposal the archives of the Legation through which all the
incidents of that operation passed, where all the facts are to be found
gathered together, facts to which he refers. I thus am in a position to review all the elements of that business and submit them to the Minister of
the Treasury's consideration. . . . The truth is as follows:

As soon as this loan of £1,200,000 was floated, Mauá began to croak at
once about the profits of the operation, making proposals to Ferraz which
the latter communicated to me and which I showed him were inadmissible.
The loan was thrown onto the market in March, 1860, and was not entirely
taken up, for a remainder was left on the agent's hands amounting to
£44,300, to be issued as occasion offered, without forcing the market.

That was the reasonable expedient, Penedo contended, especially
since the market was down because of political events in Europe.
There was no hurry since there was enough money on hand for the
government's expenses. Both he and the agents—the Rothschilds of
London—assured Ferraz of the fact. Yet on June 8, 1860, Ferraz's
orders arrived, directing the turning over of the remainder of the
loan to Mauá.

It was certain, said Penedo, that no banker had ever been so favored by the Brazilian treasury. To prove his point, he recalled the incident in 1858 when he had, he claimed, persuaded Rothschilds to refrain from protesting a bill of exchange for £50,000 issued by Mauá, Mac-Gregor and Company and thus saved the firm from bankruptcy. He alluded also to the firm support that Mauá had then received from Sousa Franco as Minister of the Treasury, in the 1860's, and from Rio Branco, Ferraz's successor:

> Ever since 1858 Mauá seems to have been accustomed to having the Treasury of Brazil at the services of his finances, and I do not know whether, on the occasion of this incident, he arranged with Ferraz for a contract concerning which neither I nor the Agents had any knowledge, in order to withdraw from their power the remainder of the securities not already issued, so that he could make money on them with which to pay the exchange fees he gave the Treasury, drawing every three and four months on his own house of Mauá, MacGregor and Company, in London!

> This, then, my dear João Lins, is the truth concerning the great services made to the *fatherland* by the Mephistopheles of the Treasury, who just today makes a public paneygeric of his own financial life!

In his *Explanation*—this self-justification of a man who, after thirty-five years of extraordinary financial and industrial undertakings, found himself called upon to account for his own bankruptcy—Mauá did frequently point out, with considerable warmth, the benefits accruing to Brazil from the many speculations he undertook which left him out-of-pocket. In that he was justified. Profits there certainly were; according to his own statement, his private fortune in 1866 was more than eight thousand contos. But what his contemporaries rarely understood and certainly underestimated were the facts that such profits were fluid and that, because he had been precluded from organizing his banking house as a corporation or limited liability company, all his assets were pledged to make good any loss.

His money was never idle, and as long as it was in use, floating new companies in new lines of business untried in Brazil before, that money was in danger of complete loss. With the resilience of a shrewd and energetic investor, he took his losses as they came, never, until the final crash, stopping to grieve over spilled milk. By 1878 he had had plenty of experience in talking other men, businessmen and public men, into taking flyers in railroads, in iron foundries, in gasworks, in steam navigation companies. He knew how to be persuasive, convincing, encouraging, especially since he himself had the imagination to grow enthusiastic over the prospects he envisaged. To him there was genuine excitement in doing what had not been done before, in making the desert bloom, as when, at the end of his active career he described his part in the plans for a railroad that would connect the sea coast with the great interior province of Mato Grosso, something today just realized:

> In spite of my having consented, before my departure for Europe in that year [1871], to take part in this idea which, as soon as it was suggested to me I saw to be one with vast and fertile possibilities (it being the first step towards the realization of a railway that some time in the future would cross South America from one side to the other), nevertheless, I had not expected such a franchise to be given to us, for I am very well acquainted with the obstructions which run-of-the-mill minds and malicious spirits opposed to the government's action on anything touching the realization of any of the many material improvements which that blessed piece of the earth's surface called the Empire of Brazil so lacks to convert into wealth the sources of prosperity and the inexhaustible resources scattered over its vast area.

> Those who lack the energy and the will power necessary to carry out commitments of such scope, attack with a mendacious severity every effort of the few among us who dare to face the difficulties and the dangers in initiating any useful idea, which because of its very size cannot be contained within the narrow limits to which mediocrity wishes always to subject what it has not the power to appreciate. For such people it is a utopian idea to have a railroad which, leaving from the most convenient point on the coast of the great bay of Paranaguá, once more conquers the formidable barrier that the Serra do Mar interposes to the establishment of an improved road system, something which would place our magnificent interior regions in a position to contribute with much greater power to the increase of the national wealth and the natural development of the living forces of the country.

A cardinal principle of his way of doing business was to maintain a good front. In floating a new company he understood thoroughly the sound psychology of laying out money to make a good impression, to attract capital for investment. Likewise, when a company was in difficulties, he knew that was not the moment to neglect appearances; a little more water might prime the pump. He had frequently to complain that the idea of reinvesting profits in a going concern in order to prolong the life of a paying enterprise was something foreign to his countrymen's way of thinking. This shrewdness, which was a commonplace of business dealings in England and France and the United States, no doubt contributed to the Emperor's mistrust of his methods. For the Emperor, well acquainted with the history of France in the nineteenth century and with the spectacle before his eyes of the rise and fall of the Second Empire, smelled a French taint in these speculative methods. The Emperor had a horror of Haussmannism in city remodeling; he would permit no rebuilding in Rio that savored of this new fad. It may well be he carried his dislike further, to Haussmannism in investment banking.

Mauá arrived at the end of his *Explanation* in a final burst of anger at his enemies:

This statement embodies, not a desire for revenge, but a cry of anguish, and such a cry is the privilege of the man who suffers; and to deny that I suffer would be to deny the truth.

It only remains for me to hope that in the half-century to come, my country may find someone who will occupy himself with the material betterment of our land with the same fervent dedication and disinterestedness (the malicious may say what they will) which has accompanied my actions throughout a similar period. . . .

And may God grant that, in the reforms that are preached as necessary to the social well-being of our fatherland, those at the head of the government may not forget that labor and the economic interests of the country are much more than worthy of the aid and protection to which they have a right.

CHAPTER XVII

PICKING UP
THE PIECES

IN 1885 an old gentleman with thick, snow-white hair closely trimmed and a short snow-white beard was frequently to be seen in the commercial and financial center of Rio. In spite of his age—he was more than seventy—and the fact that he had become somewhat more portly than he had been when younger, Mauá still walked with an upright carriage and a brisk step. He was dressed in the stout, sober black broadcloth which, in spite of the tropical climate, was then considered to be the only proper garb for a man of important affairs. He had kept the friendly sympathetic manner that had always been his towards friends and strangers, but his dark eyes, once so sparkling with visions of new enterprises, were inclined to brood or flash suddenly with resentment against the disappointments of his old age. It was a quickly changing world in which he was living out his last years. All about him there was evidence of things he had done to bring about some of that change: tramlines; at night, lighted streets; a constant flow of visitors to the capital, arriving by train from various parts of the country formerly inaccessible; news in the newspapers scarcely a day old, received by cable from the great cities of Europe and North America. Yet in the midst of all this he was almost unknown except to various elderly people who were aging with the empire and to the English businessmen come to Brazil to carry on enterprises which as likely as not had been founded by Viscount Mauá.

Thirty-five years had passed since he had been Senhor Irineu to the merchants who made up the commercial life of Rio. In those thirty-five years he had made several fortunes and spent several fortunes in a constantly growing financial and industrial domain. All that was gone now. During the years between 1878, when he had been declared a bankrupt, and 1884, when his discharge in bankruptcy had been granted, he had made earnest efforts to rally his last remaining resources. He had, at the insistence of the other shareholders, continued as manager of the prosperous Companhia Pastoril Agrícola. He had been abroad to try to collect something on the old debt owed him by the São Paulo Railway. Now he was reduced to earning commissions in the handling of exchange transactions for the customers of his modest stockbroker's office.

The contraction in his manner of living meant no great hardship for him personally. In spite of the great sums of money with which he had been accustomed to deal during his active life, he had never acquired a taste for luxurious display. Unlike most of the men ennobled by the Emperor, he built no great palaces, imported no great store of expensive house furnishings and trinkets from Europe, and when he went abroad, did not imitate the majority of the Brazilian sugar and coffee barons who in Paris gained a reputation for fabulous wealth. Not that he did not know how to use money for such adornments. When the occasion demanded, he could make a display of luxury equal to the best. Complaints were made, in fact, of the amount of money he spent on banquets for the Princess Imperial on her visit to London in the early 1870's, especially at a time when the darkest rumors were afloat about the soundness of his finances. He knew how to choose the expensive and the ornate when he made a gift to such lovers of luxury as General Urquiza or some of the Emperor's public men. But such things, in private, held little charm for him.

Chiefly the reason why the narrowness of this new life irked him
was the loss of the power to launch new enterprises. A man whose
thoughts were in the custom of ranging daily over financial affairs
covering a good part of Europe and South America was reduced to
the trivial routine of small negotiations. His discharge in bankruptcy
in 1884 was a great satisfaction to him. There were still some old
friends remaining who could sincerely rejoice with him in this removal of what he considered the deepest mark of ignominy. And the
occasion was made the sweeter by the thought that he had paid off
more than 90 percent of his debts. Few bankrupts had achieved such
a record. But though the discharge was something gained, it left him
with no future. There could be no future for a man seventy-one years
of age, who had once been the wealthiest and most powerful banker
and industrialist in Brazil and who now was forgotten and unrecog-
nized in the midst of all the tangible evidence of his achievements.

He was forgotten because, his financial world gone, he was swallowed up in the events that were hurrying the empire into its grave.
By 1885 it was not only Mauá who was reaching the end of his road.
The empire and the Emperor had entered their last decade. The Emperor had outlived most of the men upon whom he relied throughout
his long reign. Viscount Paraná, Euzébio de Queiroz, Mont'Alegre had
long since left the stage. Viscount Bom Retiro, his dearest friend and
boyhood chum, was to die within the year. The remaining old men of
the days of the Regency, Antônio Paulino Limpo de Abreu (Viscount
Abaeté, in 1883), Joaquim José Rodrigues Torres (Viscount Itaboraí,
in 1872), Pedro de Araújo Lima (Marquess Olinda, in 1870), José
Antonio Pimenta Bueno (Marquess São Vicente, in 1878), were all
dead. Luiz Alves de Lima e Silva, the Duke of Caxias, the military
mainstay of the empire, had died May 7, 1880, six months before José
Maria da Silva Paranhos, Viscount Rio Branco. These men were not
only the principal pillars of the regime of Dom Pedro II, but they
also represented the social and economic forces that supported his
throne.

Among the men who survived none was more sympathetic to the
Emperor than Baron Cotegipe, who entered politics very young and

soon found a comfortable niche in the Emperor's confidence. He was
born João Maurício Wanderley, November 1, 1815, in the province
of Pernambuco, the descendant of a Dutch nobleman who had settled
there in the seventeenth century and had married into a Brazilian family. He was educated in Baía at a time when the old northern slave
port was still the social arbiter of the country, the Baía described by
the Frenchman Alcides d'Arbigny, in 1838, as the home of a society,
"gentle, affable, and renowned in Brazil for its good manners," and
above all luxurious.

Young Wanderley had the usual gentleman's education of his day
in Brazil—Latin, French, rhetoric, rational and moral philosophy,
arithmetic and geometry. He graduated in law from the Law Faculty
at Recife, with a class of brilliant men, but he left more of a reputation as a connoisseur of the opera and the theatre than as an assiduous
student. Indeed, he did not need to study carefully to do well; his
brilliant, facile mind took in at a glance all he needed or wanted to
know of a subject. But this ease gave him negligent habits and a predilection for rule-of-thumb methods the weakness of which his political enemies were not slow to seize upon. Zacarias de Góes e Vasconcelos, for instance, found him fair game for satirical comment in parliament:

> The noble minister gets up late, more or less at ten o'clock in the morn-
> ing. He dresses with great care, which takes him the better part of an
> hour; he breakfasts at 11, chats with his friends. He arrives at the Senate
> at 12 o'clock; he goes to the House or responds here to questions concern-
> ing the cabinet's actions. He is free at four o'clock; he finds his house full
> of people; he stops to chat with his intimates; he dines at half-past seven;
> he gambles at his inevitable game of ombre; he goes to the theater at ten;
> he comes out at eleven; he goes here, there, and everywhere; and finally
> he goes home after midnight or even later.

It was obvious, was the implication of this vignette, that the noble
minister had no time in which to discharge the duties of his cabinet
post. He was an extrovert, a sybarite. His bath was perfumed; he
wore silk underwear; he smoked only the best Havana cigars. His
old friend Francisco Octaviano called him the "chief butterfly of the

empire." Yet all this did him no harm in the staid atmosphere of the imperial court, for in the Emperor's eyes his background was the right one, his political viewpoint correct, his devotion to the interests of the old slaveholding society secure. Politics was to him a game, the chief amusement of life. Rarely did the political questions of the day arouse any real warmth in him.

In 1857, at forty-one years of age and after an active political career of some years, he married, retired to his native north to be a *fazendeiro*, a power in local affairs, and father of a family. But when his wife died in 1864, he returned to Rio, to a splendid house in Botafogo, where, perhaps not as gay as he had been in his bachelor days, still he maintained the worldly court of a *grand seigneur*. Politically he shone out from among his contemporaries purely through his gifts of manner. No one else had quite his vivacity, his quickness, his grace, his fondness for solving a difficult situation by a brilliant improvisation. The Emperor rewarded these virtues with frequent political appointments of the highest importance. In 1860, when the Emperor had paid a visit to Baía, he had conferred on João Maurício the title of Baron Cotegipe.

From July to September, 1868, he was Minister of the Navy and *ad interim* Minister of Foreign Affairs in the cabinet of Viscount Itaboraí (whom, at this anxious stage of the Paraguayan war, the Emperor had called to form a Conservative cabinet after the dismissal of Zacarias). In 1875 he was for a second time (the first time had been in 1853 to 1855) the Minister of the Treasury in the Caxias cabinet which succeeded that headed by Viscount Rio Branco. In June, 1875, he added the post of Minister of Foreign Affairs to that of Minister of the Treasury, both of which he held until 1877. Finally, when he was seventy-three years of age, the Emperor named him to form a new cabinet. Thus between August 20, 1885, and March 10, 1888, he governed Brazil in a period that embraced the last critical years of the empire. The air was full of violent change—demands for absolute abolition, the rise in power of the army as an independent force, the increasing clamor for a republic. The Emperor, in ill-health and old before his time, went to Europe in search of medical treatment and some mental diversion.

Early in 1883, Carl von Koseritz, a German military man who had settled thirty years before as a colonist in Rio Grande do Sul, paid his second visit to Rio. He was a newspaperman most of his life and a principal figure in the German colony in the south of the country. He kept a diary when he visited Rio in 1883, which he published in German. His observation was sharp and his method of expressing himself candid and even caustic, and he did not think the capital of the empire came up to his home city of Pôrto Alegre.

He arrived in a Rio in which, he pointed out, sixty or seventy people died a day of yellow fever. It was April, and "the heat was insupportable, at a time when we already enjoy, in Rio Grande, a cool temperature." The noise was tremendous—horse-drawn streetcars passing in all directions, multitudes of people walking, the ubiquitous newsboys and streetvendors crying their wares in an incessant clamor; there was everything, to his mind, to prove the advantage of a small city. It was not without cause that Rio was interesting but not agreeable to live in. One could feel the pulse of the empire there—"here we find ourselves at the central and most important point of it and in the Rua do Ouvidor there may be seen daily the men who govern the country and lead public opinion; but the general character of the local society is very special and almost what I should call frivolous."

Whoever wishes to learn the manner in which Brazil is governed and public affairs conducted, has only to walk about for a few hours a day in the Rua do Ouvidor. It is one of the oldest streets in the city; it goes from the Rua Direita (where the stock exchange is), runs parallel to the Rua da Alfandega and other streets, and cuts across the Rua dos Ourives and yet more streets, all of which belong to the old part of the city and which are narrow, dirty, and crooked as they have been for the last two hundred years. Wide, regular streets, like those of the new Porto Alegre or especially pretty Pelotas [a town in Rio Grande do Sul near the Uruguayan border], there are not many such in Rio. In this narrow and almost always shady street is found the better part of the retail trade of Rio; brilliant show windows display products of European industry and innumerable articles of luxury are set out in them. The great dress-making houses, like the "Notre Dame de Paris" or the "Grande Magico" can compete with the best of Paris and Berlin; the jewelry shops are brilliant with gold, silver, and precious stones. Fruit shops exhibit fruits from all regions— pineapples and mangos side by side with grapes from Portugal and pears from Montevideo. Book shops and shops selling objets d'art call one's attention by their de luxe editions, their steel and copper tables, etc. However narow and dark the old street may be, the shops are brilliant in their contents and mode of presentation. An immense crowd of people wander about it from morning till night, and on each corner a club forms, where the talk is of politics and life abroad.

Certainly a great change had come about in the retail trade of the city since the boy Irineu had first arrived from the south sixty years earlier.

The Emperor's style of living did not impress the visitor from the south. In a city where great sums of money were carelessly spent in luxurious living, Dom Pedro lived in the greatest simplicity. His old palace near the waterfront, the Paço that had housed his grandfather and greatgrandmother when they had taken refuge in Rio, was a regular barracks, "like a government house in Pôrto Alegre, only five times bigger." It was old, ruinous, badly kept, never freshly painted. The Emperor had no personal fortune and he devoted a great share of his civil list to charity. He was averse to spending any of it in keeping up a princely state and to furbishing up his palaces. A wealthy planter like Baron Novo Friburgo might construct a mansion costing eight thousand contos, a real fairy-tale palace in the Pompeian style, with sweeping staircases, bronze statues, and seven drawingrooms on the first floor, furnished with tall looking glasses, crystal chandeliers, blue velvet carpets. [On the establishment of the republic, this palace became the new president's office building, the Catete Palace.] But Dom Pedro continued to live in a couple of old houses. Certainly this was praiseworthy in the man, but it added little to the prestige necessary to an emperor. The old Paço, for instance, had still the make-shift galleries to connect it with its adjoining buildings, hastily built before Dom João's arrival to make room for his retinue. The lower floor of these galleries was rented out to small shopkeepers and barbers, giving an odd impression to the European visitor.

Even when the Emperor went to open the new Congress, he was not able to maintain a properly splendid royal state:

Strange spectacle! First passed, at a gallop, a unit of cavalry, brandishing unused and unsheathed sabres, and soon after came four carriages of the Court, with gentlemen and ladies in waiting. Court carriages, I said, but of what a variety! Everything looked as if it belonged to the past century and was more or less in the style in which Marie Antoinette made her entrance into Paris. The gilding had become very black, the padding had come out, everything was in the saddest condition.

In fact, the whole thing made Koseritz think of carnival—the black coachmen in antiquated trappings, the elderly *grandes dames* in equally antiquated finery. The Princess Imperial and her husband, Count d'Eu, made a better impression.

One can see in him the soldier and the pride of his princely origin (which, nevertheless, does not prevent him from having a penny-pinching preoccupation with money) is written in his face. The Princess is growing old quickly and her features have acquired a certain hardness, but her blond hair always goes well with her healthy skin and her full figure. She was dressed with considerable simplicity and wore only a few diamonds. The people allowed her to pass between ranks of the most absolute silence, and only here and there could be heard some sarcastic remarks about the Count, who does not enjoy any great esteem.

Then the worthy Empress arrived. Her carriage was a little better, but it too is quite worn and dilapidated. She stepped down with effort and was conducted to the entrance by pages. She wore a low-necked dress, ceremoniously sewn with brilliants, and in her hair, which is completely white, scintillated a diadem of brilliants, while on her breast she wore the famous diamond collar which constitutes her principal treasure. On the kindly features of the Empress, who was greeted with every mark of the most profound respect, there was a shadow of fatigue. Finally the Emperor ap-

peared. Four horse-guards in new livery, on fine horses with rich trappings, and a carriage, if not new, at least completely renovated, decorated
and ornamented with silver and the imperial crown on the door, announced
his arrival. No applause greeted him, not even a simple "viva." He himself
seemed to notice this, because, after getting down from the carriage, he
straightened up to his full height and plunged a long, sharp glance over
the people surrounding him. I could not find him majestic, in his buckled
shoes, silk stockings, short breeches, cape of green velvet trimmed with
a band of feathers, under which shone his gold decorations. The curious
ornament of feathers especially produces an almost carnival-like impression. [These feathers are from the throat of the toucan bird, a brilliantly
colored inhabitant of the Brazilian jungles; the Emperor's state dress for
the opening of parliament may be seen by the modern visitor in the Imperial Museum in Petrópolis.] The Emperor walked a little bent over and
lately he has aged considerably. Also he is getting perceptibly bald, and
his great cares, perhaps also his physical sufferings, have made furrows in
his cheeks. Servants carried his crown and sceptre before him, and his
sword hung at his left side. After having thrown a long glance over the
silent people, who had been accumulating there, he directed his steps, with
considerable rapidity and his head held high, to the entrance, and with
that the spectacle was ended for us.

Later Koseritz had an opportunity for a closer view of the Emperor, when he was received in audience at the Quinta da Boa Vista,
or the palace of São Christovão in the suburbs of the city. The *quinta*
(park) itself presented pretty views, but it was not well cared for,
partly because of the Emperor's poverty and partly because he permitted hundreds of families to grow their cabbages within his grounds.
There were about twenty people, chiefly government officials, waiting to see the Emperor that afternoon. The Emperor walked into the
reception room with no ceremony, only preceded by a few minutes
by his gentleman-in-waiting for the day. He knew how to be friendly,
said Koseritz. Koseritz went to visit him again some days later and
reported:

The truth is that the Emperor is not amongst those princes who are
adored by their peoples, but he is also not hated and can live without a
guard. However, it should be realized that he is not as ingenuous as he
appears, because there are few princes in the world whose will intervenes

so much in the destiny of their nations as does Dom Pedro's, who in the true meaning of the expression "reigns, governs and administers."

Such was the pass that the empire had reached in the 1880's. The Emperor was not hated, partly because the Brazilians were not a people much given to hating and partly because they did not suffer that last degree of misery that produces hatred.

"Whoever wants to work can always get his daily bread. That worst element, neediness, is therefore lacking; a people relatively well-dressed and fed, whom the climate permits to sleep, if necessary, on a park bench, doesn't throw dynamite. They are much more likely to laugh easily, make good or bad jokes and not have much respect for kings."

Koseritz pointed out that in Europe itself the age of royalty was passing. Royalty, to be majestic, must conform to the times; the Emperor would have been better advised to have appeared on state occasions in a field marshal's uniform and in a more up-to-date equipage. Furthermore, in Brazil, monarchy had always been exotic, for Brazil was part of the New World, of the hemisphere that had revolted against the idea of kingship. Thus, to have a throne, the Emperor had been obliged to create his own nobility, to fashion his own court out of the material at hand, the sugar barons and the coffee barons. He had modified the concept of title-holding to some extent. Titles were strictly a reward for services given to the throne, and they were not inheritable; each generation had to earn its own. This odd mixture of the aristocratic and the democratic gave a distinctive flavor to Dom Pedro's peerage, as distinctive as the barbaric Indian names of many of the baronies, viscounties, counties, and marquisates he created: Baron Cotegipe, Viscount Itaboraí, Viscount Inhomerim, Marquess Paraná, Marquess Tamandaré.

It was a court, however, that lived in a glass case, well-insulated from the economic realities of the country. So long as the great landowners received princely incomes from their *fazendas*, that elegant, sophisticated world of society in Rio could survive, centering on the Emperor and his appendages, the parliament, and the cabinet. Men like Mauá might complain that in this state of affairs the country was forgotten and neglected, that all the money went to maintain the brilliance of the capital, that the provinces were left in a state of backwardness convenient to the *fazendeiros*, who, as slaveholders, saw only trouble in material improvements. A slave regime had no use for a modern economy, and as late as 1860 one quarter of the population of Brazil were slaves.

Certainly the Emperor, aware of foreign opinion concerning Brazil and sensitive to aspersions on his country as backward, must have regretted the foundation of his empire on a slave state. But the fact remained that to abolish slavery meant to disrupt the enitre economic structure of the empire, and, as Koseritz remarked, the Emperor was not as ingenuous as he sometimes appeared. He was thoroughly in agreement with Baron Cotegipe, when that clever man pointed out that the question of emancipation was dangerous. Tackling it was like rolling a rock down a mountain: "We must not give it a push or we may be hurt."

In Cotegipe, however, the Emperor had one of the few of his statesmen who were fully aware of the economic changes, emanating from the south, that were pressing so inexorably on the life fashioned by the old habits of the north. Cotegipe recognized the fact that, if the eighteenth cenury lingered longer in Brazil than in other parts of the world, the new forces of the nineteenth could not be indefinitely resisted, and it was in the south that these forces flourished.

In the south, in the province of São Paulo, there were also *fazendas*, growing coffee instead of sugar. But São Paulo was not in the tropics, and the pace of life was faster. It was too fast, in fact, for slave labor to keep up with. The climate was attractive to free white labor; it became the mecca for European immigrants, seeking better opportunity outside of an overpopulated Europe. Likewise, the growing of coffee presented problems different from those of the growing of sugar. It took more capital to begin with and it was sometimes grown on small plantations, interspersed among the great *fazendas*. It needed quick transport to the seacoast from the interior of the province, for it was more perishable than sugar. Besides, the greatest customer for Brazilian coffee was the United States, another new land that was rapidly being transformed from a purely agricultural country to one where industry flourished and where African slavery had been recently abolished, at the expense of a bloody war. All these things combined to make the *fazendeiro* of the south much more a man at home in the nineteenth century than his brother from the north. The great wealth that the Paulistas accumulated went into railroads, cities, industries, modern machinery—it created what J. F. Normano had defined as the Brazilian *homo economicus*—"that Yankee of the southern continent, whose ancestors were the *bandeirantes,* the equivalent of the pioneers of the United States."

It was the rise of a new civilization, a civilization innately at odds with the empire. The new age was not static. Koseritz declared that 25,000 immigrants came to Brazil in 1882, less than 200 of whom went to the northern provinces. Nor were they in the majority Portuguese, with a traditional respect and habit of allegiance to the Bragança dynasty. About 9,000 were Portuguese; the rest were Italians, Spaniards, Germans, Frenchmen, Englishmen, and other nationalities. These people were in search of economic independence, and, if farmers, wanted small land-holdings of their own. Slaveholding did not form an element in their plans for the future. Thus the city of São Paulo, which in 1875 had had 20,000 inhabitants, in 1884 had 35,000, at a time when Rio, the imperial capital, had prown to 500,000. By 1888 the stream of immigrants to Brazil had grown to more than 133,000 in one year, 90,000 of whom went to São Paulo.

Further south still conditions were even less favorable to the maintenance of an empire based on a slave state. The original settlers of Rio Grande do Sul had been Portuguese colonists from the Azores and migrants from the province of São Paulo. They were industrious people, used to working for themselves. Early in the nineteenth century they were joined by a constantly growing stream of German settlers, who spread out into the neighboring provinces of Paraná and Santa Catarina. In 1874 came the Italians in almost as great numbers, and Poles, and from Montevideo a constant supply of Basques. None of these people were slaveholders and as free workmen disliked and feared the slave regime.

The emancipation program was early claimed by the Liberal party as its own particular property, nor were the Liberals pleased when, to forestall more sweeping reforms, the Conservative party then in power undertook measures to bring about gradual abolition. At the close of the Paraguayan war, the Emperor named a Conservative cabinet, going counter to the popular opinion that a Liberal cabinet, with Nabuco de Araújo at its head, would be more representative of the majority view. He named first Pimenta Bueno (Viscount São Vicente). If there was any emancipating to be done—and the Paraguayan war had aroused a good deal of pro-abolitionist sentiment, strengthened by the presence of thousands of slaves who had been sent south in the imperial army on the promise of freedom—a Conservative cabinet would do the job more to the liking of the *fazendeiros*. Pimenta Bueno was soon only too glad to hand his job over to Viscount Rio Branco. Rio Branco, also, had been originally opposed to abolition, but he was preëminently a practical man and he read the signs of the times with care. Emancipation could not be ignored, so he introduced into the lower house of parliament a bill based on some of the recommendations made by the committee headed by Nabuco de Araújo. In general the bill provided that children of slave mothers should be free when they reached the age of twenty-one. This was the law of September 27, 1871, which was signed by the Princess Imperial as Regent in the absence of her father. Dom Pedro was in Europe, no doubt aware that such a law, signed by his daughter, who was known to have ardent opinions in favor of absolute abolition, would not, perhaps, draw too much unpopularity against himself, if he were far from the scene.

It was a difficult law to execute, however, especially in the remoter regions of the country. Thus, neither the *fazendeiros* nor the abilitionists were satisfied, and agitation for complete abolition, without compensation for the slaveholders, proceeded during the follow-

ing decade. Enlightened men like Baron Cotegipe favored reforms to
be carried out by local governments, such as the emancipation decrees
issued by municipalities within the various provinces. Thus the province of Ceará abolished slavery in 1881 and the province of Amazonas
in 1884. But a new problem then arose—the shipping of supplies of
slaves from one province to another within the empire. A bill prohibiting this interprovincial traffic was introduced into the parliament
during the incumbency of the Liberal cabinet under Sousa Dantas in
1884, but the opposition it stirred up among the pro-slavery group
caused the Emperor to dismiss the cabinet and call on José Antônio
Saraiva to form a new one.

Saraiva was always willing to take on a difficult task—as he had demonstrated twenty years before in the troubles in the River Plate. He
formed a new cabinet on May 6, 1885, but again the task proved too
much for simple good will. He was succeeded by Baron Cotegipe,
who with a Conservative party cabinet obtained the passage of a
new emancipation law on September 28, 1885, a law which this time
was signed by the Emperor himself. This law, like its predecessor,
satisfied neither side, for the *fazendeiros* made every effort to evade
it and the abolitionists saw no hope for effective enforcement. The
Emperor was tired of the vexed question; it had provided the most
serious problems of his whole reign, in both national and international
affairs. He was exhausted and old, suffering from diabetes, malaria,
and congestion of the liver. Again he went to Europe in search of
medical treatment, calling home his daughter, the Princess Imperial,
from Paris to take charge of the government. His popularity was
reaching its lowest point; the newspapers said he was getting old and
doddery and no longer fit to be Emperor.

Princess Isabel, his heir, lost no time in falling in step with the
spirit of the times. She was ultramontane in her sympathies, well
aware that Pope Leo XIII had made a pronouncement against slavery,
and much under the influence of her French husband, to whose European ideas slavery was an anachronism not to be tolerated. It was
obvious that she and Baron Cotegipe, whose divided sympathies made
him favor gradual emancipation, could not continue to run the gov-

ernment together for long. In March, 1888, he resigned and Princess Isabel named a new cabinet under João Alfredo Corrêa de Oliveira. The new law providing for absolute abolition was passed May 9, 1888, by an overwhelming majority in the Chamber of Deputies and signed by the Princess on May 13.

Baron Cotegipe, in the Senate, was not so joyous; he had lived a long political life and he had no illusions about the durability of the glass case under which the Emperor's government lived. Abolition, he said, would overthrow the monarchy, but his remarks were drowned out by the enthusiastic voting in favor of the bill and by the shouting of the crowds in the street outside. Cotegipe was right. No compensation had been proviled for the slaveholders, and in the north of the country, his own native land, there would be an acute labor shortage, for the free slaves would set out at once for the cities and the European immigrants were not attracted to the tropical zone as they were to the milder climate of the south of the country. Cotegipe had not long to live to see his prophecy come about. On February 13, 1889, nine months before the empire collapsed, he died the way he had lived, in ease and grace, without so much as a groan, as he stepped out of his perfumed bath.

Dom Pedro himself returned from Europe on August 22, 1888, somewhat restored in health, but not in popularity. His French son-in-law was no help in mending the situation, for Count d'Eu had always been viewed with suspicion in Brazil. He was a good soldier, but he had no great opinion of things Brazilian, was always aware of the precarious state of royalty in the world of the nineteenth century (as a relative of Louis Philippe and a descendant of the Bourbons could well be), was close with money, was deaf, and above all was a foreigner. In the newspapers and in popular complaints he was sarcastically referred to as the "Third Sovereign" and the "French Sovereign," and the idea that his wife, notably under his thumb, should succeed Dom Pedro, aroused no enthusiasm.

In this swift transformation of the Brazilian scene, in which he had played so large a role, Mauá was no longer a prominent figure. He did not regret that he did not live in a fashionable part of town, that he did not have a big house in Botafogo, overlooking the curving beach just within the shelter of the Sugarloaf. He could cast back in memory to the days of his boyhood when Botafogo had been the out-of-town residence of the English merchants in business in Rio. Now it was the choice of the very wealthy, with wide, tree-shaded, cobbled streets and big houses lost in large, iron-railed gardens. It was the focus of a far more sophisticated society than those of the Rio of his youth, an exotic reflection of the Paris of the Second Empire, a society in many ways closer to the world abroad than to the provincial life of Brazil itself. He felt no envy of it, never having had a taste for drawingroom gambling and having always been too preoccupied with business affairs to give much attention to the balls, the opera parties, the afternoon visits of ceremony, the elegant display that were such a large part of it.

He, who had always been on the move, if not to Europe, then to the River Plate, never went abroad now; there was no occasion to travel. The last trip he had paid to Europe in 1884 had been partly to consult specialists about his own health and that of his wife and eldest daughter. The European doctors had confirmed the diagnosis that he was suffering from diabetes. But in a characteristic letter from Paris to his old partner Ribeiro in Montevideo he passed by the news with the remark that the case seemed light and slow and did not inconvenience him greatly. For a number of years he had been a chronic sufferer from bronchitis, which the climate of Rio and the strain of his constant traveling had not improved.

His numerous family had dwindled, also. In 1877 his eighty-one-year-old mother had died; he said proudly, that even so, it took double pneumonia to kill her. But that physical vigor which she had passed on to him and which had been the basis of his own constructive energy had failed his son Arthur, whom he had thought to be his heir in his financial interests and who died in 1874 at the age of twenty. His eldest son and namesake, Irineu, had turned out to be a typical rich man's son, careless about money and a source of anxiety. Four other children were left to him: his second son Henrique, who had joined him in the brokerage firm he had set up; and three daughters, Maria

Carolina, who had married Baron Ibirámirim; Lísia Ricardina (the second to bear the name, in honor of his old patron Richard Carruthers); and Irene, who of all his children most resembled him in cast of mind. Besides, he was grandfather to a dozen children, for whom, in traditional grandpa fashion, his pockets were supplied with surprises. His youngest son Ricardo, whom years before he had characterized to his old friend Carruthers as "full of mind and of an excellent temper, and bound to be a master in his profession," died in 1884, a judge in Rio Grande do Sul. Always very much a family man, these domestic concerns more and more filled the narrowing world of his last days.

His native optimism did not altogether desert him. Though the last hope of a revival of his financial empire was gone, he was still able to earn a good living for his family. His spirits somewhat revived. He could be cheerful in his letters to his surviving old friends and resigned to the fact that in this new world he was no longer the great Mauá, the most powerful banker in Brazil, but only a stockbroker in a small line of business. Sometimes he visited Montevideo, to see his old partner Ribeiro, now the father-in-law of his youngest daughter. His visits there now aroused no special interest. He could remember when obscurity had not been his lot—in the late 1860's, when his affairs had been involved in the financial disasters of the River Plate. Then, when the government at Montevideo had pursued its campaign to drive his bank out of Uruguay, he had been more than once in danger of physical attack. On one occasion, in a provincial town, he and his wife had had to take refuge in the branch office of his bank, while the angry crowd outside had yelled, "down with the House of Mauá!" On another occasion they had had to take refuge in the Brazilian legation in Montevideo.

Sometimes now he visited Poços de Caldas and Lambarí, watering places in the mountains of the province of Minas Gerais, whose mineral springs he hoped would minimize his own and his wife's increasing physical discomforts. He could afford to rent a house in Petrópolis where he could spend the warm weather, for, like the Emperor, he had a particular liking for the tranquility and sophisticated simplicity of the elegant little mountain town. On days when his health permitted he went down to Rio to his office, traveling on the railway he himself had built, to the little port of Mauá, which had given its name to his title, and across the bay in the fine ferries which he had put in service and which still impressed foreign visitors. When the Emperor invited him to the palace to state functions, he did not go. He sent his wife instead; she was better able to make the polite responses necessary to the sovereign, who he felt had never been his friend. Nor did Dom Pedro fail to note and comment to the Viscountess on the absence of the man whose financial activities had always made him uneasy, whose economic views he had always suspected.

Finally these journeys down from Petrópolis stopped, for one afternoon he was to be seen returning from his office, leaning heavily on his daughter's arm and walking with uncertain, shaky steps to the ferry station. Diabetes and pneumonia killed him on October 21, 1889. Thus he missed, by a few weeks, seeing the end of the empire under which he had lived his whole professional life. For within a month the empire would be gone, the Emperor would be in exile in Europe, a new generation and a new spirit would be in charge of Brazil. The republic was at hand. In the midst of these events, his death made little noise. The Emperor did not forget to send a message of condolence to his widow and the Bank of Brazil and a number of the great commercial houses closed for the day.

Mauá's body was brought down from Petrópolis and carried across the bay in a special ferry from the port of Mauá to the water steps at Prainha, where today the Praça Mauá (Mauá Square) is situated, at the dockside end of modern Rio's principal avenue. It was accompanied on this last journey by his son Henrique and his son-in-law João Frick. As the reporter for the *Jornal do Comércio* said, "it traversed, cold and inert, the railroad which, in the ardent days of industrial enthusiasm, he had created. . . . The vicar of [the church of] Santa Rita . . . recommended to divine mercy the soul that had animated that body which, if sometimes it had erred, had on many other occasions reached sublime heights in carrying out deeds inspired by the noblest ambition."

He was buried in the family plot in the cemetery of St. Francis de Paul, in Catumbí (today an inner suburb of Rio), which he had seen founded on the outskirts of the city in his early days as a business-man. Maria Joaquina ("May") joined him there in the middle of March, 1904.

The empire had less than four more weeks to go, until November 15. When Dom Pedro became aware that his deposition was immi-nent, he accepted the suggestion of his outgoing prime minister, Vis-count Ouro Preto, that Silveira Martins was the most likely man to head a new cabinet, to postpone the collapse of the regime.

Silveira Martins, after his spectacular debut in national politics twenty years before, had first prospered. The Emperor had made him Minister of the Treasury in the Liberal party cabinet of 1878—when Silveira Martins was glad to accept Mauá's support for his policy of issuing paper money in combating the economic crisis resulting from the great drought in the northeast of the country. Within a few months he had resigned, withdrawing, according to his own state-ment, because the cabinet would not put up a firmer opposition to the Emperor's will. The Emperor retaliated by making him a senator. It was a subtly refined species of banishment from active political life in the Chamber of Deputies. In "Siberia," as the lifetime Senate was nicknamed, he would have no direct voice in imperial politics—unless the Emperor should once more see fit to make him a minister of state. It was not a welcome appointment to Silveira Martins; he did not feel, with some unrealistic people, that to enter the Senate was to achieve the highest power in the realm. He did not wish to be removed from direct contact with the electorate; he wished to be subject to the demands of the voters back home, such as he had been as a deputy. He withdrew then to provincial politics.

Now the Emperor summoned him back to Rio. On November 6, 1889, he turned over the provincial government (he was now presi-dent of the province) to a substitute, and on November 12 left for Rio. On his way north, he disappeared, for a brief period, in the prov-ince of Santa Catarina. He had in fact been arrested by the agents of the new revolutionary government that had seized the country and deposed the Emperor. He was taken to Rio and in December followed

the Emperor into exile in Europe. When he returned in 1892 he came
back to local politics in Rio Grande do Sul and finally died in volun-
tary exile in Montevideo in 1901. He had outlived Mauá and the
empire by twelve years and the Emperor by ten.

BIBLIOGRAPHY

BIBLIOGRAPHY

The following list contains only books chiefly used in the preparation of the present study. A more detailed bibliography is appended to Claudio Ganns's edition of Mauá's statement to his creditors, published as *Visconde de Mauá: Autobiografía*, 2d ed., Rio de Janeiro, Zelio Valverde, 1943.

Affonso Celso. *Oitos anos de parlamento: O poder pessoal de D. Pedro II.* New edition. São Paulo, Companhia melhoramentos de São Paulo (Weiszflog irmãos), 1929.

Agassiz, Louis. *A Journey in Brazil.* Boston, Ticknor & Fields, 1868. Other editions in 1871, 1875.

Baptista Pereira. *Figuras do imperio.* 2d ed. São Paulo, Companhio editora nacional (Brasiliana, série 5, vol. 1), 194.

Barbosa de Oliveira, Albino José. *Memórias de um magistrado do imperio.* (Edited by Américo Jacobina Lacombe.) São Paulo, Companhia editora nacional (Brasiliana, série 5, vol. 1), 1934.

Barroso, Gustavo. *A história secreta do Brasil.* 2d ed. São Paulo, Ed. da Civilização brasileira, 1937-1938.

Besouchet, Lídia. *Mauá y su época.* Buenos Aires, Ediciones America Economica, 1940.

——. *Mauá e seu tempo.* São Paulo, Ed. Anchieta, 1942.

——. *Mauá en el Río de la Plata: Prólogo a la correspendencia política: 1850-1885.* Buenos Aires, Ed. de Problemas Americanos, No. 10, 1942.

——. *Correspondência política de Mauá no Rio da Prata (1850-1885).* São

Paulo, Companhia editora nacional (Brasiliana, Série 5, vol. 227), 1943.
——. *O pensamento vivo de Mauá*. São Paulo, Livraria Martins Ed., 1944.
——. *José Ma. Paranhos, visconde do Rio Branco*. Rio de Janeiro, Zelio Valverde, 1945.
Box, Pelham Horton. *The Origins of the Paraguayan War*. Urbana, University of Illinois Press, 1930. Translated as *Los orígenes de la guerra de la triple alianza*. Asunción, La Colmena, 1936; 2d ed. Buenos Aires, Ediciones Nizza, 1958.
Camara Cascudo, Luís da. *O marques de Olinda e seu tempo*. São Paulo, Companhia editora nacional (Brasiliana, série 5, vol. 107), 1938.
Cardoso, Vicente Licino. *Á margem do história do Brasil*. São Paulo, Companhia editora nacional, (Brasiliana, séria 5, vol. 13) 1933.
Castro Rebelo, Edgardo de. *Mauá: Restaurando e verdade*. Rio de Janeiro, Editorial universo, 1932.
Cavalcanti de Albuquerque Melo, Felix. *Memórias de um Cavalcanti*. (Edited by Gilberto Freyre.) São Paulo, Companhia editora nacional (Brasiliana, série 5, vol. 196), 1940.
Costa, Renato. *Síntesis de una vida: Mauá*. Buenos Aires, Talleres gráficos "Augusta," 1943.
Faria, Alberto de. *Mauá. Irenêo Evangelista de Souza, Barão e Visconde de Mauá. 1813-1889*. 2d ed. São Paulo, Companhia editora nacional (Brasiliana, série 5, vol. 20), 1933.
Ferreira de Rezende, Francisco de Paula. *Minhas recordações*. Rio de Janeiro, José Olympio, 1944.
Ferreira Reis, Arthur Cesar. *Navegação fluvial, especialmente do Amazonas*. Vol. IV in *Panorama economico-financeiro do segundo reinado*. Rio de Janeiro, 3a. Congresso de história nacional, 1941-1942.
Franco de Almeida, Tito. *O conselheiro Francisco José Furtado*. São Paulo, Companhia editora nacional (Brasiliana, série 5, vol. 245), 1944.
Graham, Maria (Lady Callcott). *A Journal of a Voyage to Brazil and Residence there during Part of the Years 1821, 1822, 1823*. London, Longman, 1824.
Guimarães, Argeu. *Em torno do casamento de Pedro II*. Rio de Janeiro, Zelio Valverde (série *Documentos históricos*), 1942.
Harding, Bertita. *Amazon Throne: The Story of the Braganzas of Brazil*. New York, Bobbs-Merrill Co., 1941.
Hill, Lawrence. *Diplomatic Relations of the United States and Brazil*. Durham, Duke University Press. 1932.
Instituto Histórico e Geográfico Brasileiro. *O Visconde de Mauá*. Rio de Janeiro, Imprensa nacional, 1940.
Kidder, D. P. and J. C. Fletcher. *Brazil and the Brazilians*. Philadelphia, Childs and Pearson; Boston, Phillips, 1857.

Koseritz, Karl von. *Imagens do Brasil*. São Paulo, Livraria Martins, 1943. (Published in Leipzig in German in 1885.)

Lacombe, Américo Jacobina. *Paulo Barbosa e a fundação de Petrópolis*. Vol. II of the *Trabalhos da Commissão do Centenário de Petrópolis*, Petrópolis, Directoria de Educação e Cultura, 1938-1943.

Lamas, Pedro S. *Etapas de una gran política*. Sceaux, Imprenta Charaire, 1908.

Luccock, John. *Notes on Rio de Janeiro and the Southern Parts of Brazil; Taken during a Residence of Ten Years in that Country from 1808 to 1818*. London, S. Leigh, 1820.

Lyra Heitor, *História de D. Pedro II*. São Paulo, Companhia editora nacional (Brasiliana, série 5, vols. 133 and 133A), 1939.

Manchester, Alan Krebs. *British Preeminence in Brazil*. Chapel Hill, University of North Carolina Press, 1933.

Mendonça, Renato. *Um diplomata na corte do Inglaterra*. São Paulo, Companhia editora nacional. (Brasiliana, série 5, vol. 129), 1942.

Nabuco, Joaquim. *Um estadista do imperio*. Rio de Janeiro, Paris, H. Garnier, 1897. Also, São Paulo, Companhia editora nacional; Rio de Janeiro, Civilização brasileira, 1936. Also, São Paulo, Instituto Progresso Editorial, 1949.

Normano, J. F. *Brazil, a Study of Economic Types*. Chapel Hill, University of North Carolina Press, 1935. Translated as *A evolução economica do Brasil*. São Paulo, Companhia editora nacional (Brasiliana, série 5, vol. 152), 1939.

Octavio Filho, Rodrigo. *Figuras do imperio e da republica*. Rio de Janeiro, Zelio Valverde, 1944.

Orico, Oswaldo. *Silveira Martins e seu época*. Porto Alegre, Ed. da Livraria do Globo, 1933.

Osorio, Fernando Luiz. *História do General Osorio*. Vol. 1, Rio de Janeiro, Leuzinger, 1894. Vol. II, Pelotas, Ed. de Joaquim Luiz Osorio e Fernando Luis Osorio Filho, 1915.

Rangel, Alberto. *A educação do príncipe*. Rio de Janeiro, Agir, 1945.

Rebouças, André. *Diário e notas autobiográficas*. Rio de Janeiro, José Olympio, 1938.

Rio Branco, Barão de, *O visconde do Rio Branco*. Rio de Janeiro, A Noite, 1943.

Saboia de Medeiros, Fernando. *A liberdade de navegação de Amazonas*. São Paulo, Companhia editora nacional (Brasiliana, série 5, vol. 122), 1938.

Silveira Martins, J. J. *Gaspar Silveira Martins*. Rio de Janeiro, Tip. S. Benedito, 1929.

Soares de Sousa, José Antonio. *Vida do visconde de Uruguai*. São Paulo, Companhia editora nacional (Brasiliana, série 5, vol. 243), 1944.

Sodré, Nelson Werneck. *Panorama do segundo imperio*. São Paulo, Companhia editora nacional (Brasiliana, Série 5, vol. 170), 1939.

Taunay, Alfredo d'Escragnolle, Visconde de *Homens e coisas do imperio*. São Paulo, 1924.

——. *Reminiscências*. 2d ed. São Paulo, Companhia Melhoramentos, 1923.

Tavares Bastos, Aureliano Candido. *Cartas do solitário*. 3d ed. São Paulo, Companhia editora nacional (Brasiliana, série 5, vol. 115) 1938.

Walsh, Robert. *Notices of Brazil in 1828 and 1829*. Boston, Richardson, Lord & Holbrook; New York, G. and C. and H. Carvill, 1831.

Wanderley Pinho, José. *Cartas do imperador D. Pedro II ao Barão de Cotegipe*. São Paulo, Companhia editora nacional (Brasiliana, série 00, vol. 12), 1933.

——. *Cotegipe e seu tempo*. São Paulo, Companhia editora nacional (Brasiliana, série 5, vol. 85), 1937.

——. *Salões e damas do segundo reinado*. São Paulo, Livraria Martins, 1940.

Williams, Mary Wilhelmine. *Dom Pedro the Magnanimous*. Chapel Hill, University of North Carolina Press, 1937.

INDEX

INDEX

INDEX

Iron industry, 52
Isabel, Princess, 185, 265, 270, 271
Itaboraí, Viscount, Joaquim José Rodrigues Torres, 35, 73, 119, 123, 125,
171, 189, 260
João VI: arrival in Rio de Janeiro, 10;
character and achievements, 13-16;
dealings with Bank of Brazil, 115-
116; intrigues in the River Plate, 140-
141
Koeler, Frederico, 64
Koseritz, Carl von, 263-267
Lamaré, Admiral, 98-99
Lamas, Andrés: house in Petrópolis,
65; letter to, from Mauá, 100; politi-
cal activities in Montevideo, 143-144;
as agent in Rio of Montevideo, 144-
146; friendship with Mauá, 155; deal-
ings with Elizalde, 167; signs proto-
col naming Emperor as arbiter of
River Plate affairs, 167; concern for
Montevideo, 177; aids Rio Branco in
attempting to avert war, 181; tries
to reopen Mauá bank, 203; death,
239
Latorre, Colonel, 203
Lavalleja, Juan Antonio, 141
Leopoldina, Dona, 85
Leopoldina Railway, 74
Liberal party, 215-216
Lima e Silva. See Caxias
Limpo de Abreu. See Abaeté
Linhares, Count, Rodrigo de Sousa
Coutinho, 115-116
Lisboa Serra, Councilor José Duarte,
120-121
London and Brazilian Bank, 175
London, Brazilian and Mauá Bank, 136
Lópes, Carlos Antonio, 183
Lópes, Francisco Solano, 184, 190
Luccock, John, 49-51

Mangue Canal, built by Mauá at suggestion of Haddock Lobo, 60

Maria I, Queen of Portugal, 10, 16, 63-
64
Maria da Glória, wife of Joseph Büschenthal, 158-159
Maria Joaquina: educated by Mauá,
38, 43; marries Mauá, 44-46; death,
276
Marquez de Souza. See Pôrto Alegre
Mauá, Baron and Viscount, Irineu
Evangelista de Sousa: explanation of
title, 3; general reputation, 3-5; arrival in Rio, 17-18; family, 18; first
job, 19; becomes protege of Carruthers, 29-30; education and early
years as businessman, 31-34; early
political connections, 34-35; opposition to slavery, 35-37; first visit to
England, 38-39; marriage, 45-46;
views on free enterprise, 61-62; income in 1850, 79; children and family life, 79-81; working habits, 81-84;
quarrel with Nabuco de Araújo, 94;
dealings with Pedro II, 96, 99; banking philosophy, 118-120, 133; conflict with Emperor's government on
monetary theories, 124-125, 132; dealings with partners, 127-130; seat in
parliament, 133, 207-208, 219-224; first
meeting with Lamas, 207-209; founds
bank in Montevideo, 152; as creditor
of Uruguay and Argentina, 154; El
peligro brasileño, 156; banking interests in Buenos Aires, 161-162; dealings with Blancos and Colorados in
the River Plate, 176; friendship with
Rio Branco, 178; letter to São Vicente, threatening retaliation for lack of
support by Brazilian government,
193-196; enmity with Góes e Vasconcelos, 199-201; lack of typical
Brazilian cultural background, 209;
traces of English and Spanish in
manner of speech, 221-222; receives
title of Viscount, 228; agricultural
and cattle interests, 228-229; pays off
90% of his debts, 235; use of French